PRENTICE HALL

Cells and Heredity

Prentice
Hall

Needham, Massachusetts
Upper Saddle River, New Jersey
Glenview, Illinois

Cells and Heredity

Book-Specific Resources

Student Edition
Annotated Teacher's Edition
Teaching Resources with Color Transparencies
Consumable and Nonconsumable Materials Kits
Guided Reading Audio CDs
Guided Reading Audiotapes
Guided Reading and Study Workbook
Guided Reading and Study Workbook, Teacher's Edition
Lab Activity Videotapes
Science Explorer Videotapes
Science Explorer Web Site at **www.phschool.com**

Program-Wide Resources

Computer Test Bank Book with CD-ROM
How to Assess Student Work
How to Manage Instruction in the Block
Inquiry Skills Activity Book
Integrated Science Laboratory Manual
Integrated Science Laboratory Manual, Teacher's Edition
Interactive Student Tutorial CD-ROM
Prentice Hall Interdisciplinary Explorations
Probeware Lab Manual
Product Testing Activities by Consumer Reports™
Program Planning Guide
Reading in the Content Area with Literature Connections
Resource Pro® CD-ROM (Teaching Resources on CD-ROM)
Science Explorer Videodiscs
Standardized Test Preparation Book
Student-Centered Science Activity Books
Teacher's ELL Handbook: Strategies for English Language Learners

Spanish Resources

Spanish Student Edition
Spanish Guided Reading Audio CDs with Section Summaries
Spanish Guided Reading Audiotapes with Section Summaries
Spanish Science Explorer Videotapes

Science Explorer Student Editions

From Bacteria to Plants

Animals

Cells and Heredity

Human Biology and Health

Environmental Science

Inside Earth

Earth's Changing Surface

Earth's Waters

Weather and Climate

Astronomy

Chemical Building Blocks

Chemical Interactions

Motion, Forces, and Energy

Electricity and Magnetism

Sound and Light

Acknowledgments

Acknowledgment for page 172: Excerpt from *James Herriot's Dog Stories* by James Herriot. Copyright ©1986 by James Herriot. Reprinted by permission of St. Martin's Press LLC.

ISBN 0-13-054064-1
7 8 9 10 11 12 13   10 09 08 07 06 05

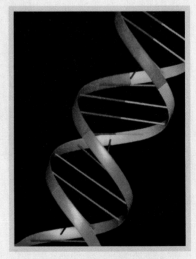

Cover: This computer image shows the structure of a DNA molecule.

Program Authors

Michael J. Padilla, Ph.D.
Professor
Department of Science Education
University of Georgia
Athens, Georgia

Michael Padilla is a leader in middle school science education. He has served as an editor and elected officer for the National Science Teachers Association. He has been principal investigator of several National Science Foundation and Eisenhower grants and served as a writer of the National Science Education Standards.

As lead author of *Science Explorer*, Mike has inspired the team in developing a program that meets the needs of middle grades students, promotes science inquiry, and is aligned with the National Science Education Standards.

Ioannis Miaoulis, Ph.D.
Dean of Engineering
College of Engineering
Tufts University
Medford, Massachusetts

Martha Cyr, Ph.D.
Director, Engineering
 Educational Outreach
College of Engineering
Tufts University
Medford, Massachusetts

Science Explorer was created in collaboration with the College of Engineering at Tufts University. Tufts has an extensive engineering outreach program that uses engineering design and construction to excite and motivate students and teachers in science and technology education.

Faculty from Tufts University participated in the development of *Science Explorer* chapter projects, reviewed the student books for content accuracy, and helped coordinate field testing.

CHAPTER PROJECT

Book Author

Donald Cronkite, Ph.D.
Professor of Biology
Hope College
Holland, Michigan

Contributing Writers

Susan Offner
Biology Teacher
Milton High School
Milton, Massachusetts

Warren Phillips
Science Teacher
Plymouth Community Intermediate School
Plymouth, Massachusetts

Thomas R. Wellnitz
Science Teacher
The Paideia School
Atlanta, Georgia

Reading Consultant

Bonnie B. Armbruster, Ph.D.
Department of Curriculum
 and Instruction
University of Illinois
Champaign, Illinois

Interdisciplinary Consultant

Heidi Hayes Jacobs, Ed.D.
Teacher's College
Columbia University
New York City, New York

Safety Consultants

W. H. Breazeale, Ph.D.
Department of Chemistry
College of Charleston
Charleston, South Carolina

Ruth Hathaway, Ph.D.
Hathaway Consulting
Cape Girardeau, Missouri

Tufts University Program Reviewers

Behrouz Abedian, Ph.D.
Department of Mechanical
Engineering

Wayne Chudyk, Ph.D.
Department of Civil and
Environmental Engineering

Eliana De Bernardez-Clark, Ph.D.
Department of Chemical Engineering

Anne Marie Desmarais, Ph.D.
Department of Civil and
Environmental Engineering

David L. Kaplan, Ph.D.
Department of Chemical Engineering

Paul Kelley, Ph.D.
Department of Electro-Optics

George S. Mumford, Ph.D.
Professor of Astronomy, Emeritus

Jan A. Pechenik, Ph.D.
Department of Biology

Livia Racz, Ph.D.
Department of Mechanical Engineering

Robert Rifkin, M.D.
School of Medicine

Jack Ridge, Ph.D.
Department of Geology

Chris Swan, Ph.D.
Department of Civil and
Environmental Engineering

Peter Y. Wong, Ph.D.
Department of Mechanical Engineering

Content Reviewers

Jack W. Beal, Ph.D.
Department of Physics
Fairfield University
Fairfield, Connecticut

W. Russell Blake, Ph.D.
Planetarium Director
Plymouth Community
Intermediate School
Plymouth, Massachusetts

Howard E. Buhse, Jr., Ph.D.
Department of Biological Sciences
University of Illinois
Chicago, Illinois

Dawn Smith Burgess, Ph.D.
Department of Geophysics
Stanford University
Stanford, California

A. Malcolm Campbell, Ph.D.
Assistant Professor
Davidson College
Davidson, North Carolina

Elizabeth A. De Stasio, Ph.D.
Associate Professor of Biology
Lawrence University
Appleton, Wisconsin

John M. Fowler, Ph.D.
Former Director of Special Projects
National Science Teacher's Association
Arlington, Virginia

Jonathan Gitlin, M.D.
School of Medicine
Washington University
St. Louis, Missouri

Dawn Graff-Haight, Ph.D., CHES
Department of Health, Human
Performance, and Athletics
Linfield College
McMinnville, Oregon

Deborah L. Gumucio, Ph.D.
Associate Professor
Department of Anatomy and Cell Biology
University of Michigan
Ann Arbor, Michigan

William S. Harwood, Ph.D.
Dean of University Division and Associate
Professor of Education
Indiana University
Bloomington, Indiana

Cyndy Henzel, Ph.D.
Department of Geography
and Regional Development
University of Arizona
Tucson, Arizona

Greg Hutton
Science and Health
Curriculum Coordinator
School Board of Sarasota County
Sarasota, Florida

Susan K. Jacobson, Ph.D.
Department of Wildlife Ecology
and Conservation
University of Florida
Gainesville, Florida

Judy Jernstedt, Ph.D.
Department of Agronomy and Range Science
University of California, Davis
Davis, California

John L. Kermond, Ph.D.
Office of Global Programs
National Oceanographic and
Atmospheric Administration
Silver Spring, Maryland

David E. LaHart, Ph.D.
Institute of Science and Public Affairs
Florida State University
Tallahassee, Florida

Joe Leverich, Ph.D.
Department of Biology
St. Louis University
St. Louis, Missouri

Dennis K. Lieu, Ph.D.
Department of Mechanical Engineering
University of California
Berkeley, California

Cynthia J. Moore, Ph.D.
Science Outreach Coordinator
Washington University
St. Louis, Missouri

Joseph M. Moran, Ph.D.
Department of Earth Science
University of Wisconsin–Green Bay
Green Bay, Wisconsin

Joseph Stukey, Ph.D.
Department of Biology
Hope College
Holland, Michigan

Seetha Subramanian
Lexington Community College
University of Kentucky
Lexington, Kentucky

Carl L. Thurman, Ph.D.
Department of Biology
University of Northern Iowa
Cedar Falls, Iowa

Edward D. Walton, Ph.D.
Department of Chemistry
California State Polytechnic University
Pomona, California

Robert S. Young, Ph.D.
Department of Geosciences and
Natural Resource Management
Western Carolina University
Cullowhee, North Carolina

Edward J. Zalisko, Ph.D.
Department of Biology
Blackburn College
Carlinville, Illinois

Teacher Reviewers

Stephanie Anderson
Sierra Vista Junior
    High School
Canyon Country, California

John W. Anson
Mesa Intermediate School
Palmdale, California

Pamela Arline
Lake Taylor Middle School
Norfolk, Virginia

Lynn Beason
College Station Jr. High School
College Station, Texas

Richard Bothmer
Hollis School District
Hollis, New Hampshire

Jeffrey C. Callister
Newburgh Free Academy
Newburgh, New York

Judy D'Albert
Harvard Day School
Corona Del Mar, California

Betty Scott Dean
Guilford County Schools
McLeansville, North Carolina

Sarah C. Duff
Baltimore City Public Schools
Baltimore, Maryland

Melody Law Ewey
Holmes Junior High School
Davis, California

Sherry L. Fisher
Lake Zurich Middle
    School North
Lake Zurich, Illinois

Melissa Gibbons
Fort Worth ISD
Fort Worth, Texas

Debra J. Goodding
Kraemer Middle School
Placentia, California

Jack Grande
Weber Middle School
Port Washington, New York

Steve Hills
Riverside Middle School
Grand Rapids, Michigan

Carol Ann Lionello
Kraemer Middle School
Placentia, California

Jaime A. Morales
Henry T. Gage Middle School
Huntington Park, California

Patsy Partin
Cameron Middle School
Nashville, Tennessee

Deedra H. Robinson
Newport News Public Schools
Newport News, Virginia

Bonnie Scott
Clack Middle School
Abilene, Texas

Charles M. Sears
Belzer Middle School
Indianapolis, Indiana

Barbara M. Strange
Ferndale Middle School
High Point, North Carolina

Jackie Louise Ulfig
Ford Middle School
Allen, Texas

Kathy Usina
Belzer Middle School
Indianapolis, Indiana

Heidi M. von Oetinger
L'Anse Creuse Public School
Harrison Township, Michigan

Pam Watson
Hill Country Middle School
Austin, Texas

Activity Field Testers

Nicki Bibbo
Russell Street School
Littleton, Massachusetts

Connie Boone
Fletcher Middle School
Jacksonville Beach, Florida

Rose-Marie Botting
Broward County
    School District
Fort Lauderdale, Florida

Colleen Campos
Laredo Middle School
Aurora, Colorado

Elizabeth Chait
W. L. Chenery Middle School
Belmont, Massachusetts

Holly Estes
Hale Middle School
Stow, Massachusetts

Laura Hapgood
Plymouth Community
    Intermediate School
Plymouth, Massachusetts

Sandra M. Harris
Winman Junior High School
Warwick, Rhode Island

Jason Ho
Walter Reed Middle School
Los Angeles, California

Joanne Jackson
Winman Junior High School
Warwick, Rhode Island

Mary F. Lavin
Plymouth Community
    Intermediate School
Plymouth, Massachusetts

James MacNeil, Ph.D.
Concord Public Schools
Concord, Massachusetts

Lauren Magruder
St. Michael's Country
    Day School
Newport, Rhode Island

Jeanne Maurand
Glen Urquhart School
Beverly Farms, Massachusetts

Warren Phillips
Plymouth Community
    Intermediate School
Plymouth, Massachusetts

Carol Pirtle
Hale Middle School
Stow, Massachusetts

Kathleen M. Poe
Kirby-Smith Middle School
Jacksonville, Florida

Cynthia B. Pope
Ruffner Middle School
Norfolk, Virginia

Anne Scammell
Geneva Middle School
Geneva, New York

Karen Riley Sievers
Callanan Middle School
Des Moines, Iowa

David M. Smith
Howard A. Eyer Middle School
Macungie, Pennsylvania

Derek Strohschneider
Plymouth Community
    Intermediate School
Plymouth, Massachusetts

Sallie Teames
Rosemont Middle School
Fort Worth, Texas

Gene Vitale
Parkland Middle School
McHenry, Illinois

Zenovia Young
Meyer Levin Junior
    High School (IS 285)
Brooklyn, New York

Contents

Cells and Heredity

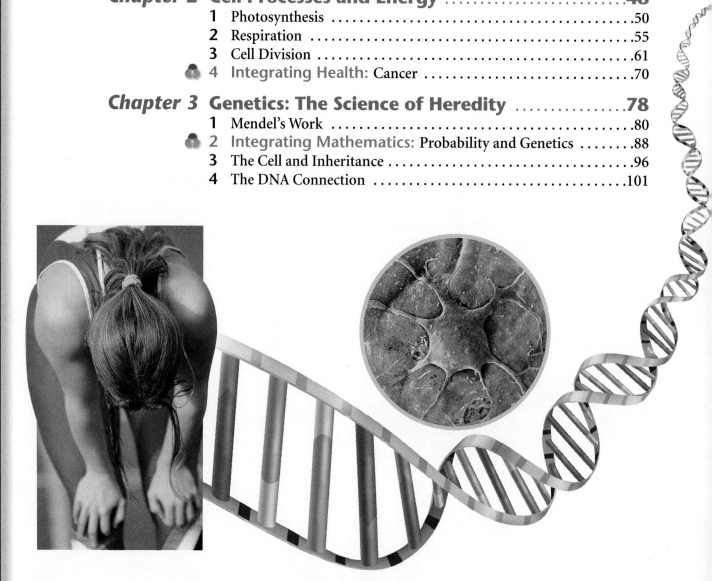

Activities

Interdisciplinary Activities

EXPLORING

Visual exploration of concepts

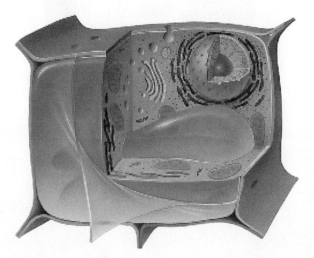

UNLOCKING THE
Secrets of Cells

It takes courage and dedication to follow your dreams. Lydia Villa-Komaroff learned that early in her career. She comes from a family of courageous Mexican American women. Her mother and both grandmothers were strong role models for her. Their support, as well as her father's, encouraged her to pursue a career in science. As a molecular biologist, Dr. Villa-Komaroff studies the role of proteins in the growth and development of living things.

In 1976, Lydia was part of a team conducting genetic engineering, a technique by which scientists transfer genes from one organism into another. Today, scientists use this technique to produce medicines, to treat diseases, and to improve crops. In the 1970s, genetic engineering was a new idea. It was feared by many people who thought it might have harmful results. In fact, the city where Lydia worked banned genetic engineering.

To continue her research, Lydia was forced to move her lab to another state. She spent a year away from many of her colleagues and friends. "It was a frustrating and lonely time," she recalls.

Lydia Villa-Komaroff is Vice President for Research at Northwestern University in Chicago, Illinois. She earned her Ph.D. in cell biology at the Massachusetts Institute of Technology. An avid skier and photographer, Lydia also loves to read, particularly mysteries and biographies.

But her hard work paid off. The ban was lifted, and soon after, Lydia helped discover a method for making insulin. Insulin is used to treat people who suffer from diabetes. Discovering a way to make insulin launched a new industry—biotechnology. It marked a personal triumph for Lydia. "Scientifically, that was the most exciting time of my life," she says. "There were any number of reasons to think we couldn't make insulin. But we planned it, we tried it, and no experiment before or since has worked so smoothly."

Many secrets of the human cell remain to be unlocked. Lydia hopes to provide some of the keys.

Talking With Dr. Lydia Villa-Komaroff

Q *How did you become interested in science?*

A My Mexican grandmother was very interested in natural history—plants in particular. She had books we used to look at with beautiful color pictures of plants. What really sparked my interest was just following her around, learning about the plants in our garden, and going out collecting wild spinach with her.

Q *What made you choose a career in biology?*

A I had an incredibly exciting developmental biology course in college. One time we camped out in the lab for 36 hours so we could watch frogs develop. Normally you study that in pictures in textbooks. But we were seeing it happen in real life. It was very exciting.

Q *What does a molecular biologist do?*

A We study development at the most basic level: what goes on within a cell. Think of the cell as a house, with many different parts—the foundation, the walls, the roof, and lots of bricks and wood and wiring. I'm interested in finding out how that structure gets built.

Dr. Villa-Komaroff explains her work to a group of students.

The gene for human insulin is isolated from its chromosome.

Plasmids, small circular rings of DNA, are removed from bacterial cells.

The insulin gene is inserted into the bacterial plasmid.

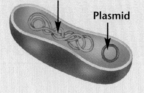

Bacterial chromosome

Plasmid

Dr. Villa-Komaroff pioneered the use of genetic engineering to produce human proteins, such as insulin.

Q *Is there a plan or blueprint for building a cell?*

A All the instructions are in the DNA. That is the material in the nucleus of a cell that carries the hereditary information that determines traits, such as your skin and hair color. The machinery, which is made up of proteins, comes in and reads bits of that information, which are called genes. Then DNA is copied into RNA, a message that travels out to the part of the cell where all the building activity goes on. Other proteins read it and start to produce the materials that the cell needs to work.

Q *Are proteins the tools or the structure of a cell?*

A Actually, they're both. Proteins are the building blocks of cells, like the bricks and mortar in a house. But they're also the machinery that builds cells, like hammers and drills. Proteins make up the cell, and build the cell.

Q *What other information does DNA contain?*

A It contains coding instructions to make sure the right information gets used at the right time. If you were building a house, you couldn't put up the roof before you had walls. In building a human, a certain amount of the head needs to be in place, for example, before you can make eyes. So it's very important for a cell to know what information to use, and when to use it.

Q *How do cells know when to start and stop building?*

A It's still not clear how that process is coordinated. There are certain genes that we understand very well. We know what signals they send the cell to say it's time to become a heart or a liver. But how does the cell know when to use that information, and when to stop? Those are some of the big questions that we're trying to answer.

4 *Plasmids with the insulin gene are taken up by the bacterial cells. The gene directs the cell to produce insulin.*

5 *The insulin is collected and used to treat people with diabetes.*

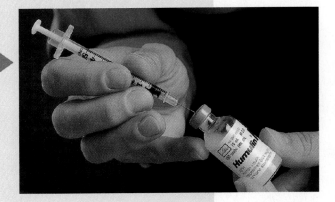

Q *What was the significance of the technique you developed to produce insulin?*

A People with diabetes used to be treated with pig insulin. But pig insulin is in short supply and therefore expensive. The work we did showed how to make a lot of insulin very cheaply, by growing it in bacteria. And it's human insulin.

Q *How did you trick the cell into making insulin?*

A We were able to isolate the gene with instructions for making insulin. We then inserted it into bacteria. Basically, we tricked the bacteria into thinking the gene was one of its own pieces of DNA. The bacteria then made the appropriate RNA, which was translated into insulin.

Q *Why didn't you give up when your research was banned?*

A We were doing very important work. To quit would have been to admit that the ban was right. We knew that others were doing the same research. You can't win a race if you quit.

Q *Were you ever discouraged?*

A There were times when I was discouraged, but I think that is true of anyone doing something where there is no guarantee of success. I think I've always approached a project with the idea that I have to give it my best shot.

Q *What advice would you give a person planning a science career?*

A You can't be entirely sure what you'll be able to do. The world is changing too fast. The important thing is to find something you like, and learn it very well. If you follow what you like, it may be different in 10 years, but it will be a logical extension of your own interests.

In Your Journal

As a young scientist, Lydia continued her research in genetic engineering in spite of obstacles that blocked her work. What does her action tell you about her as a person? Describe some character traits that you think would help a scientist to be successful. Why would those traits be important?

Cell Structure and Function

www.phschool.com

Egg-speriment With a Cell

Did you ever wonder how a baby chick can breathe when it's still inside the egg? The shell of the egg allows air through to reach the developing chick, while keeping out most other substances. Just as an egg needs to control which substances can enter, so too do all of the cells in your body.

In this chapter, you'll learn that all living things are made of cells—sometimes just one cell, sometimes trillions! You'll see the structures cells contain and how they work. You'll find out that important questions about life can be answered by understanding what happens in cells. You can start your discoveries right away by studying an everyday object that can serve as a model of a cell: an uncooked egg.

Your Goal To observe how various materials enter or leave a cell, using an egg as a model of the cell.

To complete this project, you will
◆ observe what happens when you soak an uncooked egg in vinegar, then in water, food coloring, salt water, and finally in a liquid of your choice
◆ measure the circumference of the egg every day, and graph your results
◆ explain the changes that your egg underwent
◆ follow the safety guidelines in Appendix A

Get Started Predict what might happen when you put an uncooked egg in vinegar for two days. How might other liquids affect an egg? Find a place where you can leave your egg undisturbed. Then begin your egg-speriment!

Check Your Progress You will be working on this project as you study this chapter. To keep your project on track, look for Check Your Progress boxes at the following points.

Section 1 Review, page 22: Make measurements and record data.
Section 2 Review, page 31: Experiment with different liquids.
Section 4 Review, page 44: Graph your data and draw conclusions.

Wrap Up At the end of the chapter (page 47), you will display your egg and share your results.

The thin shells of these eggs control what substances reach the developing chick inside.

SECTION
4 The Cell in Its Environment

Discover How Do Molecules Move?
Try This Diffusion in Action

1 Discovering Cells

DISCOVER • ACTIVITY • • •

Is Seeing Believing?

1. ✂ Cut a black-and-white photograph out of a page in a newspaper. With your eyes alone, closely examine the photo. Record your observations.

2. Examine the same photo with a hand lens. Record your observations.

3. Place the photo on the stage of a microscope. Use the clips to hold the photo in place. Shine a light down on the photo. Focus the microscope on part of the photo. (See Appendix B for instructions on using the microscope.) Record your observations.

Think It Over
Observing What did you see in the photo with the hand lens and the microscope that you could not see with your eyes alone?

GUIDE FOR READING

◆ How did the invention of the microscope contribute to scientists' understanding of living things?

◆ What is the cell theory?

◆ How does a lens magnify an object?

Reading Tip As you read, make a flowchart showing how the contributions of several scientists led to the development of the cell theory.

A majestic oak tree shades you on a sunny day at the park. A lumbering rhinoceros wanders over to look at you at the zoo. After a rain storm, mushrooms sprout in the damp woods. What do you think an oak tree, a rhinoceros, and a mushroom have in common? You might say that they are all living things. What makes these living things—and all other living things—alike? If you say they are made of cells, you are correct.

Cells are the basic units of structure and function in living things. Just as bricks are the building blocks of a house or school, cells are the building blocks of life. Since you are alive, you are made of cells, too. Look closely at the skin on your arm. No

Figure 1 This building is made up of individual bricks. Similarly, all living things are made up of individual cells.

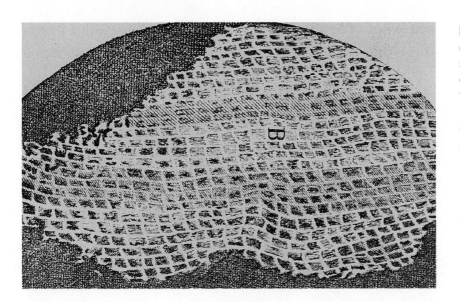

Figure 2 Robert Hooke made this drawing of dead cork cells that he saw through his microscope. Hooke called these structures *cells* because they reminded him of tiny rooms. *Comparing and Contrasting How are cells similar to the bricks in a building? How are they different?*

matter how hard you look with your eyes alone, you won't be able to see individual skin cells. The reason is that cells are very small. In fact, one square centimeter of your skin's surface contains over 100,000 cells.

First Sightings of Cells

Until the late 1500s there was no way to see cells. No one even knew that cells existed. Around 1590, the invention of the microscope enabled people to look at very small objects. **The invention of the microscope made it possible for people to discover and learn about cells.**

A **microscope** is an instrument that makes small objects look larger. Some microscopes do this by using lenses to focus light. The lenses used in light microscopes are similar to the clear curved pieces of glass used in eyeglasses. A simple microscope contains only one lens. A hand lens is an example of a simple microscope. A light microscope that has more than one lens is called a **compound microscope.**

Robert Hooke One of the first people to observe cells was the English scientist and inventor Robert Hooke. In 1663, Hooke observed the structure of a thin slice of cork using a compound microscope he had built himself. Cork, the bark of the cork oak tree, is made up of cells that are no longer alive. To Hooke, the cork looked like tiny rectangular rooms, which he called *cells*. Hooke described his observations this way: "These pores, or cells, were not very deep. . . ." You can see Hooke's drawings of cork cells in Figure 2. What most amazed Hooke was how many cells the cork contained. He calculated that in a cubic inch there were about twelve hundred million cells—a number he described as "most incredible."

Anton van Leeuwenhoek   At about the same time that Robert Hooke made his discovery, Anton van Leeuwenhoek (LAY vun hook) also began to observe tiny objects with microscopes. Leeuwenhoek was a Dutch businessman and amateur scientist who made his own lenses. He then used the lenses to construct simple microscopes.

One of the things Leeuwenhoek looked at was water from a pond. He was surprised to see one-celled organisms, which he called *animalcules* (an uh MAL kyoolz), meaning "little animals."

SCIENCE & *History*

The Microscope— Improvements Over Time

The discovery of cells would not have been possible without the microscope. Microscopes have been improved in many ways over the last 400 years.

1660
Hooke's Compound Microscope

Robert Hooke improved on the compound microscope. The stand at the right holds oil for a flame, which shines light on the specimen under the microscope.

1600   **1750**

1590
First Compound Microscope

Hans Janssen and his son Zacharias, Dutch eyeglass makers, made one of the first compound microscopes. Their microscope was simply a tube with a lens at each end.

1683
Leeuwenhoek's Simple Microscope

Although Leeuwenhoek's simple microscope used only one tiny lens, it could magnify a specimen up to 266 times. Leeuwenhoek was the first person to see many one-celled organisms, including bacteria.

Leeuwenhoek looked at many other specimens, including scrapings from teeth. When Leeuwenhoek looked at the scrapings, he became the first person to see the tiny single-celled organisms that are now called bacteria. Leeuwenhoek's many discoveries caught the attention of other researchers. Many other people began to use microscopes to see what secrets they could uncover about cells.

✓ *Checkpoint* *How does a simple microscope differ from a compound microscope?*

In Your Journal

Choose one of the microscopes. Write an advertisement for it that might appear in a popular science magazine. Be creative. Emphasize the microscope's usefulness or describe the wonders that can be seen with it.

1933
Transmission Electron Microscope (TEM)

The German physicist Ernst Ruska created the first electron microscope. TEMs make images by sending electrons through a very thinly sliced specimen. They can only examine dead specimens, but are very useful for viewing internal cell structures. TEMs can magnify a specimen up to 500,000 times.

1981
Scanning Tunneling Microscope (STM)

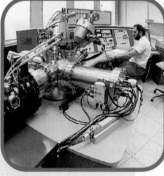

A STM measures electrons that leak, or "tunnel," from the surface of a specimen. With a STM, scientists can see individual molecules on the outer layer of a cell. STMs can magnify a specimen up to 1,000,000 times.

1900 ———————————————————————————————— **2050**

1886
Modern Compound Light Microscope

German scientists Ernst Abbé and Carl Zeiss made a compound light microscope similar to this one. The horseshoe stand keeps the microscope steady. The mirror at the bottom focuses light up through the specimen. Modern compound light microscopes can magnify a specimen up to 1,000 times.

1965
Scanning Electron Microscope (SEM)

The first commercial SEM is produced. This microscope sends a beam of electrons over the surface of a specimen, rather than through it. The result is a detailed three-dimensional image of the specimen's surface. SEMs can magnify a specimen up to 150,000 times.

Plant cells

Animal cells

Figure 3 The cell theory states that all living things, including this giraffe and the leaf it is eating, are composed of cells.

The Cell Theory

Over the years, scientists have continued to use and improve the microscope. They have discovered that all kinds of living things were made up of cells. In 1838 a German scientist named Matthias Schleiden (SHLY dun) concluded that all plants are made of cells. He based this conclusion on his own research and on the research of others before him. The next year, another German scientist, Theodor Schwann, concluded that all animals are also made up of cells. Thus, stated Schwann, all living things are made up of cells.

Schleiden and Schwann had made an important discovery about living things. However, they didn't understand where cells came from. Until their time, most people thought that living things could come from nonliving matter. In 1855, a German doctor, Rudolf Virchow (FUR koh) proposed that new cells are formed only from existing cells. "All cells come from cells," wrote Virchow.

The observations and conclusions of Hooke, Leeuwenhoek, Schleiden, Schwann, Virchow, and others led to the development of the **cell theory.** The cell theory is a widely accepted explanation of the relationship between cells and living things. **The cell theory states:**

◆ **All living things are composed of cells.**

◆ **Cells are the basic unit of structure and function in living things.**

◆ **All cells are produced from other cells.**

The cell theory holds true for all living things, no matter how big or how small. Since cells are common to all living things, they can provide information about all life. Because all cells come from other cells, scientists can study cells to learn about growth, reproduction, and all other functions that living things perform.

Checkpoint *What did Schleiden and Schwann conclude about cells?*

How a Light Microscope Works

INTEGRATING PHYSICS Microscopes use lenses to make small objects look larger. But simply enlarging a small object is not useful unless you can see the details clearly. For a microscope to be useful to a scientist, it must combine two important properties—magnification and resolution.

Magnification The first property, **magnification,** is the ability to make things look larger than they are. **The lens or lenses in a light microscope magnify an object by bending the light that passes through them.** If you examine a hand lens, you will see that the glass lens is curved, not flat. The center of the lens is thicker than the edges. A lens with this curved shape is called a **convex lens.** Look at Figure 4 to see how light is bent by a convex lens. The light passing through the sides of the lens bends inward. When this light hits the eye, the eye sees the object as larger than it really is.

Because a compound microscope uses more than one lens, it can magnify an object even more. Light passes through a specimen and then through two lenses. Figure 4 also shows the path that light takes through a compound microscope. The first lens near the specimen magnifies the object. Then a second lens near the eye further magnifies the enlarged image. The total magnification of the microscope is equal to the magnifications of the two lenses multiplied together. For example, if the first lens has a magnification of 10 and the second lens has a magnification of 40, then the total magnification of the microscope is 400.

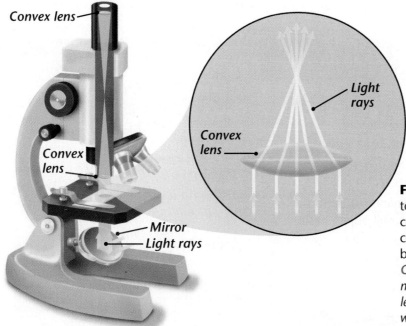

Figure 4 Microscopes use lenses to make objects look larger. A compound microscope has two convex lenses. Each convex lens bends light, making the image larger. *Calculating If one lens has a magnification of 10 and the other lens has a magnification of 50, what would the total magnification be?*

Resolution To create a useful image, a microscope must also help you see individual parts clearly. The ability to clearly distinguish the individual parts of an object is called **resolution.** Resolution is another term for the sharpness of an image.

For example, when you use your eyes to look at a photo printed in a newspaper, it looks like a complete picture from one side to the other. That picture, however, is really made up of a collection of small dots. To the unaided eye, two tiny dots close together appear as one. If you put the photo under a microscope, however, you can see the dots. You see the dots not only because they are magnified but also because the microscope improves resolution. Good resolution—being able to see fine detail—is not needed when you are reading the newspaper. But it is just what you need when you study cells.

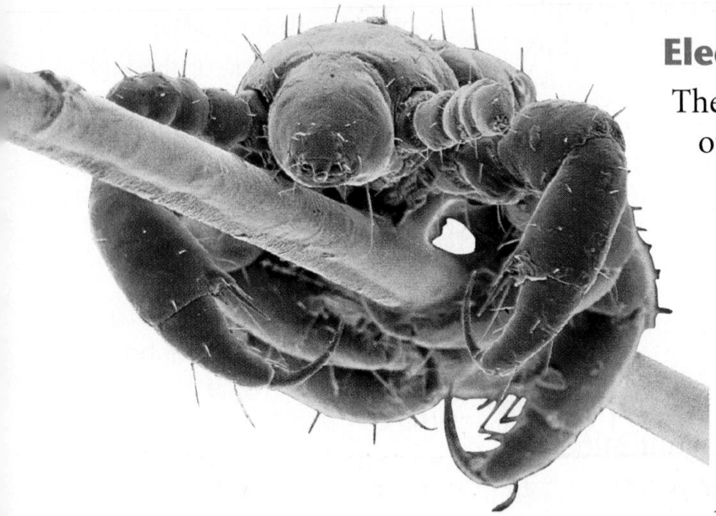

Figure 5 This head louse, shown clinging to a human hair, was photographed through a scanning electron microscope. It has been magnified to about 80 times its actual size.

Electron Microscopes

The microscopes used by Hooke, Leeuwenhoek, and other early researchers were all light microscopes. Since the 1930s, scientists have developed different types of electron microscopes. Electron microscopes use a beam of electrons instead of light to examine a specimen. Electrons are tiny particles that are smaller than atoms. Because they use tiny electrons to produce images, the resolution of electron microscopes is much better than the resolution of light microscopes. As the technology of microscopes keeps improving, scientists will continue to learn more about the structure and function of cells.

Section 1 Review

1. How did the invention of the microscope affect scientists' understanding of living things?
2. Explain the three main ideas of the cell theory.
3. How does a compound microscope use lenses to magnify an object?
4. Explain why both magnification and resolution are important when viewing a small object with a microscope.
5. **Thinking Critically Applying Concepts** Why do scientists learn more about cells each time the microscope is improved?

Check Your Progress **CHAPTER PROJECT 1**
By now you should have started your egg-speriment by soaking an uncooked egg in vinegar. Leave your egg in the vinegar for at least two days. Each day, rinse your egg in water and measure its circumference. Record all of your observations. (*Hint:* Handle the egg gently. If your egg breaks, don't give up or throw away your data. Simply start again with another egg and keep investigating.)

SECTION
② Looking Inside Cells

DISCOVER •• ACTIVITY •••

How Large Are Cells?

1. Look at the organism in the photo. The organism is an ameba, a large single-celled organism. This type of ameba is about 1 millimeter (mm) long.

2. Multiply your height in meters by 1,000 to get your height in millimeters. How many amebas would you have to stack end-to-end to equal your height?

3. Many of the cells in your body are about 0.01 mm long—one hundredth the size of an ameba. How many body cells would you have to stack end-to-end to equal your height?

Think It Over

Inferring Look at a metric ruler to see how small 1 mm is. Now imagine a distance one-hundredth as long, or 0.01 mm. Why can't you see your body's cells without the aid of a microscope?

Imagine you're in California standing next to a giant redwood tree. You have to bend your head way back to see the top of the tree. Some of these trees are over 112 meters tall and more than 10 meters in circumference! How do redwoods grow so large? How do they carry out all the functions necessary to stay alive?

To answer these questions, and to learn many other things about living things, you are about to take an imaginary journey. It will be quite an unusual trip. You will be traveling inside a living redwood tree, visiting its tiny cells. On your trip you will observe some of the structures found in plant cells. You will also learn about some of the differences between plant and animal cells.

GUIDE FOR READING

◆ What role do the cell membrane and nucleus play in the cell?

◆ What functions do other organelles in the cell perform?

◆ How do bacterial cells differ from plant and animal cells?

Reading Tip Before you read, preview *Exploring Plant and Animal Cells* on pages 26–27. Make a list of any unfamiliar terms. As you read, write a definition for each term.

◀ A giant redwood tree

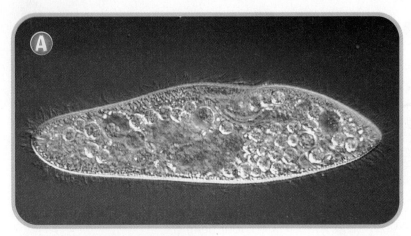

Figure 6 All cells have cell membranes, but not all cells have cell walls. **A.** The cell membrane of this single-celled paramecium controls what substances enter and leave the cell. **B.** The cell walls of these onion root cells have been stained green so you can see them clearly. Cell walls protect and support plant cells.

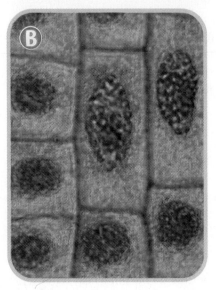

As you will discover on your journey, inside a cell are even smaller structures. These tiny cell structures, called **organelles,** carry out specific functions within the cell. Just as your stomach, lungs, and heart have different functions in your body, each organelle has a different function within the cell. You can see the organelles found in plant and animal cells in *Exploring Plant and Animal Cells* on pages 26 and 27. Now it's time to hop aboard your imaginary ship and prepare to enter a typical plant cell.

Cell Wall

Entering a plant's cell is a bit difficult. First you must pass through the cell wall. The **cell wall** is a rigid layer of nonliving material that surrounds the cells of plants and some other organisms. The cell wall is made of a tough, yet flexible, material called cellulose. If you think of a stalk of celery, you will have a good idea of what cellulose is. Celery contains a lot of cellulose.

The cells of plants and some other organisms have cell walls. In contrast, the cells of animals and some other organisms lack cell walls. A plant's cell wall helps to protect and support the cell. In woody plants, the cell walls are very rigid. This is why giant redwood trees can stand so tall. Each cell wall in the tree adds strength to the tree. Although the cell wall is stiff, many materials, including water and oxygen, can pass through the cell wall quite easily. So sail on through the cell wall and enter the cell.

Checkpoint *What is the function of the cell wall?*

Cell Membrane

As you pass through the cell wall, the next structure you encounter is the **cell membrane.** All cells have cell membranes. In cells with cell walls, the cell membrane is located just inside the cell wall. In other cells, the cell membrane forms the outside boundary that separates the cell from its environment.

As your ship nears the edge of the cell membrane, you notice that there are tiny openings, or pores, in the cell membrane. You steer toward an opening. Suddenly, your ship narrowly misses being struck by a chunk of waste material passing out of the cell. **You have discovered one of the cell membrane's main functions: the cell membrane controls what substances come into and out of a cell.**

Everything the cell needs—from food to oxygen—enters the cell through the cell membrane. Harmful waste products leave the cell through the cell membrane. For a cell to survive, the cell membrane must allow these materials to pass into and out of the cell. In a sense, the cell membrane is like a window screen. The screen keeps insects out of a room. But holes in the screen allow air to enter and leave the room.

Nucleus

As you sail inside the cell, a large, oval structure comes into view. This structure, called the **nucleus** (NOO klee us), acts as the "brain" of the cell. **You can think of the nucleus as the cell's control center, directing all of the cell's activities.**

Nuclear Membrane   Notice in Figure 7 that the nucleus is surrounded by a nuclear membrane. Just as the cell membrane protects the cell, the nuclear membrane protects the nucleus. Materials pass in and out of the nucleus through small openings, or pores, in the nuclear membrane. So aim for that pore just ahead and carefully glide into the nucleus.

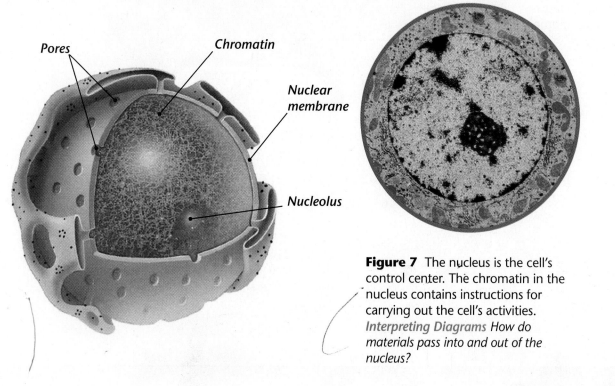

Pores

Chromatin

Nuclear membrane

Nucleolus

Figure 7 The nucleus is the cell's control center. The chromatin in the nucleus contains instructions for carrying out the cell's activities. *Interpreting Diagrams* How do materials pass into and out of the nucleus?

EXPLORING Plant and Animal Cells

On these pages, you can compare structures found in two kinds of cells: plant cells and animal cells. As you study these cells, remember that they are generalized cells. In living organisms, cells vary somewhat in shape and structure.

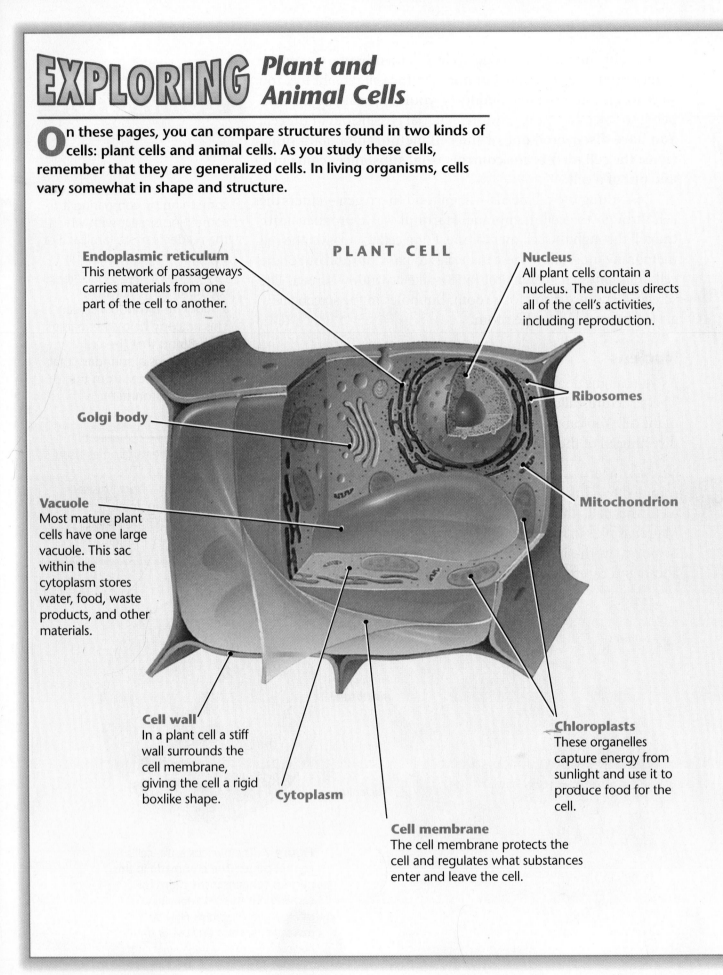

PLANT CELL

Endoplasmic reticulum
This network of passageways carries materials from one part of the cell to another.

Nucleus
All plant cells contain a nucleus. The nucleus directs all of the cell's activities, including reproduction.

Ribosomes

Golgi body

Mitochondrion

Vacuole
Most mature plant cells have one large vacuole. This sac within the cytoplasm stores water, food, waste products, and other materials.

Cell wall
In a plant cell a stiff wall surrounds the cell membrane, giving the cell a rigid boxlike shape.

Cytoplasm

Chloroplasts
These organelles capture energy from sunlight and use it to produce food for the cell.

Cell membrane
The cell membrane protects the cell and regulates what substances enter and leave the cell.

Vacuole
Some animal cells have vacuoles that store food, water, wastes, and other materials.

ANIMAL CELL

Ribosomes
These small structures function as factories to produce proteins. Ribosomes may be attached to the outer surfaces of the endoplasmic reticulum, or they may float free in the cytoplasm.

Golgi body
The Golgi bodies receive materials from the endoplasmic reticulum and send them to other parts of the cell. They also release materials outside the cell.

Cytoplasm
The cytoplasm is the area between the cell membrane and the nucleus. It contains a gel-like fluid in which many different organelles are found.

Endoplasmic reticulum

Nucleus
Almost all animal cells contain a nucleus. The nucleus directs all of the cell's activities, including reproduction.

Mitochondria
Most of the cell's energy is produced within these rod-shaped organelles.

Cell membrane
Since an animal cell does not have a cell wall, the cell membrane forms a barrier between the cytoplasm and the environment outside the cell.

Lysosomes
These small organelles found in many animal cells contain chemicals that break down food particles and worn-out cell parts.

Chromatin You might wonder how the nucleus "knows" how to direct the cell. The answer lies in those thin strands floating directly ahead in the nucleus. These strands, called **chromatin,** contain the genetic material, the instructions that direct the functions of a cell. For example, the instructions in the chromatin ensure that leaf cells grow and divide to form more leaf cells. The genetic material is passed on to each new cell when an existing cell divides. You'll learn more about how cells divide in Chapter 2.

Nucleolus As you prepare to leave the nucleus, you spot a small object floating by. This structure, the nucleolus, is where ribosomes are made. Ribosomes are the organelles where proteins are produced.

☑ Checkpoint *Where in the nucleus is genetic material found?*

Organelles in the Cytoplasm

As you leave the nucleus, you find yourself in the **cytoplasm,** the region between the cell membrane and the nucleus. Your ship floats in a clear, thick, gel-like fluid. The fluid in the cytoplasm is constantly moving, so your ship does not need to propel itself. Many cell organelles are found in the cytoplasm. **The organelles function to produce energy, build and transport needed materials, and store and recycle wastes.**

Mitochondria As you pass into the cytoplasm, you see rod-shaped structures looming ahead. These organelles are called **mitochondria** (my tuh KAHN dree uh) (singular *mitochondrion*). Mitochondria are called the "powerhouses" of the cell because they produce most of the energy the cell needs to carry out its functions. Muscle cells and other very active cells have large numbers of mitochondria.

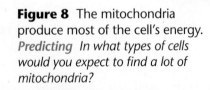

Figure 8 The mitochondria produce most of the cell's energy. *Predicting In what types of cells would you expect to find a lot of mitochondria?*

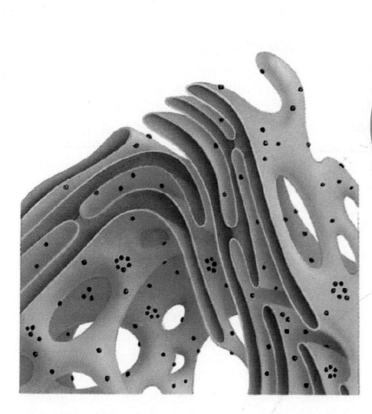

Figure 9 The endoplasmic reticulum is a passageway through which proteins and other materials move within the cell. The spots on the outside of the endoplasmic reticulum are ribosomes, structures that produce proteins.

Endoplasmic Reticulum As you sail farther into the cytoplasm, you find yourself in a maze of passageways called the **endoplasmic reticulum** (en duh PLAZ mik rih TIK yuh lum). These passageways carry proteins and other materials from one part of the cell to another.

Ribosomes Attached to the outer surface of the endoplasmic reticulum are small grainlike bodies called **ribosomes.** Other ribosomes are found floating in the cytoplasm. Ribosomes function as factories to produce proteins. The ribosomes release some proteins through the wall of the endoplasmic reticulum. From the interior of the endoplasmic reticulum, the proteins will be transported to the Golgi bodies.

Golgi Bodies As you move through the endoplasmic reticulum, you see structures that look like a flattened collection of sacs and tubes. These structures, called **Golgi bodies,** can be thought of as the cell's mailroom. The Golgi bodies receive proteins and other newly formed materials from the endoplasmic reticulum, package them, and distribute them to other parts of the cell. The Golgi bodies also release materials outside the cell.

Chloroplasts Have you noticed the many large green structures floating in the cytoplasm? Only the cells of plants and some other organisms have these structures. These organelles, called **chloroplasts,** capture energy from sunlight and use it to produce food for the cell. It is the chloroplasts that give plants their green color. You will learn more about chloroplasts in Chapter 2.

Gelatin Cell

Make your own model of a cell.

1. Dissolve a packet of colorless gelatin in warm water. Pour the gelatin into a rectangular pan (for a plant cell) or a round pan (for an animal cell).

2. Choose different materials that resemble each of the cell structures found in the cell you are modeling. Insert these materials into the gelatin before it begins to solidify.

Making Models On a sheet of paper, develop a key that identifies each cell structure in your model. Describe the function of each structure.

Vacuoles Steer past the chloroplasts and head for that large, round, water-filled sac floating in the cytoplasm. This sac, called a **vacuole** (VAK yoo ohl), is the storage area of the cell. Most plant cells have one large vacuole. Some animal cells do not have vacuoles; others do.

Vacuoles store food and other materials needed by the cell. Vacuoles can also store waste products. Most of the water in plant cells is stored in vacuoles. When the vacuoles are full of water, they make the cell plump and firm. Without much water in the vacuoles, the plant wilts.

Lysosomes Your journey through the cell is almost over. Before you leave, take another look around you. If you carefully swing your ship around the vacuole, you may be lucky enough to see a lysosome. **Lysosomes** (LY suh sohmz) are small round structures that contain chemicals that break down large food particles into smaller ones. Lysosomes also break down old cell parts and release the substances so they can be used again. In this sense, you can think of the lysosomes as the cell's cleanup crew. Lysosomes are more common in animal cells than in plant cells.

Although lysosomes contain powerful chemicals, you need not worry about your ship's safety. The membrane around a lysosome keeps these harsh chemicals from escaping and breaking down the rest of the cell.

Bacterial Cells

The plant and animal cells that you just learned about are very different from the bacterial cell you see in Figure 10. First, bacterial cells are usually smaller than plant or animal cells. A human skin cell, for example, is about 10 times as large as an average bacterial cell.

There are several other ways in which bacterial cells are different from plant and animal cells. **While a bacterial cell does have a cell wall and a cell membrane, it does not contain a nucleus.** The bacterial cell's genetic material, which looks like a thick, tangled string, is found in the cytoplasm. Bacterial cells contain ribosomes, but none of the other organelles found in plant or animal cells.

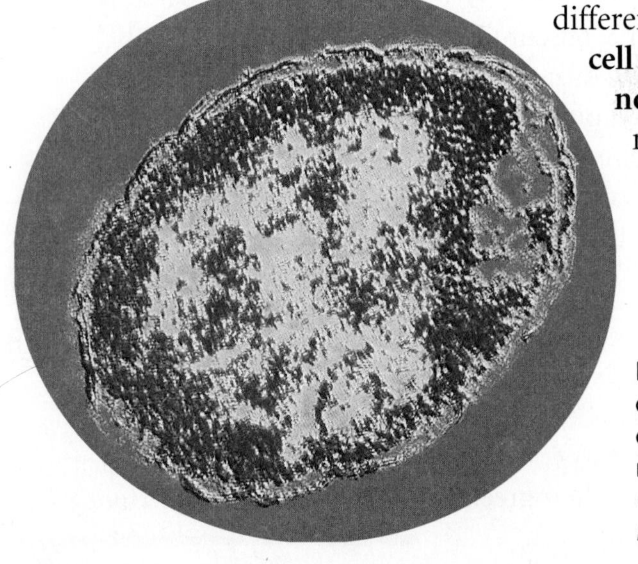

Figure 10 This single-celled organism is a type of bacteria. The cells of bacteria do not contain a nucleus or some other organelles. *Observing Where is the genetic material in a bacterial cell found?*

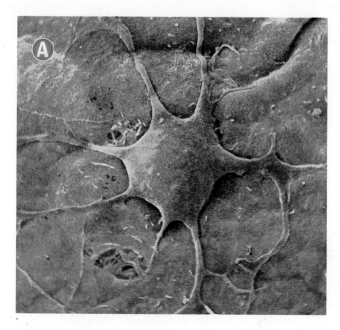

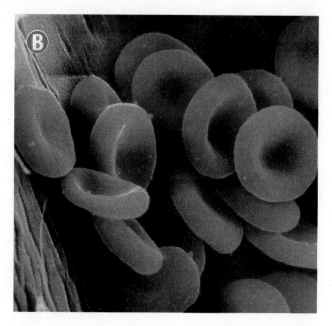

Specialized Cells

Unlike bacteria and other single-celled organisms, plants, animals (including yourself), and other organisms contain many cells. In a many-celled organism, the cells are often quite different from each other in size and structure. Think of the different parts of your body. You have skin, bones, muscles, blood, a brain, a liver, a stomach, and so on. Each of these body parts carries out a very different function. Yet all of these body parts are made up of cells. Figure 11 shows two examples of different kinds of cells in your body. The structure of each kind of cell is suited to the unique function it carries out within the organism.

Figure 11 Your body contains a variety of different types of cells. **A.** Nerve cells have long projections through which messages are sent throughout the body. **B.** Red blood cells are thin and flexible, which allows them to fit through tiny blood vessels.

Section 2 Review

1. What is the function of the cell membrane?
2. Why is the nucleus sometimes called the control center of the cell?
3. Name two plant cell parts that are not found in animal cells. What is the function of each part?
4. How do the cells of bacteria differ from those of other organisms?
5. **Thinking Critically Comparing and Contrasting** Compare the functions of the cell wall in a plant cell and the cell membrane in an animal cell. How are the functions of the two structures similar and different?

Check Your Progress

CHAPTER PROJECT 1

At this point, you should soak your egg for one or two days in water, then in water with food coloring, then in salt water, and finally in another liquid of your choice. Continue to rinse your egg and measure and record its circumference every day. Your egg should be going through some amazing changes in appearance.

A Magnified View Of Life

In this lab, you will use your observation skills to compare plant and animal cells.

Problem

How are plant and animal cells alike and different?

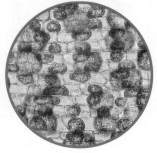

Materials

plastic dropper
water
microscope slide   *Elodea* leaf
microscope   forceps
colored pencils   coverslip
prepared slide of animal cells

Procedure

1. Before you start this lab, read *Using the Microscope* (Appendix B) on pages 190–191. Be sure you know how to use a microscope correctly and safely.

Part 1 Observing Plant Cells

2. Use a plastic dropper to place a drop of water in the center of a slide. **CAUTION:** *Slides and coverslips are fragile. Handle them carefully. Do not touch broken glass.*

3. With forceps, remove a leaf from an *Elodea* plant. Place the leaf in the drop of water on the slide. Make sure that the leaf is flat. If it is folded, straighten it with the forceps.

4. Holding a coverslip by its edges, slowly lower it onto the drop of water and *Elodea* leaf. If any air bubbles form, tap the slide gently to get rid of them.

5. Use a microscope to examine the *Elodea* leaf under low power. Then, carefully switch to high power.

6. Observe the cells of the *Elodea* leaf. Draw and label what you see, including the colors of the cell parts. Record the magnification.

7. Discard the *Elodea* leaf as directed by your teacher. Carefully clean and dry your slide and coverslip. Wash your hands thoroughly.

Part 2 Observing Animal Cells

8. Obtain a prepared slide of animal cells. The cells on the slide have been stained with an artificial color.

9. Observe the animal cells with a microscope under both low and high power. Draw and label the cell parts that you see. Record the magnification.

Analyze and Conclude

1. How are plant and animal cells alike?
2. How are plant and animal cells different?
3. What natural color appeared in the plant cells? What structures give the plant cells this color?
4. **Think About It** Why is it important to record your observations while you are examining a specimen?

More to Explore

Observe other prepared slides of animal cells. Look for ways that animal cells differ from each other. Obtain your teacher's permission before carrying out these observations.

SECTION 3 Chemical Compounds in Cells

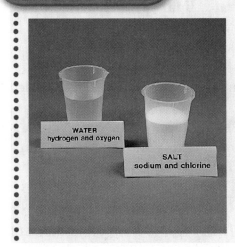

WATER
hydrogen and oxygen

SALT
sodium and chlorine

What Is a Compound?

1. Your teacher will provide you with containers filled with various substances. All of the substances are chemical compounds.

2. Examine each substance. Read the label on each container to learn what each substance is made of.

Think It Over

Forming Operational Definitions Write a definition of what you think a chemical compound is.

I f cells are the basic building blocks of living things, then what substances are the basic building blocks of cells? In what ways are the basic building blocks of cells similar to those that make up other things around you? In this section you will explore how the substances that make up living cells differ from those that make up nonliving things.

Elements and Compounds

Think about the air around you. You probably know that air is a mixture of gases, including oxygen and nitrogen. Oxygen and nitrogen are examples of elements. An **element** is any substance that cannot be broken down into simpler substances. The smallest unit of an element is called an **atom.** An element is made up of only one kind of atom. The elements found in living things include carbon, hydrogen, oxygen, nitrogen, phosphorus, and sulfur.

When two or more elements combine chemically they form a **compound.** Water, for example, is a compound made up of the elements hydrogen and oxygen. The smallest unit of most compounds is called a **molecule.** Each water molecule is made up of two hydrogen atoms and one oxygen atom.

◆ What are the four main kinds of organic molecules in living things?

◆ How is water important to the function of cells?

Reading Tip As you read, make a table of the main types of organic molecules and where in the cell each one is found.

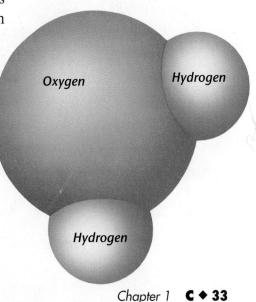

Oxygen

Hydrogen

Hydrogen

The structure of a water molecule ▶

Organic and Inorganic Compounds

Many of the compounds found in living things contain the element carbon, which is usually combined with other elements. Most compounds that contain carbon are called **organic compounds.**

The most important groups of organic compounds found in living things are carbohydrates, lipids, proteins, and nucleic acids. As you may know, many of these compounds are found in the foods you eat. This is not surprising, since the foods you eat come from living things.

Compounds that don't contain the element carbon are called **inorganic compounds.** One exception to this definition is carbon dioxide. Although carbon dioxide contains carbon, it is classified as an inorganic compound. Other inorganic compounds include water and sodium chloride, or table salt.

Carbohydrates

A **carbohydrate** is an energy-rich organic compound made of the elements carbon, hydrogen, and oxygen. Sugars and starches are examples of carbohydrates.

Sugars are produced during the food-making process that takes place in plants. Foods such as fruits and some vegetables are high in sugar content. Sugar molecules can combine, forming large molecules called starches. Plant cells store excess energy in molecules of starch. Many foods that come from plants contain starch. These foods include potatoes, noodles, rice, and bread. When you eat these foods, your body breaks down the starch into glucose, a sugar, which your cells can use to produce energy.

Carbohydrates are important components of some cell parts. The cellulose found in the cell walls of plants is a type of carbohydrate. Carbohydrates are also found in cell membranes.

Figure 12 These potatoes contain large amounts of starch, a type of carbohydrate. The blue grains you see in the closeup are starch granules in a potato. The grains have been colored blue to make them easier to see. *Classifying* What types of carbohydrates combine to form starches?

Figure 13 This bird's feathers are made up mainly of proteins. Proteins are important components of the cell membrane and many of the cell's organelles.

Proteins

What do a bird's feathers, a spider's web, and your fingernails have in common? All of these substances are made mainly of proteins. **Proteins** are large organic molecules made of carbon, hydrogen, oxygen, nitrogen, and, in some cases, sulfur. Foods that are high in protein include meat, eggs, fish, nuts, and beans.

Cells use proteins for many different things. For instance, proteins form parts of cell membranes. Proteins also make up many of the organelles within the cell. Certain cells in your body use proteins to build body parts such as hair.

Protein Structure Protein molecules are made up of smaller molecules called **amino acids.** Although there are only 20 common amino acids, cells can combine them in different ways to form thousands of different proteins. The kinds of amino acids and the order in which they link together determine the type of protein that forms. You can think of the 20 amino acids as being like the 26 letters of the alphabet. Those 26 letters can form thousands of words. The letters you use and their order determine the words you form. Even a change in one letter, for example, from *rice* to *mice*, creates a new word. Similarly, changes in the type or order of amino acids result in a different protein.

Enzymes An **enzyme** is a type of protein that speeds up a chemical reaction in a living thing. Without enzymes, many chemical reactions that are necessary for life would either take too long, or not occur at all. For example, enzymes in your saliva speed up the digestion of food by breaking down starches into sugars in your mouth.

☑ *Checkpoint* *What is the role of enzymes?*

What's That Taste?

Use this activity to discover one role that enzymes play in your body.

1. Put an unsalted soda cracker in your mouth. Chew it up, but do not swallow. Note what the cracker tastes like.

2. Continue to chew the cracker for a few minutes, mixing it well with your saliva. Note how the taste of the cracker changes.

Inferring Soda crackers are made up mainly of starch, with little sugar. How can you account for the change in taste after you chewed the cracker for a few minutes?

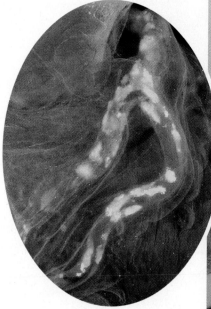

Figure 14 Cholesterol is a lipid found in foods that come from animals. Excess cholesterol in your diet can cause blood vessels to become blocked, as shown at the left.
Making Judgments Why is it a good idea to limit the amount of cholesterol you eat?

Lipids

Have you ever seen a cook trim the fat from a piece of meat before cooking it? The cook is trimming away a lipid. Fats, oils, and waxes are all **lipids.** Like carbohydrates, lipids are energy-rich organic compounds made of carbon, hydrogen, and oxygen.

Lipids contain even more energy than carbohydrates. Cells store energy in lipids for later use. For example, during winter a dormant bear lives on the energy stored as fat within its cells.

INTEGRATING HEALTH One lipid that you may have heard about is cholesterol (kuh LES tuh rawl). Cholesterol is an important component of animal cell membranes. Your body requires a certain amount of this lipid. Your liver normally produces enough cholesterol to meet your body's needs. However, many of the foods you eat also contain cholesterol. Excess amounts of cholesterol can collect along the walls of blood vessels and block the flow of blood. For this reason, many nutritionists recommend that people limit their intake of foods that are high in cholesterol. Foods that come from animals, such as meat, cheese, and eggs, are high in cholesterol.

Nucleic Acids

Nucleic acids are very large organic molecules made of carbon, oxygen, hydrogen, nitrogen, and phosphorus. Nucleic acids contain the instructions that cells need to carry out all the functions of life.

There are two kinds of nucleic acids. Deoxyribonucleic acid (dee ahk see ry boh noo KLEE ik), or **DNA,** is the genetic material that carries information about an organism that is passed from parent to offspring. The information in DNA also directs all of the cell's functions. Most of the DNA in a cell is found in the chromatin in the nucleus. Ribonucleic acid (ry boh noo KLEE ik), or **RNA,** plays an important role in the production of proteins. RNA is found in the cytoplasm, as well as in the nucleus.

Water and Living Things

Did you know that water makes up about two thirds of your body? Water plays many vital roles in cells. For example, most chemical reactions that take place in cells can occur only when substances are dissolved in water. **Without water, most chemical reactions within cells could not take place.** Also, water molecules themselves take part in many chemical reactions in cells.

Water also helps cells keep their size and shape. In fact, a cell without water would be like a balloon without air. In addition, because water changes temperature slowly, it helps keep the temperature of cells from changing rapidly. In the next section, you'll learn about the role that water plays in carrying substances into and out of cells.

Figure 15 Water is essential for all living things to survive. The cells of these tulips need water to function.

Section 3 Review

1. Name the four main groups of organic molecules in living things. Describe the function of each type of molecule.
2. What roles does water play in cells?
3. How are elements related to compounds?
4. **Thinking Critically** **Predicting** Suppose a cell did not have a supply of amino acids and could not produce them. What effect might this have on the cell?

Science at Home

With family members, look at the "Nutrition Facts" labels on a variety of food products. Identify foods that contain large amounts of the following organic compounds: carbohydrates, proteins, and fats. Discuss with your family what elements each of these compounds are made of and what roles they play in cells and in your body.

What's in Your Lunch?

You might be surprised to learn that chemists help the food industry obey the law. Most foods must carry labels listing the types of compounds they contain. In this lab, you can find out how chemists obtain that kind of information.

Problem

Which foods contain starches and lipids?

Skills Focus

predicting, drawing conclusions

Materials

cornstarch, 1 gram   water
food samples   plastic cups
plastic stirrers   plastic dropper
plastic graduated cylinder
vegetable oil, 5 milliliters
iodine solution in dropper bottle
5-centimeter squares of brown paper

Procedure

Part 1 Identifying Tests for Starches and Lipids

1. Write a prediction describing one or more differences you expect to observe between starches and lipids. Then copy the data table into your notebook, adding at least five blank rows.

2. Obtain plastic cups containing samples of cornstarch (a starch) and vegetable oil (a lipid).

3. Take a pinch of cornstarch between your thumb and index finger. Feel the substance's texture, and record your observation. Wash your hands to remove the cornstarch.

4. Take a few drops of vegetable oil between your thumb and index finger. Feel the substance's texture, and record your observation. Wash your hands to remove the vegetable oil.

5. Pour 5 milliliters of water into a plastic cup, and add about half of the cornstarch. Use a plastic stirrer to blend the contents into a starch-water mixture.

6. Obtain a brown paper square and write "S" (for "starch") in the corner. Place 3 drops of the starch mixture on the square. Record your observations. Put the square aside to observe it again in about five minutes.

7. Obtain a fresh brown paper square and write "L" (for "lipid") in the corner. Place 3 drops of vegetable oil on the square. Record your observations. Put the square aside to observe again in about five minutes.

DATA TABLE

	Substance Tested	Texture	Brown Paper Test	Iodine Test	Type of Compound
1.	Cornstarch				Starch
2.	Vegetable oil				Lipid
3.					
4.					
5.					

8. Add 4 drops of iodine to the remaining starch mixture. Use a clean plastic stirrer to mix the contents well. Record your observations. **CAUTION:** *Handle iodine carefully; it can stain skin and clothing.*

9. Add 4 drops of iodine to the remaining vegetable oil. Use a clean plastic stirrer to mix the contents well. Record your observations.

Part 2 Testing Food Samples

10. Use what you learned in Part 1 to plan starch and lipid tests for food samples such as bread, butter, onion, cooked pasta, peanut butter, potato, potato chips, and rice. If a food is in the form of a single chunk, such as a potato cube, mash it or cut it into smaller pieces. (*Hint:* You can test a sample for lipids by rubbing the sample directly on brown paper.) Be sure to submit your plan for your teacher's approval.

11. List each food you are testing in the first column of the data table. Before beginning your tests, predict what the results will be, and write a reason for each prediction. In making your predictions, consider that some foods may contain both starches and lipids.

12. Carry out the tests as in Part 1 of this lab. Record your observations in the data table. **CAUTION:** *Do not put iodine or any of the food samples in your mouth.* Wash your hands after handling the food samples.

Analyze and Conclude

1. Based on your investigation, what test results indicate the presence of starch? The presence of lipids?

2. What does it mean if one food sample reacts both to the iodine, as cornstarch did, and to the brown paper test, as the vegetable oil did?

3. What does it mean if a food does not react to either the iodine test or the brown paper test?

4. What did you discover from the tests you carried out on specific food samples? Did the results for any of the foods surprise you?

5. **Apply** Why might people want to know what kinds of organic compounds a food contains?

Design an Experiment

Some foods, such as milk and milk products, are available in both regular and low-fat forms. Plan a procedure in which you could test whether various milk products are low in fat.

SECTION
④ The Cell in Its Environment

DISCOVER •••ACTIVITY••••

How Do Molecules Move?

1. With your classmates, stand so that you are evenly spaced throughout the classroom.

2. Your teacher will spray an air freshener into the room. When you first begin to smell the air freshener, raise your hand.

3. Note how long it takes for other students in the classroom to smell the scent.

Think It Over

Developing Hypotheses How was each student's distance from the teacher related to when he or she smelled the air freshener? Develop a hypothesis about why this pattern occurred.

GUIDE FOR READING

◆ By what three methods do materials move into and out of cells?

◆ What is the difference between passive transport and active transport?

Reading Tip Before you read, use the headings to make an outline about how materials move into and out of cells. As you read, make notes about each process.

▼ The *Mir* space station

How is a cell like a space station? The walls of a space station protect the astronauts inside from the airless vacuum of space. Food, water, and other supplies must be brought to the space station by shuttles from Earth. In addition, the space station needs to be able to get rid of wastes. The doors of the space station allow the astronauts to bring materials in and move wastes out into the shuttle to be returned to Earth.

Like space stations, cells also have structures that protect them from the outside environment. As you learned, all cells are surrounded by a cell membrane that separates the cell from the outside environment. Just like the space station, the cell also has to take in needed materials and get rid of wastes. It is the cell membrane that controls what materials move into and out of the cell.

The Cell Membrane as Gatekeeper

The cell membrane is **selectively permeable,** which means that some substances can pass through it while others cannot. The term *permeable* comes from a Latin word that means "to pass through." You can think of the cell membrane as being like a gatekeeper at an ancient castle. It was the gatekeeper's job to decide when to open the gate to allow people to pass into and out of the castle. The gatekeeper made the castle wall "selectively permeable"—it was permeable to friendly folks but not to enemies.

A cell membrane is usually permeable to substances such as oxygen, water, and carbon dioxide. On the other hand, the cell membrane is usually not permeable to some large molecules and salts. **Substances that can move into and out of a cell do so by one of three methods: diffusion, osmosis, or active transport.**

Diffusion—Molecules in Motion

The main method by which small molecules move into and out of cells is diffusion. **Diffusion** (dih FYOO zhun) is the process by which molecules tend to move from an area of higher concentration to an area of lower concentration. The concentration of a substance is the amount of the substance in a given volume.

If you did the Discover activity, you observed diffusion in action. The area where the air freshener was sprayed had many molecules of freshener. The molecules gradually moved from this area of higher concentration to the other parts of the classroom, where there were few molecules of freshener, and thus a lower concentration.

What Causes Diffusion? Molecules are always moving. As

INTEGRATING CHEMISTRY they move, the molecules bump into one another. The more molecules there are in an area, the more collisions there will be. Collisions cause molecules to push away from one another. Over time, the molecules of a substance will continue to spread out. Eventually they will be spread evenly throughout the area.

Diffusion in Cells Have you ever used a microscope to observe one-celled organisms in pond water? These organisms obtain the oxygen they need to survive from the water around them. Luckily for them, there are many more molecules of oxygen in the water outside the cell than there are inside the cell. In other words, there is a higher concentration of oxygen molecules in the water than inside the cell. Remember that the cell membrane is permeable to oxygen molecules. The oxygen molecules diffuse from the area of higher concentration—the pond water—through the cell membrane to the area of lower concentration—the inside of the cell.

Figure 16 Molecules move by diffusion from an area of higher concentration to an area of lower concentration. **A.** There is a higher concentration of molecules outside the cell than inside the cell. **B.** The molecules diffuse into the cell. Eventually, there is an equal concentration of molecules inside and outside the cell.
Predicting What would happen if the concentration of the molecules outside the cell was lower than the concentration inside?

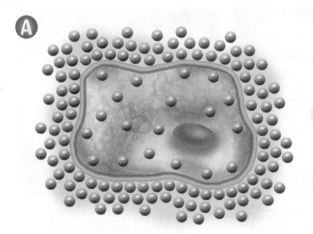

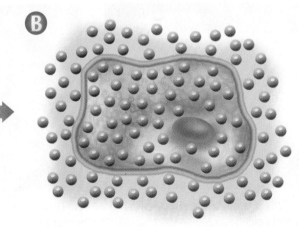

Diffusion in Action

Here's how you can observe the effects of diffusion. **ACTIVITY**

1. Fill a small clear plastic cup with cold water. Place the cup on a table and allow it to sit until there is no movement in the water.

2. Use a plastic dropper to add one large drop of food coloring to the water.

3. Observe the water every minute. Note any changes that take place. Continue to observe until you can no longer see any changes.

Inferring What role did diffusion play in the changes you observed?

Osmosis—The Diffusion of Water Molecules

Like oxygen, water passes easily into and out of cells through the cell membrane. The diffusion of water molecules through a selectively permeable membrane is called **osmosis.** Osmosis is important to cells because cells cannot function properly without adequate water.

Remember that molecules tend to move from an area of higher concentration to an area of lower concentration. In osmosis, water molecules move by diffusion from an area where they are highly concentrated through the cell membrane to an area where they are less concentrated. This can have important consequences for the cell.

Look at Figure 17 to see the effect of osmosis on cells. In Figure 17 A, red blood cells are bathed in a solution in which the concentration of water is the same as it is inside the cells. This is the normal shape of a red blood cell.

Now look at Figure 17 B. The red blood cells are floating in water that contains a lot of salt. The concentration of water molecules outside the cells is lower than the concentration of water molecules inside the cells. This is because the salt takes up space in the salt water, so there are fewer water molecules. As a result, water moves out of the cells by osmosis, and the cells shrink.

Finally, consider Figure 17 C. The red blood cells are floating in water that contains a very small amount of salt. The water inside the cells contains more salt than the solution they are floating in. Thus, the concentration of water outside the cell is greater than it is inside the cell. The water moves into the cell, causing it to swell.

✓ *Checkpoint* How is osmosis related to diffusion?

Figure 17 Osmosis is the diffusion of water molecules through a selectively permeable membrane.

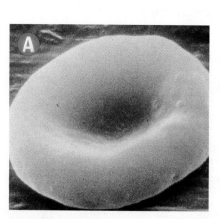

A. This is the normal shape of a red blood cell.

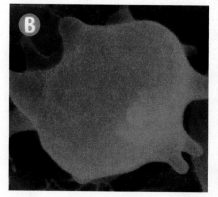

B. This cell has shrunk because water moved out of it by osmosis.

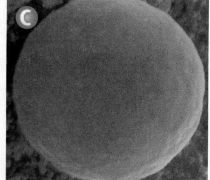

C. This cell is swollen with water that has moved into it by osmosis.

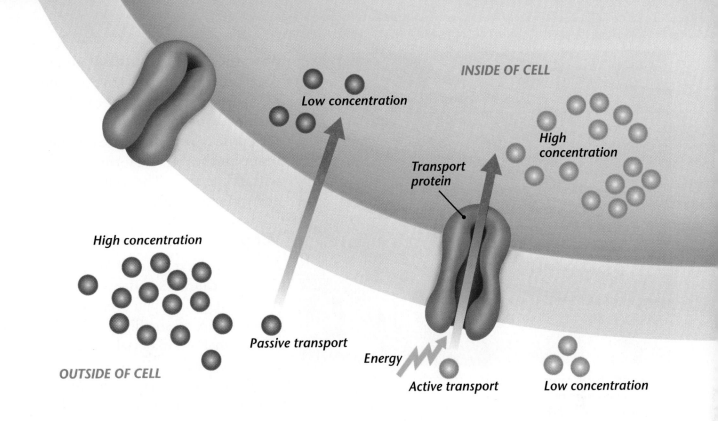

INSIDE OF CELL

Low concentration

High concentration

Transport protein

High concentration

Passive transport

OUTSIDE OF CELL

Energy

Active transport

Low concentration

Active Transport

If you have ever ridden a bicycle down a long hill, you know that it doesn't take any of your energy to go fast. But pedaling back up the hill does take energy. For a cell, moving materials through the cell membrane by diffusion and osmosis is like cycling downhill. These processes do not require the cell to use any energy. The movement of materials through a cell membrane without using energy is called **passive transport.**

What if a cell needs to take in a substance that is in higher concentration inside the cell than outside? The cell would have to move the molecules in the opposite direction than they naturally move by diffusion. Cells can do this, but they have to use energy—just as you would use energy to pedal back up the hill. **Active transport** is the movement of materials through a cell membrane using energy. **The main difference between passive transport and active transport is that active transport requires the cell to use energy while passive transport does not.**

Transport Proteins A cell has several ways of moving materials by active transport. In one method, transport proteins in the cell membrane "pick up" molecules outside the cell and carry them in, using energy in the process. Transport proteins also carry molecules out of cells in a similar way. Some substances that are carried into and out of cells in this way include calcium, potassium, and sodium.

Figure 18 Diffusion and osmosis are forms of passive transport. These processes do not require the cell to use any energy. Active transport, on the other hand, requires the use of energy.
Interpreting Diagrams How are passive and active transport related to the concentrations of the molecules inside and outside the cell?

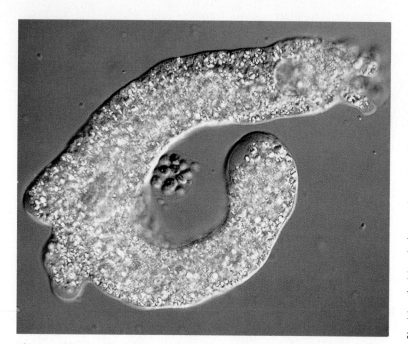

Figure 19 A cell can move some materials into the cell by engulfing them. This single-celled ameba is engulfing a smaller single-celled organism.

Transport by Engulfing You can see another method of active transport in Figure 19. First the cell membrane surrounds, or engulfs, a particle. Once the particle is engulfed, the cell membrane pinches off and forms a vacuole within the cell. The cell must use energy in this process.

Why Are Cells Small?

As you know, most cells are so small that you cannot see them without a microscope. Have you ever wondered why cells are so small? One reason is related to how materials move into and out of cells.

As a cell's size increases, more of its cytoplasm is located farther from the cell membrane. Once a molecule enters a cell, it is carried to its destination by a stream of moving cytoplasm, somewhat like the way currents of water in the ocean move a raft. But in a very large cell, the streams of cytoplasm must travel farther to bring materials to all parts of the cell. It would take much longer for a molecule to reach the center of a very large cell than it would in a small cell. Likewise, it would take a long time for wastes to be removed. If a cell grew too large, it could not function well enough to survive. When a cell reaches a certain size, it divides into two new cells. You will learn more about cell division in Chapter 2.

Section 4 Review

1. Describe three methods by which substances can move into and out of cells.
2. How are passive transport and active transport similar? How do they differ?
3. Why is small size an advantage to a cell?
4. **Thinking Critically** **Predicting** A single-celled organism is transferred from a tank of fresh water into a tank of salt water. How will the cell change? Explain.

Check Your Progress
CHAPTER
PROJECT
1

Begin to think about why the egg changed as it did at each stage of the project. Consider how each of the different substances affected your egg. (*Hint:* Water plays a crucial role in the activities of a cell. How has water been involved in your investigation?) Organize your results into a report and make a graph of your egg's changing circumference. You may want to include diagrams to explain the processes that took place.

SECTION 1 Discovering Cells

Key Ideas

◆ The invention of the microscope made the discovery of the cell possible.

◆ The cell theory states that: all living things are made of cells; cells are the basic units of life; all cells come from other cells.

Key Terms

cell
microscope
compound microscope
cell theory

magnification
convex lens
resolution

SECTION 2 Looking Inside Cells

Key Ideas

◆ The cell membrane protects the cell and controls what substances enter and leave it.

◆ The nucleus is the cell's control center.

◆ Organelles in the cytoplasm perform many vital functions.

Key Terms

organelle
cell wall
cell membrane
nucleus
chromatin

cytoplasm
mitochondrion
endoplasmic
  reticulum
ribosome

Golgi body
chloroplast
vacuole
lysosome

SECTION 3 Chemical Compounds in Cells

INTEGRATING CHEMISTRY

Key Ideas

◆ The main groups of organic compounds found in living things are carbohydrates, lipids, proteins, and nucleic acids.

◆ Without water, most chemical reactions within cells could not take place.

Key Terms

element
atom
compound
molecule
organic compound

inorganic
  compound
carbohydrate
protein
amino acid

enzyme
lipid
nucleic acid
DNA
RNA

SECTION 4 The Cell in Its Environment

Key Ideas

◆ Substances can move into and out of a cell by diffusion, osmosis, or active transport.

◆ Diffusion is the process by which molecules move from an area of higher concentration to an area of lower concentration. Osmosis is the diffusion of water molecules through a selectively permeable membrane.

◆ Active transport requires the cell to use energy while passive transport does not.

◆ If a cell grew too large, it could not function well enough to survive.

Key Terms

selectively permeable
diffusion
osmosis

passive transport
active transport

Organizing Information

Concept Map Copy the concept map onto a separate sheet of paper. Then complete the map and add a title. (For more about concept maps, see the Skills Handbook.)

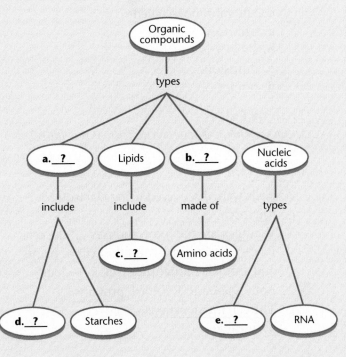

Reviewing Content

 For more review of key concepts, see the Interactive Student Tutorial CD-ROM.

Multiple Choice

Choose the letter of the best answer.

1. The ability of microscopes to distinguish fine details is called
   a. resolution.
   b. bending.
   c. magnification.
   d. active transport.
2. In plant and animal cells, the control center of the cell is the
   a. chloroplast.
   b. ribosome.
   c. nucleus.
   d. Golgi body.
3. The storage compartment of a cell is the
   a. cell wall.
   b. lysosome.
   c. endoplasmic reticulum.
   d. vacuole.
4. Starch is an example of a
   a. nucleic acid.
   b. protein.
   c. lipid.
   d. carbohydrate.
5. The process by which water moves across a cell membrane is called
   a. osmosis.
   b. active transport.
   c. diffusion.
   d. resolution.

True or False

If the statement is true, write true. If it is false, change the underlined word or words to make the statement true.

6. Cells were discovered using <u>electron</u> microscopes.
7. <u>Vacuoles</u> are the "powerhouses" of the cell.
8. Bacterial cells differ from the cells of plants and animals in that they lack a <u>nucleus</u>.
9. Both DNA and RNA are <u>proteins</u>.
10. The <u>cell membrane</u> is selectively permeable.

Checking Concepts

11. What role did the microscope play in the development of the cell theory?
12. Describe the function of the cell wall in the cells that have these structures.
13. Explain the difference between organic and inorganic compounds.
14. How are enzymes important to living things?
15. What is diffusion? What role does diffusion play in the cell?
16. **Writing to Learn** Suppose you had been a reporter assigned to cover early scientists' discoveries about cells. Write a brief article for your daily newspaper that explains one scientist's discoveries. Be sure to explain both how the discoveries were made and why they are important.

Thinking Critically

17. **Applying Concepts** Explain how the cell theory applies to a dog.
18. **Relating Cause and Effect** Suppose a microscope is invented that scientists could use to see molecules inside a cell's organelles. How could the microscope contribute to their understanding of the cell?
19. **Predicting** Could a cell survive without a cell membrane? Give reasons to support your answer.
20. **Comparing and Contrasting** How are plant and animal cells similar? How are they different? To answer these questions, make a list of the different organelles in each cell. Explain how each organelle is vital to the life and function of a plant or animal.
21. **Making Generalizations** Why is the study of chemistry important to the understanding of living things?
22. **Comparing and Contrasting** Explain how active transport is different from osmosis.

Applying Skills

A scientist watered the plant in Figure A with salt water. After 30 minutes, the plant looked as you see it in Figure B. Use the drawings to answer Questions 23–25.

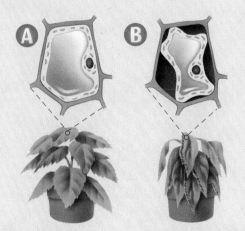

23. **Observing** How did the plant cells change after the plant was watered?
24. **Inferring** Describe a process that would lead to the changes in the plant cells.

25. **Predicting** Suppose the scientist were to water the plant in B with fresh water. Predict what would happen to the plant. Explain your prediction.

Performance ▼ Assessment
CHAPTER PROJECT 1

Project Wrap Up Bring in your egg, your graph, and any diagrams you made. As a class or in groups, discuss your results and conclusions. Then, as a group, try to agree on answers to these questions: What happened to the eggshell? What process took place at each stage of the experiment?

Reflect and Record In your notebook, describe what you learned from doing this egg-speriment. Which part of the project was the most surprising? When did you begin to understand what was happening to the egg?

Test Preparation

Use these questions to prepare for standardized tests.

Study the table. Then answer Questions 26–30.

Cell	Nucleus	Cell Wall	Cell Membrane
Cell A	Yes	Yes	Yes
Cell B	Yes	No	Yes
Cell C	No	Yes	Yes

26. Which cell is probably an animal cell?
    a. cell A   b. cell B
    c. cell C   d. none of the above
27. Which cell is probably a plant cell?
    a. cell A   b. cell B
    c. cell C   d. none of the above

28. Which cell is a bacterial cell?
    a. cell A   b. cell B
    c. cell C   d. none of the above
29. In Cell B, where would the genetic material be found?
    a. in the mitochondria
    b. in the vacuoles
    c. in the nucleus
    d. in the cell membrane
30. Which cell(s) would most likely contain chloroplasts?
    a. cell A   b. cell B
    c. cell C   d. cell B and cell C

WEB ACTIVITY

www.phschool.com

Shine On!

Every morning at sunrise, tiny living factories start a manufacturing process. These "factories" are cells that contain chloroplasts. The power they use is sunlight. The manufacturing process is called photosynthesis.

In this chapter, you'll learn what cells make during photosynthesis, and why nearly all organisms depend on this process. To begin your study, you'll investigate how light affects one familiar group of photosynthesizers—plants.

Your Goal To determine how different lighting conditions affect the health and growth of plants.

To complete the project you will
◆ write up a plan to grow plants under different lighting conditions
◆ care for your plants daily, and keep careful records of their health and growth for three weeks
◆ graph your data, and draw conclusions about the effect of light on plant growth
◆ follow the safety guidelines in Appendix A

Get Started Brainstorm with classmates to answer these questions: What different light conditions might you test? What plants will you use? How will you measure health and growth? How can you be sure your results are due to the light conditions? Write up your plan and submit it to your teacher.

Check Your Progress You'll be working on this project as you study this chapter. To keep your project on track, look for Check Your Progress boxes at the following points.

Section 1 Review: page 54: Place your plants in different light conditions.

Section 3 Review, page 68: Observe your plants daily.

Section 4 Review, page 73: Analyze and graph your results.

Wrap Up At the end of the chapter (page 77), you'll present your results to your classmates.

These paintbrush and dwarf fireweed plants in Glacier Bay National Park in Alaska depend on the sun for energy.

SECTION
4
Integrating Health
Cancer

Discover What Happens When There Are Too Many Cells?

SECTION 1 Photosynthesis

DISCOVER ·· ACTIVITY····

Where Does the Energy Come From?

1. Obtain a solar-powered calculator that does not use batteries. Place the calculator in direct light.

2. Cover the solar cells with your finger. Note how your action affects the number display.

3. Uncover the solar cells. What happens to the number display?

4. Now cover all but one of the solar cells. How does that affect the number display?

Think It Over
Inferring From your observations, what can you infer about the energy that powers the calculator?

GUIDE FOR READING

◆ What happens during the process of photosynthesis?

◆ How does the sun supply living things with the energy they need?

Reading Tip As you read, create a flowchart that shows the steps involved in the process of photosynthesis.

It's a beautiful summer afternoon—a perfect day for a picnic in the park. The aroma of chicken cooking on the grill fills the air. Your dog is busy chasing sticks under a nearby tree. Up above, bluejays swoop down from the tree's branches, hunting for food. "Let's go for a bike ride before lunch," suggests your cousin. "Great idea," you say, and you ride off down the path.

Dogs running, birds flying, people biking—all of these activities require energy. Where do you think this energy comes from? Believe it or not, all the energy used to perform such activities comes from the sun. In fact, the sun provides almost all the energy used by living things on Earth.

What Is Photosynthesis?

Every living thing needs energy. All cells need energy to carry out their functions, such as making proteins and transporting substances into and out of the cell. Your picnic lunch supplies your cells with the energy they need. But plants and other organisms, such as algae and some bacteria, obtain their energy in a different way. These organisms use the energy in sunlight to make their own food.

The process by which a cell captures the energy in sunlight and uses it to make food is called **photosynthesis** (foh toh SIN thuh sis). The term *photosynthesis* comes from the root words *photo,* which means "light," and *synthesis,* which means "putting together." Photosynthesis means using light to make food.

A Two-Stage Process

Photosynthesis is a very complicated process. **During photosynthesis, plants and some other organisms use energy from the sun to convert carbon dioxide and water into oxygen and sugars, including glucose.** You can think of photosynthesis as taking place in two stages: capturing the sun's energy and producing sugars. You're probably familiar with many two-stage processes. To make a cake, for example, the first stage is to combine the ingredients to make the batter. The second stage is to bake the batter in an oven. To get the desired result—the cake—both stages must occur in the correct order.

Capturing the Sun's Energy The first stage of photosynthesis involves capturing the energy in sunlight. In plants, this energy-capturing process occurs in the leaves and other green parts of the plant. Recall from Chapter 1 that chloroplasts are green organelles inside plant cells. In most plants, leaf cells contain more chloroplasts than do cells in other parts of the plant.

Figure 1 Photosynthesis occurs inside chloroplasts in the cells of plants and some other organisms. The chloroplasts are the green structures in the cell in the inset. *Applying Concepts Where in a plant are cells with many chloroplasts found?*

Sharpen your Skills

Inferring

In this activity, you will observe the pigments in a leaf.

1. Cut a strip 5 cm by 20 cm out of a coffee filter.

2. 🔳 Place a leaf on top of the paper strip, about 2 cm from the bottom.

3. Roll the edge of a dime over a section of the leaf, leaving a narrow band of color on the paper strip.

4. ☠️🔥 Pour rubbing alcohol into a plastic cup to a depth of 1 cm. Stand the paper strip in the cup so the color band is about 1 cm above the alcohol. Hook the other end of the strip over the top of the cup.

5. After 10 minutes, remove the paper strip and let it dry. Observe the strip.

6. Wash your hands.

What does the appearance of your paper strip reveal about the presence of pigments in the leaf?

The chloroplasts in plant cells give plants their green color. The green color comes from **pigments,** colored chemical compounds that absorb light. The main pigment found in the chloroplasts of plants is **chlorophyll.** Chloroplasts may also contain yellow and orange pigments, but they are usually masked by the green color of chlorophyll.

Chlorophyll and the other pigments function in a manner similar to that of the solar "cells" in a solar-powered calculator. Solar cells capture the energy in light and use it to power the calculator. Similarly, the pigments capture light energy and use it to power the second stage of photosynthesis.

Using Energy to Make Food In the second stage of photosynthesis, the cell uses the captured energy to produce sugars. The cell needs two raw materials for this stage: water (H_2O) and carbon dioxide (CO_2). In plants, the roots absorb water from the soil. The water then moves up through the plant's stem to the leaves. Carbon dioxide is one of the gases in the air. Carbon dioxide enters the plant through small openings on the undersides of the leaves called **stomata** (STOH muh tuh)(singular *stoma*). Once in the leaves, the water and carbon dioxide move into the chloroplasts.

Inside the chloroplasts, the water and carbon dioxide undergo a complex series of chemical reactions. The reactions are powered by the energy captured in the first stage. One of the products of the reactions is oxygen (O_2). The other products are sugars, including glucose ($C_6H_{12}O_6$). Recall from Chapter 1 that sugars are a type of carbohydrate. Cells can use the energy in the sugars to carry out important cell functions.

✓ *Checkpoint* *Why are plants green?*

Figure 2 Stomata are small openings on the undersides of leaves. Stomata can open (left) or close (right) to control the movement of carbon dioxide, oxygen, and water vapor.

Figure 3 During photosynthesis, chlorophyll and other pigments capture energy from sunlight. The cells then use this energy, along with water and carbon dioxide, to produce sugars and oxygen. *Interpreting Diagrams* What happens to the oxygen produced during photosynthesis?

The Photosynthesis Equation

The events of photosynthesis can be summed up by the following chemical equation:

$$6\,CO_2 \;+\; 6\,H_2O \;\xrightarrow{\text{light energy}}\; C_6H_{12}O_6 \;+\; 6\,O_2$$

carbon dioxide water glucose oxygen

INTEGRATING CHEMISTRY Notice that the raw materials—six molecules of carbon dioxide and six molecules of water—are on the left side of the equation. The products—one molecule of glucose and six molecules of oxygen—are on the right side of the equation. An arrow, which is read as "yields," connects the raw materials to the products. Light energy, which is necessary for the chemical reaction to occur, is written above the arrow.

What happens to the products of photosynthesis? Plant cells use some of the sugar for food. The cells break down the sugar molecules to release the energy they contain. This energy can then be used to carry out the plant's functions. Some sugar molecules are converted into other compounds, such as cellulose. Other sugar molecules may be stored in the plant's cells for later use. When you eat food from plants, such as potatoes or carrots, you are eating the plant's stored food.

The other product of photosynthesis is oxygen. Most of the oxygen passes out of the plant through the stomata and into the air. All organisms that carry out photosynthesis release oxygen.

Photosynthesis and Life

INTEGRATING ENVIRONMENTAL SCIENCE If you were a caterpillar, you might be sitting on a plant chewing on a leaf. The plant is an **autotroph** (AW toh trohf), an organism that makes its own food. The plant's leaves contain sugars made during photosynthesis. Leaves also contain starches, cellulose, and other compounds made from sugars. The energy in these compounds originally came from the sun.

The caterpillar is a **heterotroph** (HET uh roh trohf), an organism that cannot make its own food. To live, grow, and perform other caterpillar functions, it needs the energy in the plant's sugars. By eating plants, the caterpillar gets its energy from the sun, although in an indirect way.

Watch out—there's a bird! The bird, a heterotroph, gets its energy by eating caterpillars. Since the energy in caterpillars indirectly comes from the sun, the bird too is living off the sun's energy. **Nearly all living things obtain energy either directly or indirectly from the energy of sunlight captured during photosynthesis.**

Photosynthesis is also essential for the air you breathe. Most living things need oxygen to survive. About 21% of Earth's atmosphere is oxygen—thanks to plants and other organisms that carry out photosynthesis. Almost all the oxygen in Earth's atmosphere was produced by living things through the process of photosynthesis.

Figure 4 Both the caterpillar and the western bluebird obtain their energy indirectly from the sun.

Section 1 Review

1. What are the raw materials needed for photosynthesis? What are the products?
2. How do plants get energy? How do animals get energy?
3. What role does chlorophyll play in photosynthesis? Where is chlorophyll found?
4. **Thinking Critically Applying Concepts** List three ways that autotrophs were important to you today.

Check Your Progress CHAPTER PROJECT 2
Make any necessary revisions to your experimental plan. Then create a data table in which to record your observations each day. Now it's time to place your plants in the different lighting conditions. (*Hint:* Be sure to keep all other conditions the same throughout the project. For example, give all your plants the same amount of water.)

SECTION
2 Respiration

What Is a Product of Respiration?

1. [goggles icon] Put on your goggles. Fill two test tubes half full of warm water. Add 5 milliliters of sugar to one of the test tubes. Put the tubes in a test tube rack.

2. Add 0.5 milliliter of dried yeast (a single-celled organism) to each tube. Stir the contents of each tube with a straw. Place a stopper snugly in the top of each tube.

3. Observe any changes that occur in the two test tubes over the next 10 to 15 minutes.

Think It Over

Observing What changes occurred in each test tube? How can you account for any differences that you observed?

Your friend stops along the trail ahead of you and calls out, "Let's eat!" He looks around for a flat rock to sit on. You're ready for lunch. You didn't have much breakfast this morning, and you've been hiking for the past hour. As you look around you, you see that the steepest part of the trail is still ahead of you. You'll need a lot of energy to make it to the top.

Everyone knows that food provides energy. But not everyone knows *how* food provides energy. The food you eat does not provide your body with energy immediately after you eat it. First, the food must pass through your digestive system. There, the food is broken down into small molecules. These small molecules can then pass out of the digestive system and into your bloodstream. Next, the molecules travel through the bloodstream to the cells of your body. Inside the cells, the energy in the molecules is released. In this section, you'll learn how your body's cells obtain energy from the food you eat.

GUIDE FOR READING

◆ What events occur during respiration?

◆ How are photosynthesis and respiration related?

◆ What is fermentation?

Reading Tip Before you read, write a definition of *respiration*. As you read, revise your definition based on what you have learned.

Figure 5 All organisms need energy to live. **A.** This leopard frog uses the energy stored in carbohydrates to leap great distances. **B.** Although these mushrooms don't move, they still need a continuous supply of energy to grow and reproduce. *Applying Concepts What is the name of the process by which cells obtain the energy they need?*

Storing and Releasing Energy

To understand how cells use energy, think about how people save money in a bank. You might, for example, put some money in a savings account. Then, when you want to buy something, you withdraw some of the money. Cells store and use energy in a similar way. During photosynthesis, plants capture the energy from sunlight and "save" it in the form of carbohydrates, including sugars and starches. When the cells need energy, they "withdraw" it by breaking down the carbohydrates. This process releases energy. Similarly, when you eat a meal, you add to your body's energy savings account. When your cells need energy, they make a withdrawal and break down the food to release energy.

Respiration

After you eat a meal, your body converts the carbohydrates in the food into glucose, a type of sugar. The process by which cells "withdraw" energy from glucose is called **respiration. During respiration, cells break down simple food molecules such as glucose and release the energy they contain.** Because living things need a continuous supply of energy, the cells of all living things carry out respiration continuously.

The term *respiration* might be confusing. You have probably used it to mean breathing, that is, moving air in and out of your lungs. Because of this confusion, the respiration process that takes place inside cells is sometimes called cellular respiration.

The double use of the term *respiration* does point out a connection that you should keep in mind. Breathing brings oxygen into your lungs, and oxygen is necessary for cellular respiration to occur in most cells. Some cells can obtain energy from glucose without using oxygen. But the most efficient means of obtaining energy from glucose requires the presence of oxygen.

The Respiration Equation Although respiration occurs in a series of complex steps, the overall process can be summarized in the following equation:

$$C_6H_{12}O_6 \ + \ 6\,O_2 \ \longrightarrow \ 6\,CO_2 \ + \ 6\,H_2O \ + \ energy$$
$$\text{glucose} \qquad \text{oxygen} \qquad\quad \text{carbon dioxide} \quad \text{water}$$

Notice that the raw materials for respiration are glucose and oxygen. Plants and other organisms that undergo photosynthesis make their own glucose. The glucose in the cells of animals and other organisms comes from the food they consume. The oxygen comes from the air or water surrounding the organism.

The Two Stages of Respiration Like photosynthesis, respiration is a two-stage process. The first stage takes place in the cytoplasm of the organism's cells. There, glucose molecules are broken down into smaller molecules. Oxygen is not involved in this stage of respiration. Only a small amount of the energy in glucose is released during this stage.

The second stage of respiration takes place in the mitochondria. There, the small molecules are broken down into even smaller molecules. These chemical reactions require oxygen, and a great deal of energy is released. This is why the mitochondria are sometimes called the "powerhouses" of the cell.

Figure 6 summarizes the process of respiration. If you trace the steps in the breakdown of glucose, you'll see that energy is released in both stages. Two other products of respiration are carbon dioxide and water. These products diffuse out of the cell. In animals, the carbon dioxide and some water leave the body when they breathe out. Thus, when you breathe in, you take in oxygen, a raw material for respiration. When you breathe out, you release carbon dioxide and water, products of respiration.

Checkpoint *What are the raw materials for respiration?*

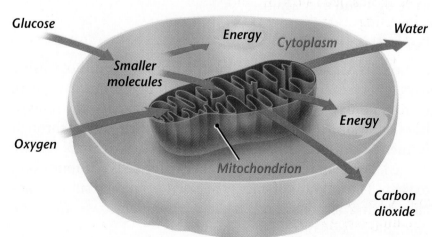

Figure 6 The first stage of respiration, which takes place in the cytoplasm, releases a small amount of energy. The second stage takes place in the mitochondria. A large amount of energy is released at this stage.

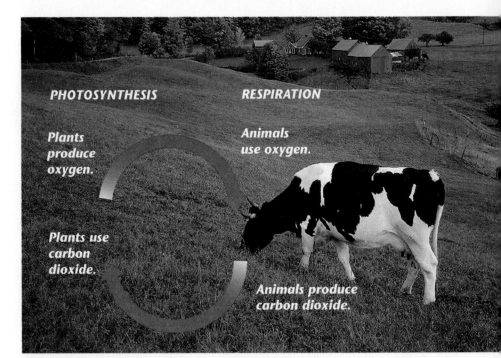

PHOTOSYNTHESIS

Plants produce oxygen.

Plants use carbon dioxide.

RESPIRATION

Animals use oxygen.

Animals produce carbon dioxide.

Figure 7 Photosynthesis and respiration can be thought of as opposite processes. *Interpreting Photographs How do these two processes keep the levels of oxygen and carbon dioxide in the atmosphere fairly constant?*

Comparing Photosynthesis and Respiration

Do you notice anything familiar about the equation for respiration? You are quite right if you said it is the opposite of the equation for photosynthesis. This is an important point to remember. During photosynthesis, carbon dioxide and water are used to produce sugars and oxygen. During respiration, glucose (a sugar) and oxygen are used to produce carbon dioxide and water. **Photosynthesis and respiration can be thought of as opposite processes.** Together, these two processes form a cycle that keeps the levels of oxygen and carbon dioxide fairly constant in the atmosphere. As you can see in Figure 7, living things use both gases over and over again.

Fermentation

Some cells are able to obtain energy from food without using oxygen. For example, some single-celled organisms live where there is no oxygen, such as deep in the ocean or in the mud of lakes or swamps. These organisms obtain their energy through **fermentation,** an energy-releasing process that does not require oxygen. **Fermentation provides energy for cells without using oxygen.** The amount of energy released from each sugar molecule during fermentation, however, is much lower than the amount released during respiration.

Alcoholic Fermentation One type of fermentation occurs in yeast and some other single-celled organisms. This process is sometimes called alcoholic fermentation because alcohol is one of the products made when these organisms break down sugars. The other products are carbon dioxide and a small amount of energy.

The products of alcoholic fermentation are important to bakers and brewers. The carbon dioxide produced by yeast causes dough to rise, and it creates the air pockets you see in bread. Carbon dioxide is also the source of bubbles in alcoholic drinks such as beer and sparkling wine.

Lactic-Acid Fermentation Another type of

INTEGRATING HEALTH fermentation takes place at times in your body, and you've probably felt its effects. Think of a time when you've run as fast as you could for as long as you could. Your leg muscles were pushing hard against the pavement, and you were breathing quickly. Eventually, however, your legs became tired and you couldn't run any more.

No matter how hard you breathed, your muscle cells used up the oxygen faster than it could be replaced. Because your cells lacked oxygen, fermentation occurred. One product of this type of fermentation is an acid known as lactic acid. When lactic acid builds up, you feel a painful sensation in your muscles. Your muscles feel weak and sore.

Figure 8 When an athlete's muscles run out of oxygen, lactic-acid fermentation occurs. The athlete's muscles feel tired and sore.

Section 2 Review

1. Why is respiration important for a cell?
2. Explain the relationship between photosynthesis and respiration.
3. Which raw material is *not* needed for fermentation to occur?
4. How do plants and animals maintain the level of oxygen in the atmosphere?
5. **Thinking Critically Applying Concepts** Do plant cells need to carry out respiration? Explain.

Science at Home

With an adult family member, follow a recipe in a cookbook to make a loaf of bread using yeast. Explain to your family what causes the dough to rise. After you bake the bread, observe a slice and look for evidence that fermentation occurred.

Gases in Balance

Problem

How are photosynthesis and respiration related?

Skills Focus

controlling variables, interpreting data

Materials

marking pens
2 *Elodea* plants
plastic graduated cylinder, 100-mL
bromthymol blue solution
3 flasks with stoppers, 250-mL

straws
light source

Procedure

1. Bromthymol blue can be used to test for carbon dioxide. To see how this dye works, pour 100 mL of bromthymol blue solution into a flask. Record its color. **CAUTION:** *Bromthymol blue can stain skin and clothing. Avoid spilling or splashing it on yourself.*

2. Provide a supply of carbon dioxide by gently blowing into the solution through a straw until the dye changes color. Record the new color. **CAUTION:** *Do not inhale any of the solution through the straw.*

3. Copy the data table into your notebook. Add 100 mL of bromthymol blue to the other flasks. Then blow through clean straws into each solution until the color changes.

4. Now you will test to see what gas is used by a plant in the presence of light. Obtain two *Elodea* plants of about the same size.

5. Place one plant into the first flask. Label the flask "L" for light. Place the other plant in the second flask. Label the flask "D" for darkness. Label the third flask "C" for control. Put stoppers in all three flasks.

DATA TABLE

| Flask | Color of Solution | |
	Day 1	Day 2
L (light)		
D (dark)		
C (control)		

6. Record the colors of the three solutions under Day 1 in your data table.

7. Place the flasks labeled L and C in a lighted location as directed by your teacher. Place the flask labeled D in a dark location as directed by your teacher. Wash your hands thoroughly when you have finished.

8. On Day 2, examine the flasks and record the colors of the solutions in your data table.

Analyze and Conclude

1. Explain why the color of each solution did or did not change from Day 1 to Day 2.

2. Why was it important to include the flask labeled C as part of this experiment?

3. Predict what would happen if you blew into the flask labeled L after you completed Step 8. Explain your prediction.

4. **Apply** How does this lab show that photosynthesis and respiration are opposite processes? Why are both processes necessary to maintain an environment suitable for living things?

More to Explore

Suppose you were to put an *Elodea* plant and a small fish in a stoppered flask. Predict what would happen to the levels of oxygen and carbon dioxide in the flask. Explain your prediction.

What Are the Cells Doing?

1. 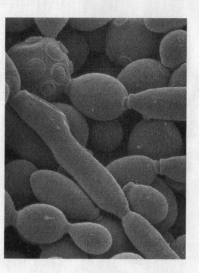 Use a plastic dropper to transfer some yeast cells from a yeast culture to a microscope slide. Your teacher has prepared the slide by drying methylene blue stain onto it. Add a cover-slip and place the slide under a microscope.

2. Examine the cells on the slide. Use low power first, then high power. Look for what appears to be two cells attached to each other. One cell may be larger than the other. Draw what you see.

Think It Over

Developing Hypotheses What process do you think the "double cells" are undergoing? Develop a hypothesis that might explain what you see.

I n the early autumn, many local fairs run pumpkin contests. Proud growers enter their largest pumpkins, hoping to win a prize. If you've never seen these prize-winning pumpkins, you would be amazed. Some have masses close to 400 kilograms and can be as big as a doghouse. What's even more amazing is that these giant pumpkins began as small flowers on pumpkin plants. How did the pumpkins grow so big?

A pumpkin grows in size by increasing both the size and the number of its cells. A single cell divides, forming two cells. Then two cells divide, forming four, and so on. This process of cell division does not occur only in pumpkins, though. In fact, many cells in your body are undergoing cell division as you read this page.

GUIDE FOR READING

◆ What events take place during the three stages of the cell cycle?

◆ What is the role of DNA replication?

Reading Tip Before you read, use the headings to outline the process of cell division. As you read, fill in information under each heading.

The Cell Cycle

Think about the cells you learned about in Chapter 1. Each cell contains many different structures, including a cell membrane, a nucleus, mitochondria, and ribosomes. To divide into two equal parts, the cell would need to either duplicate the structures or divide them equally between the two new cells. Both cells would then contain everything they need in order to survive and carry out their life functions.

The regular sequence of growth and division that cells undergo is known as the **cell cycle.** You can see details of the cell cycle in *Exploring the Cell Cycle* on pages 64 and 65. Notice that the cell cycle is divided into three main stages. As you read about each stage, follow the events that occur as one "parent" cell divides to form two identical "daughter" cells.

Figure 9 The cells that make up this young monkey are the same size as those that make up its mother. However, the adult has many more cells in its body.

Stage 1: Interphase

The first stage of the cell cycle is called **interphase.** Interphase is the period before cell division occurs. Even though it is not dividing, the cell is quite active during this stage. **During interphase, the cell grows to its mature size, makes a copy of its DNA, and prepares to divide into two cells.**

Growth During the first part of interphase, the cell doubles in size and produces all the structures needed to carry out its functions. For example, the cell enlarges its endoplasmic reticulum, makes new ribosomes, and produces enzymes. Both mitochondria and chloroplasts make copies of themselves during the growth stage. The cell matures to its full size and structure.

DNA Replication After a cell has grown to its mature size, the next part of interphase begins. The cell makes a copy of the DNA in its nucleus in a process called **replication.** Recall that DNA is a nucleic acid found in the chromatin in a cell's nucleus. DNA holds all the information that the cell needs to carry out its functions. The replication of a cell's DNA is very important, since each daughter cell must have a complete set of DNA to survive. At the end of DNA replication, the cell contains two identical sets of DNA. One set will be distributed to each daughter cell. You will learn the details of DNA replication later in this section.

Preparation for Division Once the cell's DNA has replicated, preparation for cell division begins. The cell produces structures that it will use to divide during the rest of the cell cycle. At the end of interphase, the cell is ready to divide.

Stage 2: Mitosis

Once interphase is complete, the second stage of the cell cycle begins. **Mitosis** (my TOH sis) is the stage during which the cell's nucleus divides into two new nuclei. **During mitosis, one copy of the DNA is distributed into each of the two daughter cells.**

Scientists divide mitosis into four parts, or phases: prophase, metaphase, anaphase, and telophase. During prophase, the threadlike chromatin in the cell's nucleus begins to condense and coil, like fishing line wrapping around a ball. Under a light microscope, the condensed chromatin looks like tiny rods, as you can see in Figure 10. Since the cell's DNA has replicated, each rod has doubled. Each is an exact copy of the other. Scientists call each doubled rod of condensed chromatin a **chromosome.** Each identical rod, or strand, of the chromosome is called a **chromatid.** The two strands are held together by a structure called a centromere.

As the cell progresses through metaphase, anaphase, and telophase, the chromatids separate from each other and move to opposite ends of the cell. Then two nuclei form around the chromatids at the two ends of the cell. You can follow this process in *Exploring the Cell Cycle.*

☑ *Checkpoint* *During which stage of mitosis does the chromatin condense and form rodlike structures?*

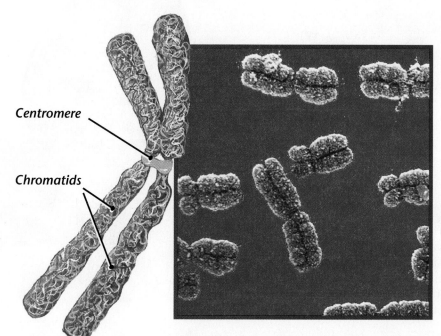

Centromere

Chromatids

Figure 10 During mitosis, the chromatin condenses to form rodlike chromosomes. Each chromosome consists of two identical strands, or chromatids. *Interpreting Diagrams What is the name of the structure that holds the chromatids together?*

EXPLORING the Cell Cycle

ells undergo an orderly sequence of events as they grow and divide. The sequence shown here is a typical cell cycle in an animal cell. Plant cells have somewhat different cell cycles.

1 INTERPHASE
The cell grows to its mature size, makes a copy of its DNA, and prepares to divide into two cells.

3 CYTOKINESIS
The cell membrane pinches in around the middle of the cell. Eventually, the cell pinches in two. Each daughter cell ends up with the same number of identical chromosomes and about half the organelles and cytoplasm.

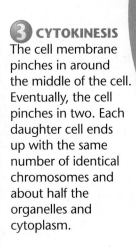

2 D MITOSIS: Telophase
The chromosomes begin to stretch out and lose their rodlike appearance. This occurs in the two regions at the ends of the cell. A new nuclear membrane forms around each region of chromosomes.

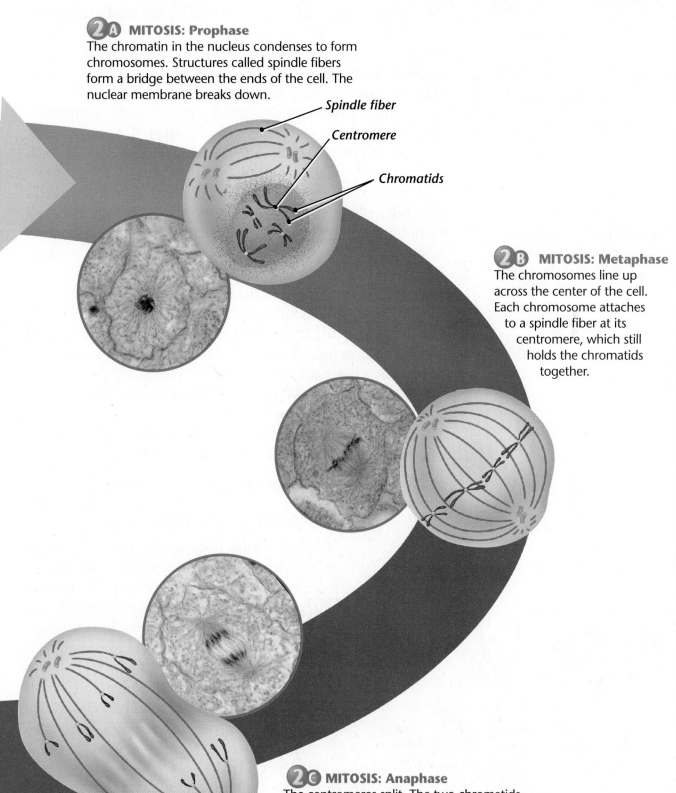

2Ⓐ MITOSIS: Prophase

The chromatin in the nucleus condenses to form chromosomes. Structures called spindle fibers form a bridge between the ends of the cell. The nuclear membrane breaks down.

Spindle fiber

Centromere

Chromatids

2Ⓑ MITOSIS: Metaphase

The chromosomes line up across the center of the cell. Each chromosome attaches to a spindle fiber at its centromere, which still holds the chromatids together.

2Ⓒ MITOSIS: Anaphase

The centromeres split. The two chromatids separate. One chromatid moves along the spindle fiber to one end of the cell. The other chromatid moves to the opposite end. The cell becomes stretched out as the opposite ends pull apart.

Interpreting Data

Use the circle graph shown in Figure 11 to answer the following questions.

1. How long is the cell cycle shown in the graph?

2. Which stage of the cell cycle would you expect more of the cells to be in at any given time—interphase, mitosis, or cytokinesis? Explain.

Stage 3: Cytokinesis

After mitosis, the final stage of the cell cycle, called **cytokinesis** (sy toh kih NEE sis), completes the process of cell division. **During cytokinesis, the cytoplasm divides, distributing the organelles into each of the two new cells.** Cytokinesis usually starts at about the same time as telophase.

During cytokinesis in animal cells, the cell membrane squeezes together around the middle of the cell. The cytoplasm pinches into two cells with about half of the organelles in each daughter cell.

Cytokinesis is somewhat different in plant cells. A plant cell's rigid cell wall cannot squeeze together in the same way that a cell membrane can. Instead, a structure called a cell plate forms across the middle of the cell. The cell plate gradually develops into new cell membranes between the two daughter cells. New cell walls then form around the cell membranes.

There are many variations of the basic pattern of cytokinesis. For example, yeast cells divide, though not equally. A small daughter cell, or bud, pinches off of the parent cell. The bud then grows into a full-sized yeast cell.

Cytokinesis marks the end of the cell cycle. Two new cells have formed. Each daughter cell has the same number of chromosomes as the original parent cell. At the end of cytokinesis, each cell enters interphase, and the cycle begins again.

✓ *Checkpoint* *When in the cell cycle does cytokinesis begin?*

Length of the Cell Cycle

How long does it take for a cell to go through one cell cycle? The answer depends on the type of cell. In a young sea urchin, for example, one cell cycle takes about 2 hours. In contrast, a human liver cell completes one cell cycle in about 22 hours, as shown in Figure 11. The length of each stage in the cell cycle also varies greatly from cell to cell. Some cells, such as human brain cells, never divide—they remain in the first part of interphase for as long as they live.

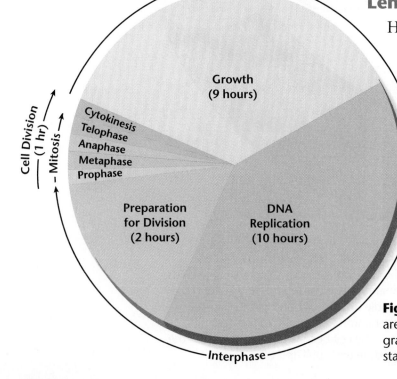

Figure 11 The main stages of the cell cycle are interphase, mitosis, and cytokinesis. This graph shows the average length of each stage in a human liver cell.

DNA Replication

A cell makes a copy of its DNA before mitosis occurs. **DNA replication ensures that each daughter cell will have all of the genetic information it needs to carry out its activities.**

Only in the last 50 years have scientists understood the importance of DNA. By the early 1950s, the work of several scientists showed that DNA carries all of the cell's instructions. They also learned that DNA is passed from a parent cell to its daughter cells. In 1953, two scientists, James Watson and Francis Crick, figured out the structure of DNA. This discovery revealed important information about how DNA copies itself.

The Structure of DNA Notice in Figure 12 that a DNA molecule looks like a twisted ladder, or spiral staircase. Because of its shape, a DNA molecule is often called a "double helix." A helix is a shape that twists like the threads of a screw.

The two sides of the DNA ladder are made up of molecules of a sugar called deoxyribose, alternating with molecules known as phosphates. Each rung of the DNA ladder is made up of a pair of molecules called nitrogen bases. Nitrogen bases are molecules that contain the element nitrogen and other elements. There are four kinds of nitrogen bases: adenine (AD uh neen), thymine (THY meen), guanine (GWAH neen), and cytosine (SY tuh seen). The capital letters A, T, G, and C are used to represent the four bases.

Look closely at Figure 12. Notice that the bases on one side of the ladder match up in a specific way with the bases on the other side. Adenine (A) only pairs with thymine (T), while guanine (G) only pairs with cytosine (C). This pairing pattern is the key to understanding how DNA replication occurs.

Figure 12 A DNA molecule is shaped like a twisted ladder. The sides are made up of sugar and phosphate molecules. The rungs are formed by pairs of nitrogen bases. *Classifying Which base always pairs with adenine?*

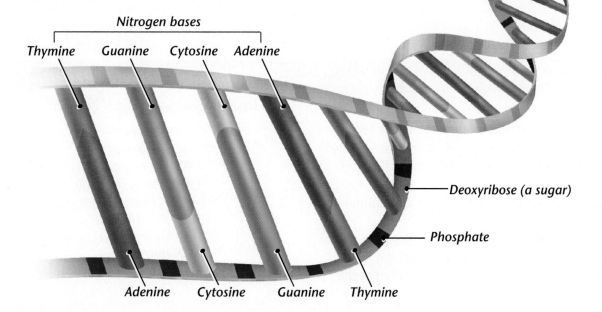

Nitrogen bases

Thymine   Guanine   Cytosine   Adenine

Deoxyribose (a sugar)

Phosphate

Adenine   Cytosine   Guanine   Thymine

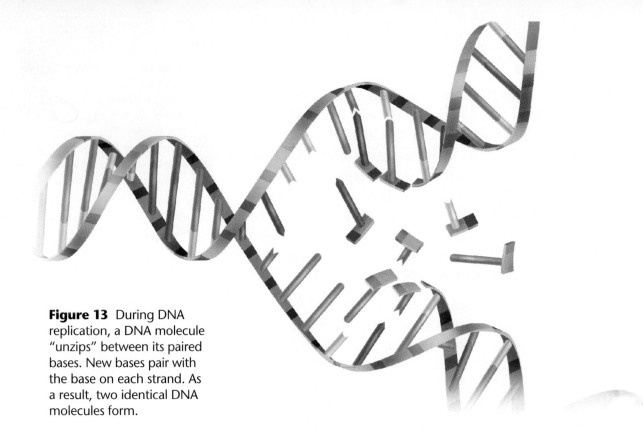

Figure 13 During DNA replication, a DNA molecule "unzips" between its paired bases. New bases pair with the base on each strand. As a result, two identical DNA molecules form.

The Replication Process DNA replication begins when the two sides of the DNA molecule unwind and separate, like a zipper unzipping. As you can see in Figure 13, the molecule separates between the paired nitrogen bases on each rung. Next, nitrogen bases that are floating in the nucleus pair up with the bases on each half of the DNA molecule. Remember that the pairing of bases follows definite rules: A always pairs with T, while G always pairs with C. Once the new bases are attached, two new DNA molecules are formed. The order of the bases in each new DNA molecule will exactly match the order in the original DNA molecule.

Section 3 Review

1. What are the three main stages of the cell cycle? Briefly describe the events that occur at each stage.
2. Why must the DNA in a cell replicate before the cell divides?
3. How does cytokinesis differ in plant and animal cells?
4. **Thinking Critically** **Predicting** Suppose that during anaphase, the centromeres did not split and the chromatids did not separate. Predict the results.

Check Your Progress CHAPTER PROJECT 2
At this point, you should be observing the health of your plants, and measuring their growth. Make drawings to show the appearance of the plants at different stages of the project. (*Hint:* In addition to overall height, you may wish to note the number and length of stems, and the number, size, color, and firmness of the leaves.)

Multiplying by Dividing

Problem

How long do the stages of the cell cycle take?

Materials

microscope
colored pencils
calculator (optional)
prepared slides of onion root tip cells
   undergoing cell division

Procedure

1. Place the slide on the stage of a microscope. Use low power to locate a cell in interphase. Then switch to high power, and make a labeled drawing of the cell. **CAUTION:** *Slides and coverslips break easily. Do not allow the objective to touch the slide. If the slide breaks, notify your teacher. Do not touch broken glass.*

2. Repeat Step 1 to find cells in prophase, metaphase, anaphase, and telophase. Then copy the data table into your notebook.

3. Return to low power. Find an area of the slide with many cells undergoing cell division. Switch to the magnification that lets you see about 50 cells at once (for example, 100 ×).

4. Examine the cells row by row, and count the cells that are in interphase. Record that number in the data table under *First Sample.*

5. Examine the cells row-by-row four more times to count the cells in prophase, metaphase, anaphase, and telophase. Record the results.

6. Move to a new area on the slide. Repeat Steps 3–5 and record your counts in the column labeled *Second Sample.*

7. Fill in the column labeled *Total Number* by adding the numbers across each row in your data table.

8. Add the totals for the five stages to find the total number of cells counted.

Analyze and Conclude

1. Which stage of the cell cycle did you observe most often?

2. The cell cycle for onion root tips takes about 720 minutes (12 hours). Use your data and the formula below to find the number of minutes each stage takes.

$$\text{Time for each stage} = \frac{\text{Number of cells at each stage}}{\text{Total number of cells counted}} \times 720 \text{ min}$$

3. **Think About It** Use the data to compare the amount of time spent in mitosis with the total time for the whole cell cycle.

More to Explore

Examine prepared slides of animal cells undergoing cell division. Use drawings and descriptions to compare plant and animal mitosis.

DATA TABLE

Stage of Cell Cycle	First Sample	Second Sample	Total Number
Interphase			
Mitosis: Prophase			
Metaphase			
Anaphase			
Telophase			
Total number of cells counted			

SECTION 4 Cancer

DISCOVER

What Happens When There Are Too Many Cells?

1. Use tape to mark off a one meter-by-one meter square on the floor. The square represents an area inside the human body. Have two students stand in the square to represent cells.

2. Suppose each cell divides every 30 seconds, and then one cell dies. With a group of students, model this situation. After 30 seconds, two new students should enter the square and one student should leave the square.

3. Model another round of cell division by having three new students enter the square while one student leaves. Continue this process until no more students can fit in the square.

Think It Over

Predicting Use this activity to predict what would happen if some cells in a person's body divided faster than they should.

GUIDE FOR READING

◆ How is cancer related to the cell cycle?

◆ What are some ways that cancer can be treated?

Reading Tip As you read, make a list of the main causes of cancer and how to prevent them.

Imagine that you are planting a flower garden near your home. After careful planning, you plant snapdragons, geraniums, and petunias exactly where you think they will look best. You also plant a ground ivy that you think will look nice between the flowers. You water your garden and wait for it to grow.

Much to your dismay, after a few months you notice that the ground ivy has taken over the garden. Where there should be flowers, there is nothing but a tangle of vines. Only a few flowers have survived. The ivy has used up more than its share of garden space and soil nutrients. A neighbor remarks, "That vine is so out of control, it's like a cancer."

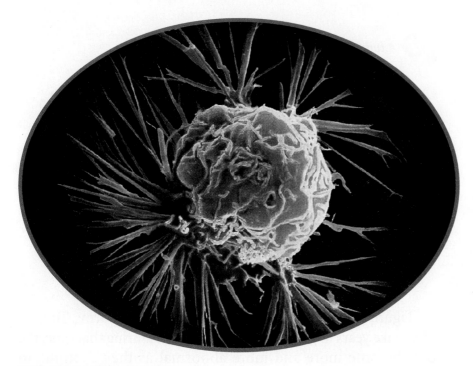

Figure 14 A cancer tumor begins as a single abnormal cell, like this breast cancer cell. A mutation occurs in the cell's DNA and disrupts the normal cell cycle.
Relating Cause and Effect
How does the cell behave as a result of the mutation?

What Is Cancer?

Your neighbor compared the ground ivy to a cancer because it grew uncontrollably and destroyed the other plants. **Cancer** is a disease in which cells grow and divide uncontrollably, damaging the parts of the body around them.

Cancer is actually not just one disease. In fact, there are more than 100 types of cancer. Cancer can occur in almost any part of the body. Cancers are often named by the place in the body where they begin. In the United States today, lung cancer is the leading cause of cancer deaths among both men and women.

How Cancer Begins Scientists think that cancer begins when something damages a portion of the DNA in a chromosome. The damage causes a change in the DNA called a **mutation.** Remember that DNA contains all the instructions necessary for life. Damage to the DNA can cause cells to function abnormally.

Normally, the cells in one part of the body live in harmony with the cells around them. Cells that go through the cell cycle divide in a controlled way. Other cells don't divide at all. **Cancer begins when mutations disrupt the normal cell cycle, causing cells to divide in an uncontrolled way.** The cells stop behaving as they normally do. Without the normal controls on the cell cycle, the cells grow too large and divide too often.

How Cancer Spreads At first, one cell develops in an abnormal way. As the cell divides, more and more abnormal cells like it grow near it. In time, these cells form a tumor. A **tumor** is a mass of abnormal cells that develops when cancerous cells divide and grow uncontrollably.

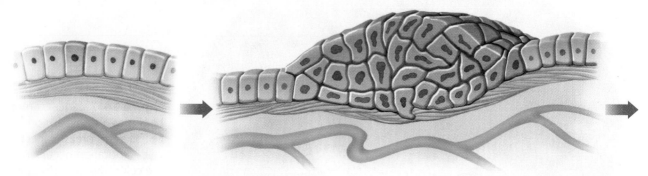

① *A mutation occurs in a cell.*

② *A tumor forms.*

Figure 15 A tumor is a mass of cells that divide uncontrollably. It may take years for a tumor to grow large enough to be noticed. *Interpreting Diagrams How can cancer spread from one part of the body to another?*

Figure 15 shows the process by which a tumor forms. Tumors often take years to grow to a noticeable size. During that time, the cells become more and more abnormal as they continue to divide. Some of the cancerous cells may break off the tumor and enter the bloodstream. In this way, the cancer can spread to other areas of the body.

☑ *Checkpoint* *What is the first step that leads to the development of a tumor?*

Treating Cancer

If a person is stricken with cancer, there are a variety of treatments that may be effective in fighting the disease. **Doctors usually treat cancer in one or more of three ways: surgery, radiation, or drugs that destroy the cancer cells.**

When a cancer is detected before it has spread to other parts of the body, surgery is usually the best treatment. If doctors can completely remove the cancerous tumor, a person may be cured of the disease. If, however, the cancer has spread or if the tumor cannot be removed, doctors may use radiation, beams of high-energy waves. Fast-growing cancer cells are more likely than normal cells to be destroyed by radiation.

Chemotherapy, or the use of drugs to kill cancer cells, is another form of treatment. Chemotherapy is effective because the drugs spread throughout the body, killing cancer cells or slowing their growth.

Unfortunately, none of these cancer treatments is perfect. Most have unpleasant, or even dangerous, side effects. Scientists continue to look for new ways to treat cancer. If, for example, scientists can discover how the cell cycle is controlled, they may find ways to stop cancer cells from going through the cell cycle.

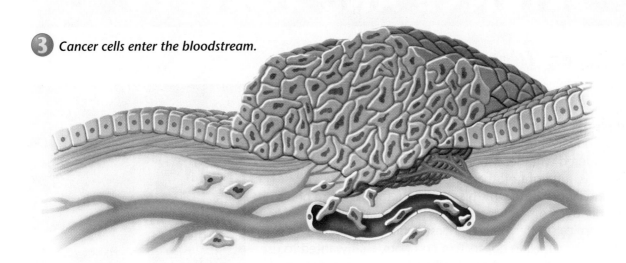

3 *Cancer cells enter the bloodstream.*

They might be able to "turn off" cancer before it causes too much damage to the body. Another possible treatment for cancer is to use drugs that block the flow of blood to tumors. Without a blood supply, tumors might not be able to continue growing.

Cancer Prevention

Scientists estimate that almost two thirds of all cancer deaths are caused either by tobacco use or unhealthful diets. Smoking is the main cause of lung cancer. When people repeatedly expose their bodies to the chemicals in tobacco, their cells will likely become damaged. Cancer may result.

It might surprise you to learn that unhealthful diets may lead to almost as many cancer deaths as does tobacco. A diet high in fat is especially harmful. Regularly eating high-fat foods, such as fatty meats and fried foods, can put a person at risk for cancer. A diet that includes a lot of fruits, vegetables, and grain products can help lower a person's risk of some types of cancer.

Section 4 Review

1. Explain the relationship between cancer and the cell cycle.
2. Describe three ways that cancer can be treated.
3. What two health habits can help prevent cancer?
4. **Thinking Critically Relating Cause and Effect** How could smoking tobacco cause cancer to develop inside the lungs?

Check Your Progress

CHAPTER PROJECT
2

It is now time to make your final observations of your plants. Then examine all of the data that you have collected. Which data can you present in graphs? Which of your diagrams show the major differences between your two plants? Write a brief summary that describes your experimental plan and your results.

Who Owns Your Cells?

John Moore was seriously ill. He had leukemia—cancer of the blood cells—and his spleen was in danger of bursting. Doctors removed his spleen, but Moore's condition was still serious. Surprisingly, however, Moore made a remarkable recovery. The doctors wondered whether Moore's body produced disease-fighting cells that fought off the cancer.

Without telling Moore why, his doctors gathered more of his cells. They discovered that Moore's cells were a natural "factory" of lifesaving chemicals. After years of investigation, the doctors sold the cells for several million dollars to a company that wanted to use the cells to manufacture medicines. When Moore found out, he sued the doctors, claiming that he owned his cells. Who do you think was right?

The Issues

Do Patients Have a Right to Their Cells?

Once a person's cells are outside his or her body, the person usually can no longer control what is done with them. For example, people who donate blood cannot tell blood banks what to do with their blood. On the other hand, people are able to decide whether or not to donate their organs when they die. Similarly, many people think they should be able to decide whether their cells can be used in medical research.

Do Doctors Have the Right to Use People's Cells?

If people could control what was done with their cells, some doctors think it would be harder to find new cures for diseases. Scientists need to be free to experiment and to learn from their research. But who should make money from life-saving research? The doctors argued that the profits from Moore's cells belonged to them. Moore had signed a consent form that gave the doctors permission to operate and remove his cells. It was the doctors' hard work and knowledge that turned the cells into something valuable.

Other people argue that there is not enough protection for patients. When Moore agreed to have the operation, he wasn't thinking about what would happen to his cells. His only concern was his need for the life-saving operation.

What Decision Was Reached?

In Moore's case, the California Supreme Court ruled that the doctors owned the cells once they were out of Moore's body. However, the Court also said that Moore's doctors should have specifically asked for permission to use his cells. Moore was awarded a small amount of money, barely enough to pay his legal fees.

You Decide

1. Identify the Problem

In your own words, describe the controversy raised in John Moore's lawsuit against his doctors.

2. Analyze the Options

List some of the options the California Supreme Court might have considered in their decision. Be sure to include solutions in which neither Moore nor his doctors would get everything they want.

3. Find a Solution

Suppose you were one of the judges in Moore's court case. Choose a solution that you think is fair to both Moore and his doctors, and is best for society. Give reasons to support your decision.

SECTION 1 Photosynthesis

Key Ideas
◆ During photosynthesis, plants and some other organisms use energy from the sun to convert carbon dioxide and water into oxygen and sugars, including glucose.
◆ In the first stage of photosynthesis, chlorophyll and other plant pigments capture energy from sunlight. In the second stage, the cell uses the energy to produce sugars from carbon dioxide and water.
◆ Nearly all living things obtain the energy they need either directly or indirectly from the sun.

Key Terms
photosynthesis   chlorophyll   autotroph
pigment   stomata   heterotroph

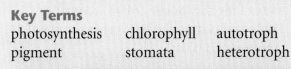

SECTION 2 Respiration

Key Ideas
◆ Respiration is a process in which cells break down simple food substances, such as glucose, and release the energy they contain.
◆ During respiration, glucose and oxygen are converted into carbon dioxide and water.
◆ Photosynthesis and respiration can be thought of as opposite processes. These two processes form a cycle that keeps the levels of oxygen and carbon dioxide fairly constant in the atmosphere.
◆ Fermentation provides energy for cells without using oxygen.

Key Terms
respiration   fermentation

SECTION 3 Cell Division

Key Ideas
◆ Cells go through a cycle of growth and division called the cell cycle. The phases of the cell cycle are interphase, mitosis, and cytokinesis.
◆ DNA replication ensures that each cell will have all of the genetic information it needs.

Key Terms
cell cycle   mitosis   chromatid
interphase   chromosome   cytokinesis
replication

SECTION 4 Cancer

INTEGRATING HEALTH

Key Ideas
◆ Cancer begins when the normal cell cycle is disrupted by mutations, causing cells to divide in an uncontrolled way.
◆ Cancer is usually treated with surgery, radiation, or chemotherapy.

Key Terms
cancer   tumor
mutation   chemotherapy

Organizing Information

Cycle Diagram Copy the cycle diagram about the cell cycle onto a separate sheet of paper. Then complete it and add a title.

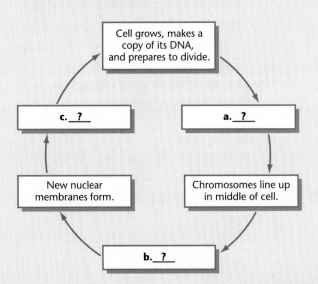

Reviewing Content

 For more review of key concepts, see the Interactive Student Tutorial CD-ROM.

Multiple Choice

Choose the letter of the best answer.

1. The organelle in which photosynthesis takes place is the
   a. mitochondrion.
   b. chloroplast.
   c. chlorophyll.
   d. nucleus.
2. What process is responsible for producing most of Earth's oxygen?
   a. photosynthesis
   b. replication
   c. mutation
   d. respiration
3. The process in which a cell makes an exact copy of its DNA is called
   a. fermentation.
   b. respiration.
   c. replication.
   d. reproduction.
4. Chromatids are held together by a
   a. spindle.
   b. chloroplast.
   c. centromere.
   d. cell membrane.
5. A mass of cancer cells is called a
   a. tumor.
   b. chromosome.
   c. mutation.
   d. mitochondrion.

True or False

If the statement is true, write true. If it is false, change the underlined word or words to make the statement true.

6. An organism that makes its own food is an <u>autotroph</u>.
7. The process of respiration takes place mainly in the <u>mitochondria</u>.
8. An energy-releasing process that does not require oxygen is <u>replication</u>.
9. The stage of the cell cycle when DNA replication occurs is <u>telophase</u>.
10. Uncontrolled cell division is a characteristic of <u>cancer</u>.

Checking Concepts

11. Briefly explain what happens to energy from the sun during photosynthesis.
12. Explain how heterotrophs depend on the sun for energy.
13. Why do organisms need to carry out the process of respiration?
14. Describe what happens during interphase.
15. How do the events of the cell cycle ensure that the daughter cells will be identical to the parent cell?
16. Describe how cancer usually begins to develop in the body.
17. **Writing to Learn** Write a paragraph describing the journey of an oxygen molecule as it moves between a plant and another organism.

Thinking Critically

18. **Predicting** Suppose a volcano spewed so much ash into the air that it blocked most of the sunlight that usually strikes Earth. How might this affect the ability of animals to obtain the energy they need to live?
19. **Applying Concepts** Explain the relationship between the processes of breathing and respiration.
20. **Comparing and Contrasting** Compare and contrast photosynthesis and respiration in terms of raw materials, products, and where each occurs.
21. **Inferring** Suppose one strand of a DNA molecule contained the following bases: A C G T C T G. What would the bases on the other strand be?
22. **Making Generalizations** Suppose you want to reduce your risks for getting cancer. Outline three steps you could take to lower your risk.

Applying Skills

Use the table below to answer Questions 23–25.

Percentages of Nitrogen Bases In the DNA of Various Organisms

Nitrogen Base	Human	Wheat	E. coli bacterium
Adenine	30%	27%	24%
Guanine	20%	23%	26%
Thymine	30%	27%	24%
Cytosine	20%	23%	26%

23. **Graphing** For each organism, draw a bar graph to show the percentages of each nitrogen base in its DNA.

24. **Interpreting Data** What is the relationship between the amounts of adenine and thymine in the DNA of each organism? Between the amounts of guanine and cytosine?

25. **Inferring** Based on your answer to Question 23, what can you infer about the structure of DNA in these three organisms?

Performance CHAPTER PROJECT 2 **Assessment**

Project Wrap Up Bring in your plants, recorded observations, and graphs to share with the class. Be prepared to describe your experimental plan and explain your results. What did you learn about photosynthesis and light from the experiment you performed?

Reflect and Record How well were you able to follow your experimental plan? Describe any difficulties or surprises you encountered. If you had to do another study of plants and light, what would you do differently? Why?

Test Preparation

Use these questions to prepare for standardized tests.

Study the equations. Then answer Questions 26–28.

Photosynthesis

$$6 \, CO_2 + 6 \, H_2O \xrightarrow{\text{light energy}} C_6H_{12}O_6 + 6 \, O_2$$

Respiration

$$C_6H_{12}O_6 + 6 \, O_2 \rightarrow 6 \, CO_2 + 6 \, H_2O + \text{energy}$$

26. What products are produced during photosynthesis?
    a. carbon dioxide and water
    b. light energy and carbon dioxide
    c. carbon dioxide and sugar
    d. sugar and oxygen

27. What raw materials are needed for respiration to occur?
    a. energy and water
    b. carbon dioxide, water, and energy
    c. sugar and oxygen
    d. sugar and carbon dioxide

28. Why are the words "light energy" written above the arrow in the photosynthesis equation?
    a. Light energy is necessary for the reaction to occur.
    b. Light energy is produced during the reaction.
    c. Oxygen can exist only in the presence of light.
    d. Sugar can exist only in the presence of light.

WEB
ACTIVITY

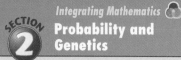

www.phschool.com

All In The Family

Did you ever wonder why some offspring resemble their parents while others do not? In this chapter, you'll learn how offspring come to have traits similar to those of their parents. In this project, you'll create a family of "paper pets" to explore how traits pass from parents to offspring.

Your Goal To create a "paper pet" that will be crossed with a pet belonging to a classmate, and to determine what traits the offspring will have.

To complete this project successfully, you must
◆ create your own unique paper pet with five different traits
◆ cross your pet with another pet to produce six offspring
◆ determine what traits the offspring will have, and explain how they came to have those traits

Get Started Cut out your pet from either blue or yellow construction paper. Choose other traits for your pet from this list: female or male; square eyes or round eyes; oval nose or triangular nose; pointed teeth or square teeth. Then create your pet using materials of your choice.

Check Your Progress You'll be working on this project as you study this chapter. To keep your project on track, look for Check Your Progress boxes at the following points.
   Section 1 Review, page 85: Identify your pet's genotype.
   Section 3 Review, page 100: Determine what traits your pet's offspring have.
   Section 4 Review, page 106: Make a display of your pet's family.

Wrap Up At the end of the chapter (page 109), you and your partner will display your pet's family and analyze the inheritance patterns.

These boxer puppies and their mother resemble each other in many ways. However, there are also noticeable differences between one dog and the next.

1 Mendel's Work

What Does the Father Look Like?

1. Observe the colors of each kitten in the photo. Record each kitten's coat colors and patterns. Include as many details as you can.

2. Observe the mother cat in the photo. Record her coat color and pattern.

Think It Over

Inferring Based on your observations, describe what you think the kittens' father might look like. Identify the evidence on which you based your inference.

Gregor Mendel in the monastery garden ▼

The year was 1851. Gregor Mendel, a young priest from a monastery in Central Europe, entered the University of Vienna to study mathematics and science. Two years later, Mendel returned to the monastery and began teaching at a nearby high school.

Mendel also cared for the monastery's garden, where he grew hundreds of pea plants. He became curious about why some of the plants had different physical characteristics, or **traits.** Some pea plants grew tall while others were short. Some plants produced green seeds, while others had yellow seeds.

Mendel observed that the pea plants' traits were often similar to those of their parents. Sometimes, however, the pea plants had different traits than their parents. The passing of traits from parents to offspring is called **heredity.** For more than ten years, Mendel experimented with thousands of pea plants to understand the process of heredity. Mendel's work formed the foundation of **genetics,** the scientific study of heredity.

Mendel's Peas

Mendel made a wise decision when he chose to study peas rather than other plants in the monastery garden. Pea plants are easy to study because they have many traits that exist in only two forms. For example, pea plant stems are either tall or short, but not medium height. Also, garden peas produce a large number of offspring in one generation. Thus, it is easy to collect large amounts of data to analyze.

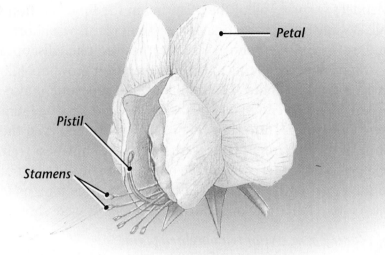

Petal

Pistil

Stamens

Figure 1 Garden peas usually reproduce by self-pollination. Pollen from a flower's stamens lands on the pistil of the same flower. Plants that result from self-pollination inherit all of their characteristics from the single parent plant. *Applying Concepts How did Mendel prevent his pea plants from self-pollinating?*

Figure 1 shows a flowering pea plant. Notice that the flower's petals surround the pistil and the stamens. The pistil produces female sex cells, or eggs, while the stamens produce pollen, which contains the male sex cells.

In nature, pea plants are usually self-pollinating. This means that pollen from one flower lands on the pistil of the same flower. Mendel developed a method by which he could cross-pollinate, or "cross," pea plants. To cross two plants, he removed pollen from a flower on one plant and brushed it onto a flower on a second plant. To prevent the pea plants from self-pollinating, he carefully removed the stamens from the flowers on the second plant.

Mendel's Experiments

Suppose you had a garden full of pea plants, and you wanted to study the inheritance of traits. What would you do? Mendel decided to cross plants with opposite forms of a trait, for example, tall plants and short plants. He started his experiments with purebred plants. A **purebred** plant is one that always produces offspring with the same form of a trait as the parent. For example, purebred short pea plants always produce short offspring. Purebred tall pea plants always produce tall offspring. To produce purebred plants, Mendel allowed peas with one particular trait to self-pollinate for many generations. By using purebred plants, Mendel knew that the offspring's trait would always be identical to that of the parents.

In his first experiment, Mendel crossed purebred tall plants with purebred short plants. He called these parent plants the parental generation, or P generation. He called the offspring from this cross the first filial (FIL ee ul) generation, or the F_1 generation. The word *filial* means "son" in Latin.

Gregor Mendel presented a detailed description of his observations in a scientific paper in 1866. In the excerpt that follows, notice how clearly he describes his observations of the two different seed shapes in peas.

"These are either round or roundish, the depressions, if any, occur on the surface, being always only shallow; or they are irregularly angular and deeply wrinkled."

In Your Journal

Choose an everyday object, such as a piece of fruit or a pen. Make a list of the object's features. Then write a short paragraph describing the object. Use clear, precise language in your description.

You can see the results of Mendel's first cross in Figure 2. To Mendel's surprise, all of the offspring in the F_1 generation were tall. Despite the fact that one of the parent plants was short, none of the offspring were short. The shortness trait had disappeared!

Mendel let the plants in the F_1 generation grow and allowed them to self-pollinate. The results of this experiment also surprised Mendel. The plants in the F_2 (second filial) generation were a mix of tall and short plants. This occurred even though none of the F_1 parent plants were short. The shortness trait had reappeared. Mendel counted the number of tall and short plants in the F_2 generation. He found that about three fourths of the plants were tall, while one fourth of the plants were short.

☑ *Checkpoint* **What is a purebred plant?**

Other Traits

In addition to stem height, Mendel studied six other traits in garden peas: seed shape, seed color, seed coat color, pod shape, pod color, and flower position. Compare the two forms of each trait in Figure 3. Mendel crossed plants with these traits in the same manner as he did for stem height. The results in each experiment were similar to those that he observed with stem height. Only one form of the trait appeared in the F_1 generation. However, in the F_2 generation the "lost" form of the trait always reappeared in about one fourth of the plants.

Figure 2 When Mendel crossed purebred tall and short pea plants, all the offspring in the F_1 generation were tall. In the F_2 generation, three fourths of the plants were tall, while one fourth were short.

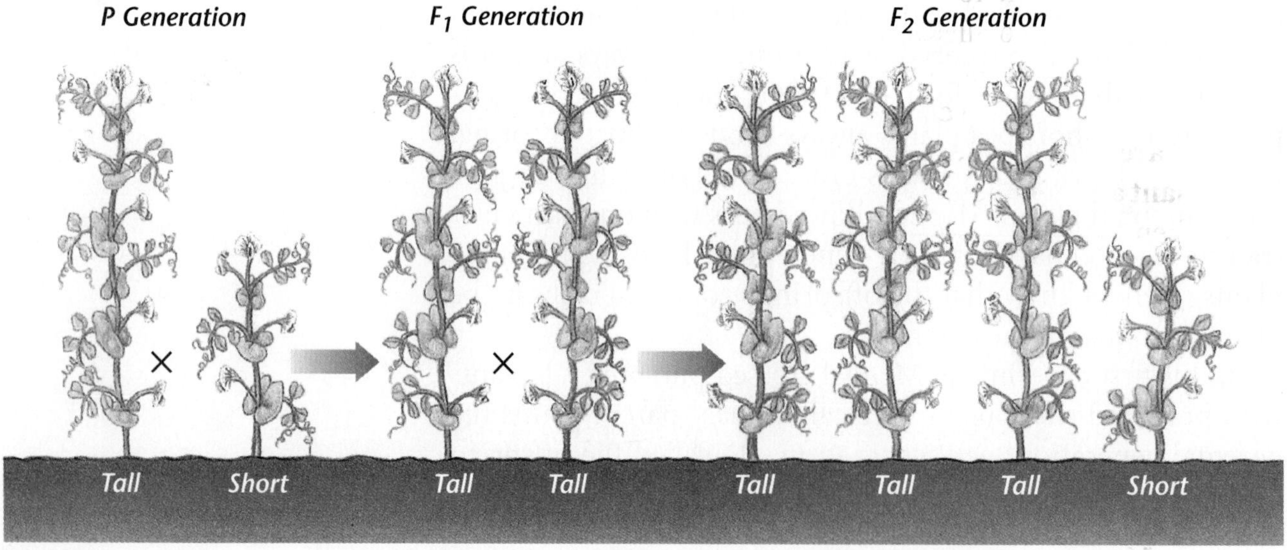

P Generation   F₁ Generation   F₂ Generation

Tall   Short   Tall   Tall   Tall   Tall   Tall   Short

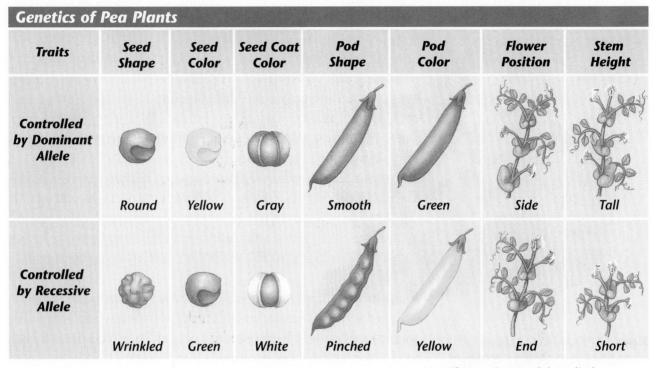

Genetics of Pea Plants

Traits	Seed Shape	Seed Color	Seed Coat Color	Pod Shape	Pod Color	Flower Position	Stem Height
Controlled by Dominant Allele	Round	Yellow	Gray	Smooth	Green	Side	Tall
Controlled by Recessive Allele	Wrinkled	Green	White	Pinched	Yellow	End	Short

Figure 3 Mendel studied seven different traits in pea plants. Each trait has two different forms. *Interpreting Diagrams Is yellow seed color controlled by a dominant allele or a recessive allele? What type of allele controls pinched pod shape?*

Dominant and Recessive Alleles

From his results, Mendel reasoned that individual factors must control the inheritance of traits in peas. The factors that control each trait exist in pairs. The female parent contributes one factor, while the male parent contributes the other factor.

Mendel went on to reason that one factor in a pair can mask, or hide, the other factor. The tallness factor, for example, masked the shortness factor in the F_1 generation.

Today, scientists call the factors that control traits **genes.** They call the different forms of a gene **alleles** (uh LEELZ). The gene that controls stem height in peas, for example, has one allele for tall stems and one allele for short stems. Each pea plant inherits a combination of two alleles from its parents—either two alleles for tall stems, two alleles for short stems, or one of each.

Individual alleles control the inheritance of traits. Some alleles are dominant, while other alleles are recessive. A **dominant allele** is one whose trait always shows up in the organism when the allele is present. A **recessive allele,** on the other hand, is masked, or covered up, whenever the dominant allele is present. A trait controlled by a recessive allele will only show up if the organism does not have the dominant allele.

In pea plants, the allele for tall stems is dominant over the allele for short stems. Pea plants with one allele for tall stems and one allele for short stems will be tall. The allele for tall stems masks the allele for short stems. Only pea plants that inherit two recessive alleles for short stems will be short.

Figure 4 These rabbits have some traits controlled by dominant alleles and other traits controlled by recessive alleles. For example, the allele for black fur is dominant over the allele for white fur. *Inferring What combination of alleles must the white rabbit have?*

Understanding Mendel's Crosses

You can understand Mendel's results by tracing the inheritance of alleles in his experiments. The purebred plants in the P generation had two identical alleles for stem height. The purebred tall plants had two alleles for tall stems. The purebred short plants had two alleles for short stems. In the F_1 generation, all of the plants received one allele for tall stems from the tall parent. They received one allele for short stems from the short parent. The F_1 plants are called **hybrids** (HY bridz) because they have two different alleles for the trait. All the F_1 plants are tall because the dominant allele for tall stems masks the recessive allele for short stems.

When Mendel crossed the hybrid plants in the F_1 generation, some of the plants inherited two dominant alleles for tall stems. These plants were tall. Other plants inherited one dominant allele for tall stems and one recessive allele for short stems. These plants were also tall. Other plants inherited two recessive alleles for short stems. These plants were short.

☑ *Checkpoint If a pea plant has a tall stem, what possible combinations of alleles could it have?*

Using Symbols in Genetics

Geneticists today use a standard shorthand method to write about alleles in genetic crosses. Instead of using words such as "tall stems" to represent alleles, they simply use letters. A dominant allele is represented by a capital letter. For example, the allele for tall stems is represented by *T*. A recessive allele is represented by the lowercase version of the letter. So, the allele for short stems would be represented by *t*. When a plant inherits two dominant alleles for tall stems, its alleles are written as *TT*. When a plant inherits two recessive alleles for short stems, its alleles are written as *tt*. When a plant inherits one allele for tall stems and one allele for short stems, its alleles are written as *Tt*.

Mendel's Contribution

In 1866, Mendel presented his results to a scientific society that met regularly near the monastery. In his paper, Mendel described the principles of heredity he had discovered. Unfortunately, other scientists did not understand the importance of Mendel's work. Some scientists thought that Mendel had oversimplified the process of inheritance. Others never read his paper, or even heard about his work. At that time, scientists in different parts of the world were isolated from each other. Mendel was especially isolated because he wasn't at a university. Remember, there were no telephones, and no computers to send electronic mail.

Mendel's work was forgotten for 34 years. In 1900, three different scientists rediscovered Mendel's work. They had made many of the same observations as Mendel had. The scientists quickly recognized the importance of Mendel's work. Many of the genetic principles that Mendel discovered still stand to this day. Because of his work, Mendel is often called the Father of Genetics.

Figure 5 The dominant allele for yellow skin color in summer squash is represented by the letter *Y*. The recessive allele for green skin color is represented by the letter *y*.

Section 1 Review

1. Explain how the inheritance of traits is controlled in organisms. Use the terms *genes* and *alleles* in your explanation.
2. What is a dominant allele? What is a recessive allele? Give an example of each.
3. The allele for round seeds is represented by *R*. Suppose that a pea plant inherited two recessive alleles for wrinkled seeds. How would you write the symbols for its alleles?
4. **Thinking Critically Applying Concepts** Can a short pea plant ever be a hybrid? Why or why not?

Check Your Progress

CHAPTER PROJECT 3

By now you should have constructed your paper pet. On the back, write what alleles your pet has for each trait. Use XX for a female, and XY for a male. The dominant alleles for the other four traits are: *B* (blue skin), *R* (round eyes), *T* (triangular nose), and *P* (pointed teeth). (*Hint:* If your pet has a trait controlled by a dominant allele, you can choose which of the possible combinations of alleles your pet has.)

Developing Hypotheses

Take a Class Survey

In this lab, you'll explore how greatly traits can vary in a group of people—your classmates.

Problem

Are traits controlled by dominant alleles more common than traits controlled by recessive alleles?

Materials

mirror (optional)

Procedure

Part 1 Dominant and Recessive Alleles

1. Write a hypothesis reflecting your ideas about the problem question. Then copy the data table.

2. For each of the traits listed in the data table, work with a partner to determine which trait you have. Circle that trait in your data table.

3. Count the number of students who have each trait. Record that number in your data table. Also record the total number of students.

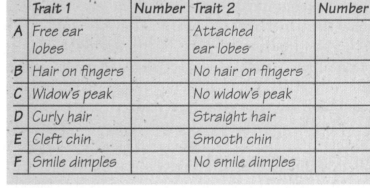

DATA TABLE				
Total Number _____				
	Trait 1	Number	Trait 2	Number
A	Free ear lobes		Attached ear lobes	
B	Hair on fingers		No hair on fingers	
C	Widow's peak		No widow's peak	
D	Curly hair		Straight hair	
E	Cleft chin		Smooth chin	
F	Smile dimples		No smile dimples	

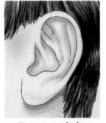
Free ear lobe

Hair on fingers

Widow's peak

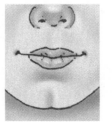
Cleft chin

Smile dimples

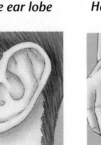
Attached ear lobe

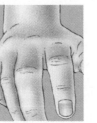
No hair on fingers

No widow's peak

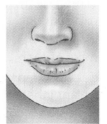
No cleft chin

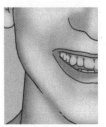
No smile dimples

Part 2 Are Your Traits Unique?

4. Look at the circle of traits below. All the traits in your data table appear in the circle. Place the eraser end of your pencil on the trait in the small central circle that applies to you—either free ear lobes or attached ear lobes.

5. Look at the two traits touching the space your eraser is on. Move your eraser onto the next description that applies to you. Continue using your eraser to trace your traits until you reach a number on the outside rim of the circle. Share that number with your classmates.

Analyze and Conclude

1. The traits listed under Trait 1 in the data table are controlled by dominant alleles. The traits listed under Trait 2 are controlled by recessive alleles. Which traits controlled by dominant alleles were shown by a majority of students? Which traits controlled by recessive alleles were shown by a majority of students?

2. How many students ended up on the same number on the circle of traits? How many students were the only ones to have their number? What do the results suggest about each person's combination of traits?

3. Think About It Do your data support the hypothesis you proposed in Step 1? Explain your answer with examples.

Design an Experiment

Do people who are related to each other show more genetic similarity than unrelated people? Write a hypothesis. Then design an experiment to test your hypothesis.

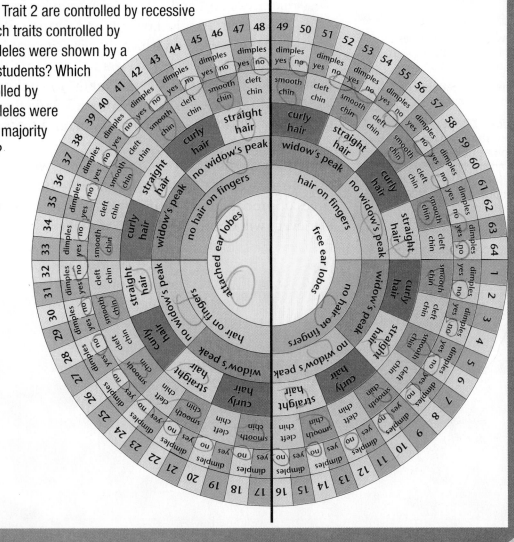

SECTION 2 Probability and Genetics

DISCOVER •••••••••••••••••••••••••••••••• ACTIVITY ••••

What's the Chance?

1. Suppose you were to toss a coin 20 times. Predict how many times the coin would land "heads up" and how many times it would land "tails up."

2. Now test your prediction by tossing a coin 20 times. Record the number of times the coin lands heads up and the number of times it lands tails up.

3. Combine the data from the entire class. Record the total number of tosses, the number of heads, and the number of tails.

Think It Over
Predicting How did your results in Step 2 compare to your prediction? How can you account for any differences between your results and the class results?

GUIDE FOR READING

◆ How do the principles of probability help explain Mendel's results?

◆ How do geneticists use Punnett squares?

Reading Tip Before you read, rewrite the headings in the section as questions that begin with *how, what,* or *why.* As you read, look for answers to these questions.

The city of Portland, Oregon, was founded in the mid-1800s. Two men, Asa L. Lovejoy and Francis W. Pettygrove, owned the land on which the new city was built. Lovejoy, who was from Massachusetts, wanted to name the new town Boston. Pettygrove, however, thought the town should be named after his hometown, Portland, Maine. To settle the dispute, they decided to toss a coin. Pettygrove won, and the new town was named Portland.

What was the chance that Pettygrove would win the coin toss? To answer this question, you need to understand the principles of probability. **Probability** is the likelihood that a particular event will occur.

Principles of Probability

If you did the Discover activity, you used the principles of probability to predict the results of a particular event. Each time you toss a coin, there are two possible ways that the coin can land—heads up or tails up. Each of these two events is equally likely to occur. In mathematical terms, you can say that the probability that a tossed coin will land heads up is 1 in 2. There is also a 1 in 2 probability that the coin will land tails up. A 1 in 2 probability can also be expressed as the fraction $\frac{1}{2}$ or as a percent—50 percent.

If you tossed a coin 20 times, you might expect it to land heads up 10 times and tails up 10 times. However, you might not actually get these results. You might get 11 heads and 9 tails, or 8 heads and 12 tails. Remember that the laws of probability predict what is likely to occur, not necessarily what will occur. However, the more tosses you make, the closer your actual results will be to the results predicted by probability.

When you toss a coin more than once, the results of one toss do not affect the results of the next toss. Each event occurs independently. For example, suppose you toss a coin five times and it lands heads up each time. What is the probability that it will land heads up on the next toss? Because the coin landed heads up on the previous five tosses, you might think that it would be likely to land heads up on the next toss. However, this is not the case. The probability of the coin landing heads up on the next toss is still 1 in 2, or 50 percent. The results of the first five tosses do not affect the results of the sixth toss.

✔️ *Checkpoint* *Why is there a 1 in 2 probability that a tossed coin will land heads up?*

Calculating Percent

One way you can express a probability is as a percent. A percent (%) is a number compared to 100. For example, 50% means 50 out of 100.

Suppose that 3 out of 5 tossed coins landed heads up. Here's how you can calculate what percent of the coins landed heads up.

1. Write the comparison as a fraction.

$$3 \text{ out of } 5 = \frac{3}{5}$$

2. Multiply the fraction by 100% to express it as a percent.

$$\frac{3}{5} \times \frac{100\%}{1} = 60\%$$

60% of the coins landed heads up.

Now, suppose 3 out of 12 coins landed tails up. How can you express this as a percent?

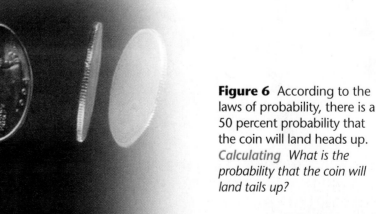

Figure 6 According to the laws of probability, there is a 50 percent probability that the coin will land heads up. *Calculating* What is the probability that the coin will land tails up?

Mendel and Probability

How is probability related to genetics? To answer this question, think back to Mendel's experiments with peas. Remember that Mendel carefully counted the offspring from every cross that he carried out. When Mendel crossed two plants that were hybrid for stem height (Tt), three fourths of the F_1 plants had tall stems. One fourth of the plants had short stems.

Each time Mendel repeated the cross, he obtained similar results. Mendel realized that the mathematical principles of probability applied to his work. He could say that the probability of such a cross producing a tall plant was 3 in 4. The probability of producing a short plant was 1 in 4. **Mendel was the first scientist to recognize that the principles of probability can be used to predict the results of genetic crosses.**

Punnett Squares

A tool that can help you understand how the laws of probability apply to genetics is called a Punnett square. A **Punnett square** is a chart that shows all the possible combinations of alleles that can result from a genetic cross. **Geneticists use Punnett squares to show all the possible outcomes of a genetic cross and to determine the probability of a particular outcome.**

The Punnett square in Figure 7 shows a cross between two hybrid tall pea plants (Tt). Each parent can pass either of its alleles, T or t, to its offspring. The possible alleles that one parent can pass on are written across the top of the Punnett square. The possible alleles that the other parent can pass on are written down the left side of the Punnett square. The boxes in the Punnett square represent the possible combinations of alleles that the offspring can inherit. The boxes are filled in like a multiplication problem, with one allele contributed by each parent.

Using a Punnett Square You can use a Punnett square to calculate the probability that offspring with a certain combination of alleles will result. The allele that each parent will pass on is based on chance, just like the toss of a coin. Thus, there are four possible combinations of alleles that can result. The

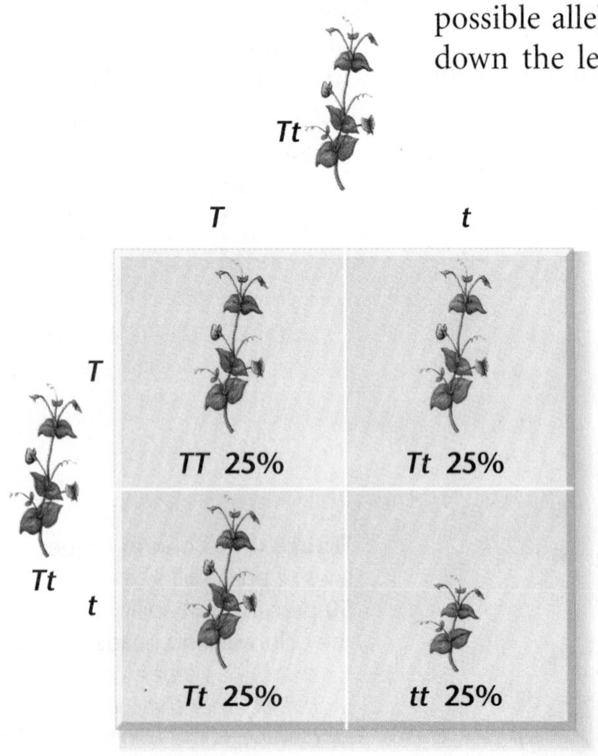

Tt

	T	**t**
T	TT 25%	Tt 25%
t	Tt 25%	tt 25%

Tt

Figure 7 This Punnett square shows a cross between two hybrid tall pea plants. *Interpreting Charts Which allele combinations will result in tall offspring?*

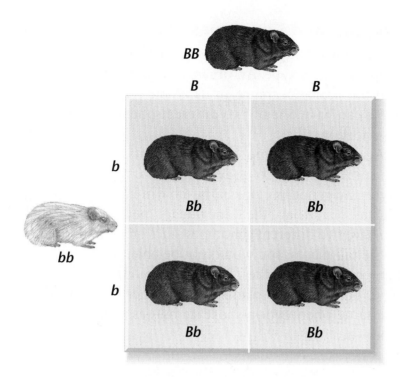

BB

B   *B*

b   *Bb*   *Bb*

b   *Bb*   *Bb*

bb

Figure 8 This Punnett square shows a cross between a black guinea pig (*BB*) and a white guinea pig (*bb*). *Calculating* What is the probability that an offspring will have white fur?

probability that an offspring will be *TT* is 1 in 4, or 25 percent. The probability that an offspring will be *tt* is also 1 in 4, or 25 percent. Notice, however, that the *Tt* allele combination appears in two boxes in the Punnett square. This is because there are two possible ways in which this combination can occur. The probability, then, that an offspring will be *Tt* is 2 in 4, or 50 percent.

Recall that when Mendel performed this cross, he discovered that about three fourths of the plants (75%) had tall stems. The remaining one fourth of the plants (25%) had short stems. Now you can understand why that was true. Plants with the *TT* allele combination would be tall. So too would those plants with the *Tt* allele combination. Remember that the dominant allele masks the recessive allele. Only those plants with the *tt* allele combination would be short.

Predicting Probabilities You can also use a Punnett square to predict probabilities. For example, Figure 8 shows a cross between a purebred black guinea pig and a purebred white guinea pig. The allele for black fur is dominant over the allele for white fur. Notice that only one allele combination is possible in the offspring—*Bb*. All of the offspring will inherit the dominant allele for black fur. Because of this, all of the offspring will have black fur. You can predict that there is a 100% probability that the offspring will have black fur.

☑ *Checkpoint* *If two guinea pigs with the alleles* Bb *are crossed, what is the probability that an offspring will have white fur?*

Coin Crosses

Here's how you can use coins to model Mendel's cross between two *Tt* pea plants.

1. Place a small piece of masking tape on each side of two coins.

2. Write a *T* (for tall) on one side of each coin and a *t* (for short) on the other.

3. Toss both coins together 20 times. Record the letter combinations that you obtain from each toss.

Interpreting Data How many of the offspring would be tall plants? (*Hint:* What different letter combinations would result in a tall plant?) How many would be short? Convert your results to percents. Then compare your results to Mendel's.

Phenotypes and Genotypes	
Phenotype	**Genotype**
Tall	*TT*
Tall	*Tt*
Short	*tt*

Figure 9 The phenotype of an organism is its physical appearance. Its genotype is its genetic makeup.

Phenotypes and Genotypes

Two useful terms that geneticists use to describe organisms are phenotype and genotype. An organism's **phenotype** (FEE noh typ) is its physical appearance, or its visible traits. For example, pea plants can have one of two different phenotypes for stem height—short or tall.

An organism's **genotype** (JEN uh typ) is its genetic makeup, or allele combinations. To understand the difference between phenotype and genotype, look at the table in Figure 9. Although all of the tall plants have the same phenotype (they are all tall), they can have two different genotypes—*TT* or *Tt*. If you were to look at the tall plants, you would not be able to tell the difference between those with the *TT* genotype and those with the *Tt* genotype. The short pea plants, on the other hand, would all have the same phenotype—short stems—as well as the same genotype—*tt*.

Geneticists use two additional terms to describe an organism's genotype. An organism that has two identical alleles for a trait is said to be **homozygous** (hoh moh ZY gus) for that trait. A tall pea plant that has the alleles *TT* and a short pea plant with the alleles *tt* are both homozygous. An organism that has two different alleles for a trait is said to be **heterozygous** (het ur oh ZY gus) for that trait. A tall pea plant with the alleles *Tt* is heterozygous. Mendel used the term *hybrid* to describe heterozygous pea plants.

☑ *Checkpoint* *If a pea plant's genotype is* Tt, *what is its phenotype?*

Codominance

For all of the traits that Mendel studied, one allele was dominant while the other was recessive. This is not always the case. For some alleles, an inheritance pattern called codominance exists. In **codominance,** the alleles are neither dominant nor recessive. As a result, both alleles are expressed in the offspring.

Look at the Punnett square in Figure 11. Mendel's principle of dominant and recessive alleles does not explain why the heterozygous chickens have both black and white feathers. The alleles for feather color are

Figure 10 In Erminette chickens, the alleles for black feathers and white feathers are codominant.

Figure 11 The offspring from the cross in this Punnett square will have both black and white feathers. *Classifying Will the offspring be heterozygous or homozygous? Explain your answer.*

codominant—neither dominant nor recessive. As you can see, neither allele is masked in the heterozygous chickens. Notice also that the codominant alleles are written as capital letters with superscripts—F^B for black feathers and F^W for white feathers. As the Punnett square shows, heterozygous chickens have the $F^B F^W$ allele combination.

Another example of codominance can be found in cattle. Red hair and white hair are codominant. Heterozygous cattle have coats with both white hairs and red hairs. From a distance, heterozygous cattle look pinkish brown, a color called roan.

Section 2 Review

1. What is meant by the term *probability*? How is probability related to genetics?
2. How are Punnett squares useful to geneticists?
3. What is the difference between a phenotype and a genotype? Give an example of each.
4. A white cow is crossed with a red bull. The calf is neither white nor red, but roan. Explain how this happens.
5. **Thinking Critically Problem Solving** In pea plants, the allele for round seeds (*R*) is dominant over the allele for wrinkled seeds (*r*). Construct a Punnett square that shows a cross between a heterozygous plant with round seeds (*Rr*) and a homozygous plant with wrinkled seeds (*rr*). What is the probability that an offspring will have wrinkled seeds?

Science at Home

Have a family member think of a number between 1 and 5. Then try to guess the number. Discuss the probability of guessing the correct number. Then repeat the guessing activity four more times. How did your success rate compare to the probability of guessing correctly? How can you account for any difference between your success rate and the results predicted by probability?

MAKE THE RIGHT CALL!

You know that making predictions is an important part of science. An accurate prediction can be a sign that you understand the event you are studying. In this lab, you will make predictions as you model the events involved in genetic crosses.

Problem

How can you predict the possible results of genetic crosses?

Materials

2 small paper bags
marking pen
3 blue marbles
3 white marbles

Procedure

1. Label one bag "Bag 1, Female Parent." Label the other bag "Bag 2, Male Parent." Then read over Part 1, Part 2, and Part 3 of this lab. Write a prediction about the kinds of offspring you expect from each cross.

Part 1 Crossing Two Homozygous Parents

2. Copy the data table and label it *Data Table Number 1*. Then place two blue marbles in Bag 1. This pair of marbles represents the female parent's alleles. Use the letter *B* to represent the dominant allele for blue color.

3. Place two white marbles in Bag 2. Use the letter *b* to represent the recessive allele for white color.

4. For Trial 1, remove one marble from Bag 1 without looking in the bag. Record the result in your data table. Return the marble to the bag. Again, without looking in the bag, remove one marble from Bag 2. Record the result in your data table. Return the marble to the bag.

5. In the column labeled *Offspring's Alleles*, write *BB* if you removed two blue marbles, *bb* if you removed two white marbles, or *Bb* if you removed one blue marble and one white marble.

6. Repeat Steps 4 and 5 nine more times.

DATA TABLE

Number _____

Trial	Allele From Bag 1 (Female Parent)	Allele From Bag 2 (Male Parent)	Offspring's Alleles
1			
2			
3			
4			
5			
6			

Part 2 Crossing a Homozygous Parent With a Heterozygous Parent

7. Place two blue marbles in Bag 1. Place one white marble and one blue marble in Bag 2. Copy the data table again, and label it *Data Table Number 2.*

8. Repeat Steps 4 and 5 ten times.

Part 3 Crossing Two Heterozygous Parents

9. Place one blue marble and one white marble in Bag 1. Place one blue marble and one white marble in Bag 2. Copy the data table again and label it *Data Table Number 3.*

10. Repeat Steps 4 and 5 ten times.

Analyze and Conclude

1. Make a Punnett square for each of the crosses you modeled in Part 1, Part 2, and Part 3.

2. According to your results in Part 1, how many different kinds of offspring are possible when the homozygous parents (*BB* and *bb*) are crossed? Do the results you obtained using the marble model agree with the results shown by a Punnett square?

3. According to your results in Part 2, what percent of offspring are likely to be homozygous when a homozygous parent (*BB*) and a heterozygous parent (*Bb*) are crossed? What percent of offspring are likely to be heterozygous? Does the model agree with the results shown by a Punnett square?

4. According to your results in Part 3, what different kinds of offspring are possible when two heterozygous parents (*Bb* × *Bb*) are crossed? What percent of each type of offspring are likely to be produced? Does the model agree with the results of a Punnett square?

5. For Part 3, if you did 100 trials instead of 10 trials, would your results be closer to the results shown in a Punnett square? Explain.

6. **Think About It** How does the marble model compare with a Punnett square? How are the two methods alike? How are they different?

More to Explore

In peas, the allele for yellow seeds (*Y*) is dominant over the allele for green seeds (*y*). What possible crosses do you think could produce a heterozygous plant with yellow seeds (*Yy*)? Use the marble model and Punnett squares to test your predictions.

SECTION
③ The Cell and Inheritance

DISCOVER • ACTIVITY • • •

Which Chromosome Is Which?

Mendel did not know that chromosomes play a role in genetics. Today we know that genes are located on chromosomes.

1. Label two craft sticks with the letter *A*. The craft sticks represent a pair of chromosomes in the female parent. Turn the sticks face down on a piece of paper.

2. Label two more craft sticks with the letter *a*. These represent a pair of chromosomes in the male parent. Turn the sticks face down on another piece of paper.

3. Turn over one craft stick "chromosome" from each piece of paper. Move both sticks to a third piece of paper. These represent a pair of chromosomes in the offspring. Note the allele combination that the offspring received.

Think It Over
Inferring Use this model to explain how chromosomes are involved in the inheritance of alleles.

GUIDE FOR READING

◆ What role do chromosomes play in inheritance?

◆ What events occur during meiosis?

Reading Tip Before you read, preview *Exploring Meiosis* on page 99. Predict what role chromosomes play in the inheritance of traits.

Sperm cells ▼

When Mendel's results were rediscovered in 1900, scientists around the world became excited about Mendel's principles of inheritance. They were eager to identify the structures inside of cells that carried Mendel's hereditary factors, or genes.

In 1903, Walter Sutton, an American geneticist, added an important piece of information to scientists' understanding of genetics. Sutton was studying the cells of grasshoppers. He was trying to understand how sex cells—sperm and egg—form. During his studies, Sutton examined sex cells in many different stages of formation. He became particularly interested in the movement of chromosomes during the formation of sex cells. Sutton hypothesized that chromosomes were the key to understanding how offspring come to have traits similar to those of their parents.

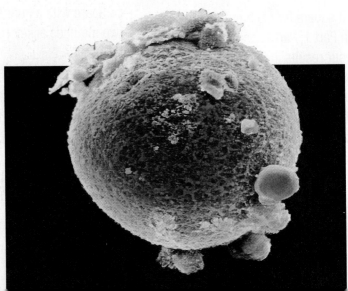

◄ Egg cell

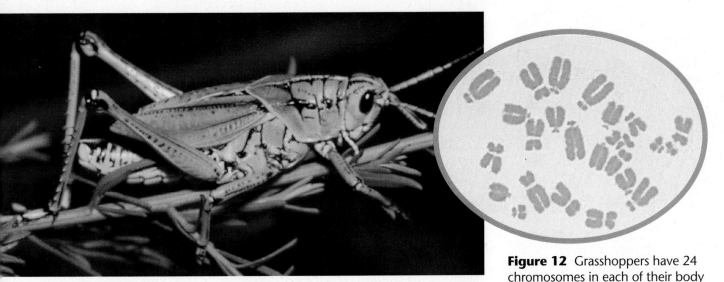

Figure 12 Grasshoppers have 24 chromosomes in each of their body cells. *Applying Concepts How many chromosomes did Sutton observe in the sperm cells and egg cells of grasshoppers?*

Chromosomes and Inheritance

Sutton knew that structures inside cells must be responsible for the inheritance of genes. He needed evidence to support his hypothesis that chromosomes were those structures. Sutton compared the number of chromosomes in a grasshopper's sex cells with the number of chromosomes in the other cells in the grasshopper's body. As you can see in Figure 12, the body cells of grasshoppers have 24 chromosomes. To his surprise, Sutton found that the grasshopper's sex cells have only 12 chromosomes. In other words, a grasshopper's sex cells have exactly half the number of chromosomes found in its body cells.

Sutton knew that he had discovered something important. He observed what happened when a sperm cell (with 12 chromosomes) and an egg cell (with 12 chromosomes) joined. The fertilized egg that formed had 24 chromosomes—the original number. As a result, the grasshopper offspring had exactly the same number of chromosomes in its cells as did each of its parents. The 24 chromosomes existed in 12 pairs. One chromosome in each pair came from the male parent, while the other chromosome came from the female parent.

Sutton concluded that the chromosomes carried Mendel's hereditary factors, or genes, from one generation to the next. In other words, genes are located on chromosomes. Sutton's idea came to be known as the chromosome theory of inheritance. **According to the chromosome theory of inheritance, genes are carried from parents to their offspring on chromosomes.**

☑ *Checkpoint How does the number of chromosomes in a grasshopper's sex cells compare to the number in its body cells?*

Meiosis

How do sex cells end up with half the number of chromosomes as body cells? To answer this question, you need to understand the events that occur during meiosis. **Meiosis** (my OH sis) is the process by which the number of chromosomes is reduced by half to form sex cells—sperm and eggs.

You can trace the events of meiosis in *Exploring Meiosis*. In this example, each parent cell has four chromosomes arranged in two pairs. **During meiosis, the chromosome pairs separate and are distributed to two different cells. The resulting sex cells have only half as many chromosomes as the other cells in the organism.** In *Exploring Meiosis,* notice that the sex cells end up with only two chromosomes each—half the number found in the parent cell. Only one chromosome from each chromosome pair ends up in each sex cell.

When sex cells combine to produce offspring, each sex cell will contribute half the normal number of chromosomes. Thus, the offspring gets the normal number of chromosomes—half from each parent.

☑ *Checkpoint* *What types of cells form by meiosis?*

Meiosis and Punnett Squares

The Punnett squares that you learned about earlier in this chapter are actually a shorthand way to show the events that occur at meiosis. When the chromosome pairs separate into two different sex cells, so do the alleles carried on each chromosome. One allele from each pair goes to each sex cell. In Figure 13, you can see how the Punnett square accounts for the separation of alleles during meiosis.

As shown across the top of the Punnett square, half of the sperm cells from the male parent will receive the chromosome with the *T* allele. The other half of the sperm cells will receive the chromosome with the *t* allele. In this example, the same is true for the egg cells from the female parent, as shown down the left side of the Punnett square. Depending on which sperm cell combines with which egg cell, one of the allele combinations shown in the boxes will result.

Figure 13 This Punnett square shows how alleles separate when sex cells form during meiosis. It also shows the possible allele combinations that can result after fertilization occurs. *Interpreting Charts What is the probability that a sperm cell will contain a T allele?*

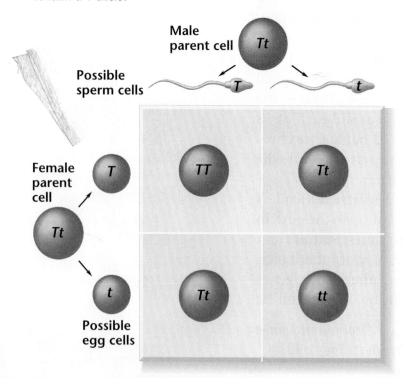

Male parent cell — Tt
Possible sperm cells — T — t
Female parent cell — Tt
Possible egg cells — T — t

TT | Tt
Tt | tt

EXPLORING Meiosis

During meiosis, a cell undergoes two divisions to produce sex cells that have half the number of chromosomes.

1 Beginning of Meiosis
Before meiosis begins, every chromosome in the cell is copied. As in mitosis, centromeres hold the double-stranded chromosomes together.

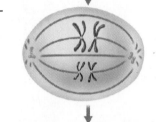

2 Meiosis I
The chromosome pairs line up next to each other in the center of the cell. The pairs then separate from each other and move to opposite ends of the cell. Two cells form, each with half the number of chromosomes. Each chromosome is still double-stranded.

3 Meiosis II
The double-stranded chromosomes move to the center of the cell. The centromeres split and the two strands of each chromosome separate. The two strands move to opposite ends of the cell.

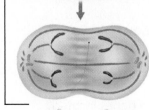

4 End of Meiosis
Four sex cells have been produced. Each cell has only half the number of chromosomes that the parent cell had at the beginning of meiosis. Each cell has only one chromosome from each original pair.

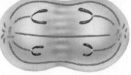

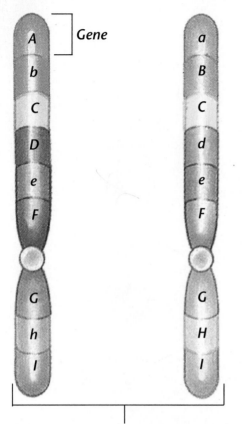

Gene

A chromosome pair

Figure 14 Genes are located on chromosomes. The chromosomes in a pair may have different alleles for some genes and the same alleles for others. *Classifying For which genes is this organism homozygous? For which genes is it heterozygous?*

Chromosomes

Since Sutton's time, scientists have studied the chromosomes of many different organisms. The body cells of humans, for example, contain 23 pairs, or 46 chromosomes. The body cells of dogs have 78 chromosomes, while the body cells of silkworms have 56 chromosomes. As you can see, larger organisms don't always have more chromosomes.

Chromosomes are made up of many genes joined together like beads on a string. Sutton reasoned that chromosomes must contain a large number of genes because organisms have so many traits. Although you have only 23 pairs of chromosomes, your body cells contain more than 60,000 genes. Each of the genes controls a particular trait.

Look at the pair of chromosomes in Figure 14. One chromosome in the pair came from the female parent. The other chromosome came from the male parent. Notice that each chromosome in the pair has the same genes. The genes are lined up in the same order from one end of the chromosome to the other. However, the alleles for some of the genes might be different. For example, the organism has the *A* allele on one chromosome and the *a* allele on the other. As you can see, this organism is heterozygous for some traits and homozygous for others.

Section 3 Review

1. Explain the role that chromosomes play in inheritance.
2. Briefly describe what happens to chromosomes during meiosis.
3. On what structures in a cell are genes located?
4. How is a Punnett square a model for what happens during meiosis?
5. **Thinking Critically** **Inferring** The body cells of hamsters have 44 chromosomes. How many chromosomes would the sex cells of a hamster have?

Check Your Progress CHAPTER PROJECT 3
At this point, you should find a classmate with a paper pet of the opposite sex. Suppose the two pets were crossed and produced six offspring. For each trait, use coin tosses to determine which allele the offspring will inherit from each parent. Construct a paper pet for each offspring, showing the traits that each one has inherited. Write the genotype for each trait on their backs.

Can You Crack the Code?

A • –	N – •
B – • • •	O – – –
C – • – •	P • – – •
D – • •	Q – – • –
E •	R • – •
F • • – •	S • • •
G – – •	T –
H • • • •	U • • –
I • •	V • • • –
J • – – –	W • – –
K – • –	X – • • –
L • – • •	Y – • – –
M – –	Z – – • •

1. Use the Morse code in the chart to decode the question in the message below. The letters are separated by slash marks.

• – – / • • • • / • / • – • / • / • – / • – • / • / – – • / • / – • /
• / • • • / • – • • / – – – / – • – • / • – / – / • / – • • /

2. Write your answer to the question in Morse code.

3. Exchange your coded answer with a partner. Then decode your partner's answer.

Think It Over

Forming Operational Definitions Based on your results from this activity, write a definition of the word *code*. Then compare your definition to one in a dictionary.

A white buffalo calf was born on Childs Place Farm near Hanover, Michigan, in 1998. White buffaloes are extremely rare, occurring only once in every 10 million births. Why was this calf born with such an uncommon phenotype? To answer this question, you need to know how the genes on a chromosome control an organism's traits.

The Genetic Code

Today scientists know that the main function of genes is to control the production of proteins in the organism's cells. Proteins help to determine the size, shape, and many other traits of an organism.

GUIDE FOR READING

◆ What is meant by the term "genetic code"?

◆ How does a cell produce proteins?

◆ How do mutations affect an organism?

Reading Tip As you read, create a flowchart that shows how a cell produces proteins.

Figure 15 The white color of this buffalo calf is very unusual. Both of the calf's parents had brown coats.

Recall from Chapter 2 that chromosomes are composed mostly of DNA. In Figure 16, you can see the relationship between chromosomes and DNA. Notice that a DNA molecule is made up of four different nitrogen bases—adenine (A), thymine (T), guanine (G), and cytosine (C). These bases form the rungs of the DNA "ladder." A single gene on a chromosome may contain anywhere from several hundred to a million or more of these bases. The bases are arranged in a specific order— for example, ATGACGTAC.

The order of the nitrogen bases along a gene forms a genetic code that specifies what type of protein will be produced. In the genetic code, a group of three bases codes for the attachment of a specific amino acid. Amino acids are the building blocks of proteins. The order of the bases determines the order in which amino acids are put together to form a protein. You can think of the bases as three-letter code words. The code words tell the cell which amino acid to add to the growing protein chain.

☑ *Checkpoint* *What is the main function of genes?*

How Cells Make Proteins

The production of proteins is called protein synthesis. **During protein synthesis, the cell uses information from a gene on a chromosome to produce a specific protein.** Protein synthesis takes place on the ribosomes in the cytoplasm of the cell. As you know, the cytoplasm is outside the nucleus. The chromosomes, however, are found inside the nucleus. How, then, does the information needed to produce proteins get out of the nucleus and into the cytoplasm?

Figure 16 A chromosome contains thousands of genes along its length. The sequence of bases along a gene forms a code that tells the cell what protein to produce. *Interpreting Diagrams Where in the cell are the chromosomes located?*

Chromosome

Cell

The Role of RNA Before protein synthesis can take place, a "messenger" must first carry the genetic code from the DNA inside the nucleus into the cytoplasm. This genetic messenger is called ribonucleic acid, or RNA.

Although RNA is similar to DNA, the two molecules differ in some important ways. Unlike DNA, which looks like a twisted ladder, an RNA molecule almost always looks like only one side, or strand, of the ladder. RNA also contains a different sugar molecule from the sugar found in DNA. Another difference between DNA and RNA is in their nitrogen bases. Like DNA, RNA contains adenine, guanine, and cytosine. However, instead of thymine, RNA contains uracil (YOOR uh sil).

There are several types of RNA involved in protein synthesis. **Messenger RNA** copies the coded message from the DNA in the nucleus, and carries the message into the cytoplasm. Another type of RNA, called **transfer RNA**, carries amino acids and adds them to the growing protein.

Translating the Code The process of protein synthesis is shown in *Exploring Protein Synthesis* on the next page. The first step is for a DNA molecule to "unzip" between its base pairs. Then one of the strands of DNA directs the production of a strand of messenger RNA. To form the RNA strand, RNA bases pair up with the DNA bases. Instead of thymine, however, uracil pairs with adenine. The messenger RNA then leaves the nucleus and attaches to a ribosome in the cytoplasm. There, molecules of transfer RNA pick up the amino acids specified by each three-letter code word. Each transfer RNA molecule puts the amino acid it is carrying in the correct order along the growing protein chain.

☑ *Checkpoint* *What is the function of transfer RNA?*

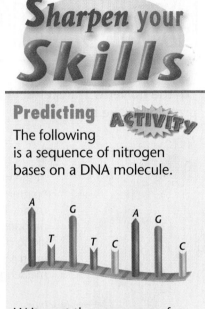

Sharpen your **Skills**

Predicting ACTIVITY
The following is a sequence of nitrogen bases on a DNA molecule.

Write out the sequence of RNA bases that would pair up with the DNA bases.

DNA molecule

Nitrogen bases

EXPLORING Protein Synthesis

To make proteins, messenger RNA copies information from DNA in the nucleus. Transfer RNA then uses this information to produce proteins in the ribosomes.

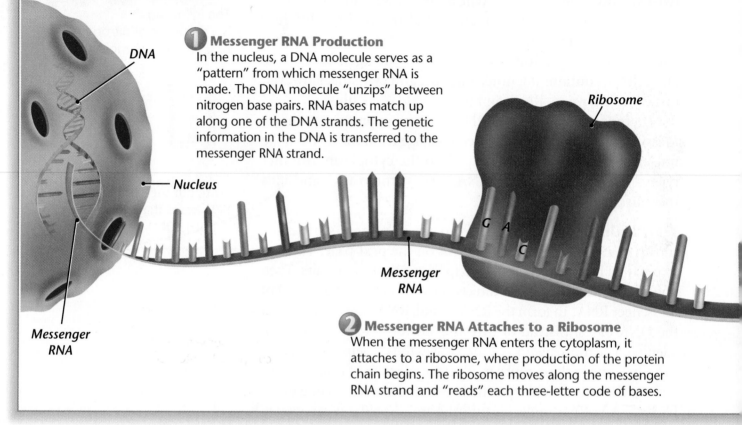

1 **Messenger RNA Production**
In the nucleus, a DNA molecule serves as a "pattern" from which messenger RNA is made. The DNA molecule "unzips" between nitrogen base pairs. RNA bases match up along one of the DNA strands. The genetic information in the DNA is transferred to the messenger RNA strand.

DNA

Ribosome

Nucleus

G A
C

Messenger RNA

Messenger RNA

2 **Messenger RNA Attaches to a Ribosome**
When the messenger RNA enters the cytoplasm, it attaches to a ribosome, where production of the protein chain begins. The ribosome moves along the messenger RNA strand and "reads" each three-letter code of bases.

Mutations

Suppose that a mistake occurred in one gene of a chromosome. Instead of the base A, for example, the DNA molecule might have the base G. Such a mistake is one type of mutation that can occur in a cell's hereditary material. Recall from Chapter 2 that a mutation is any change in a gene or chromosome. Mutations can cause a cell to produce an incorrect protein during protein synthesis. As a result, the organism's traits, or phenotype, will be different from what it normally would have been. In fact, the term *mutation* comes from a Latin word that means "change."

Types of Mutations Some mutations are the result of small changes in an organism's hereditary material, such as the substitution of a single base for another. This type of mutation can occur during the DNA replication process. The white coat on the

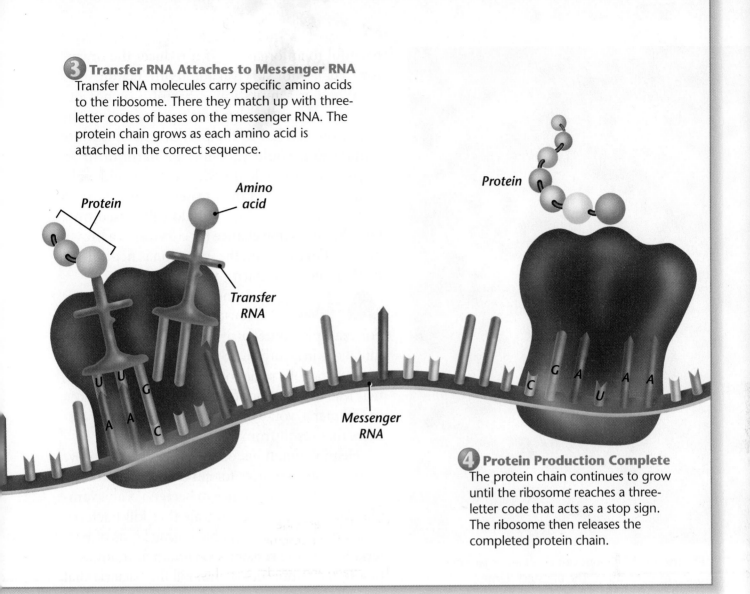

③ Transfer RNA Attaches to Messenger RNA

Transfer RNA molecules carry specific amino acids to the ribosome. There they match up with three-letter codes of bases on the messenger RNA. The protein chain grows as each amino acid is attached in the correct sequence.

Protein

Amino acid

Protein

Transfer RNA

Messenger RNA

④ Protein Production Complete

The protein chain continues to grow until the ribosome reaches a three-letter code that acts as a stop sign. The ribosome then releases the completed protein chain.

buffalo calf you read about at the start of this section might have resulted from this type of mutation. Other mutations may occur when chromosomes don't separate correctly during meiosis. When this type of mutation occurs, a cell can end up with too many or too few chromosomes. The cell could also end up with extra segments of chromosomes.

If a mutation occurs in a body cell, such as a skin cell, the mutation will affect only the cell that carries it. If, however, a mutation occurs in a sex cell, the mutation can be passed on to an offspring and affect the offspring's phenotype.

The Effects of Mutations Because mutations can introduce changes in an organism, they can be a source of genetic variety. **Some of the changes brought about by mutations are harmful to an organism. Other mutations, however, are helpful, and still others are neither harmful nor helpful.** A mutation is

Figure 17 Mutations can affect an organism's traits, or phenotype. The unusually large strawberries on the left are the result of a mutation. The cells of these strawberries have extra sets of chromosomes.

harmful to an organism if it reduces the organism's chance for survival and reproduction.

Whether a mutation is harmful or not depends partly on the organism's environment. The mutation that led to the production of a white buffalo calf would probably be harmful to an organism in the wild. Its white color would make it more visible, and thus easier for predators to find. However, a white buffalo calf raised on a farm has the same chance for survival as a brown buffalo. On the farm, the mutation is neutral—it neither helps nor harms the buffalo.

INTEGRATING HEALTH Some diseases in humans are caused by harmful mutations. For example, some forms of cancer are caused by mutations in an organism's body cells. Overexposure to the ultraviolet radiation in sunlight, for example, may lead to mutations that could cause skin cancer. In Chapter 4, you will learn more about other diseases that result from harmful mutations.

Helpful mutations, on the other hand, improve an organism's chances for survival and reproduction. Antibiotic resistance in bacteria is an example. Antibiotics are chemicals that kill bacteria. Gene mutations have enabled some kinds of bacteria to become resistant to certain antibiotics—that is, the antibiotics do not kill the bacteria that have the mutations. Since the antibiotic-resistant bacteria are not killed by the antibiotics, the mutations have improved the bacteria's ability to survive and reproduce.

Section 4 Review

1. How do the nitrogen bases along a gene serve as a genetic code?
2. Briefly describe the process by which a cell produces proteins.
3. What possible effects can a mutation have on an organism?
4. Where in a cell does protein synthesis take place?
5. **Thinking Critically** Relating Cause and Effect Why are mutations that occur in an organism's body cells not passed on to its offspring?

Check Your Progress **CHAPTER PROJECT 3**
With your partner, plan a display of your pet's family. Label the parents the P generation. Label the offspring the F_1 generation. Construct a Punnett square for each trait to help explain the inheritance pattern in your pet's family. (Hint: Attach your pets to the display in a way that lets viewers turn the pets over to read their genotypes.)

SECTION 1 — Mendel's Work

Key Ideas
- Gregor Mendel's work was the foundation for understanding why offspring have traits similar to those of their parents.
- Traits are controlled by alleles of genes. Organisms inherit one allele from each parent.
- Some alleles are dominant and some alleles are recessive.

Key Terms
trait	purebred	dominant allele
heredity	gene	recessive allele
genetics	allele	hybrid

SECTION 2 — Probability and Genetics

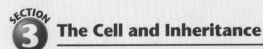
INTEGRATING MATHEMATICS

Key Ideas
- Probability is the likelihood that a particular event will happen.
- Mendel was the first scientist to interpret his data using the principles of probability.
- Geneticists use Punnett squares to show all the possible outcomes of a genetic cross.

Key Terms
probability	homozygous
Punnett square	heterozygous
phenotype	codominance
genotype	

SECTION 3 — The Cell and Inheritance

Key Ideas
- According to the chromosome theory of inheritance, genes are carried from parents to their offspring on chromosomes.
- During meiosis, chromosome pairs separate to form sex cells. Only one chromosome from each pair ends up in each sex cell. The sex cells have half the number of chromosomes as the body cells.

Key Term
meiosis

SECTION 4 — The DNA Connection

Key Ideas
- The nitrogen bases along a gene form a code that specifies the order in which amino acids will be put together to produce a protein.
- During protein synthesis, messenger RNA copies the coded message from the DNA in the nucleus and carries the message into the cytoplasm. Transfer RNA adds amino acids to the growing protein.
- A mutation is a change in a gene or chromosome. Some mutations are harmful, some are helpful, and some are neutral.

Key Terms
messenger RNA
transfer RNA

Organizing Information

Compare/Contrast Table Copy the table comparing DNA and messenger RNA onto a separate sheet of paper. Then complete the table. (For more about compare/contrast tables, see the Skills Handbook.)

Characteristic	DNA	Messenger RNA
Nitrogen bases	a. ? , b. ? , c. ? , d. ?	Adenine, uracil, guanine, cytosine
Structure	Twisted ladder	e. ?
Function	Forms a genetic code that specifies what type of protein will be produced	f. ?

Reviewing Content

For more review of key concepts, see the Interactive Student Tutorial CD-ROM.

Multiple Choice

Choose the letter of the best answer.

1. The different forms of a gene are called
   a. alleles.
   b. chromosomes.
   c. phenotypes.
   d. genotypes.

2. In a coin toss, the probability of the coin landing heads up is
   a. 100 percent.
   b. 75 percent.
   c. 50 percent.
   d. 25 percent.

3. An organism with two identical alleles for a trait is
   a. heterozygous.
   b. homozygous.
   c. recessive.
   d. dominant.

4. If the body cells of an organism have 10 chromosomes, then its sex cells would have
   a. 5 chromosomes.
   b. 10 chromosomes.
   c. 15 chromosomes.
   d. 20 chromosomes.

5. During protein synthesis, messenger RNA
   a. "reads" each three-letter code of bases.
   b. releases the completed protein chain.
   c. copies information from DNA in the nucleus.
   d. carries amino acids to the ribosome.

True or False

If the statement is true, write true. If it is false, change the underlined word or words to make the statement true.

6. The scientific study of heredity is called <u>genetics</u>.

7. An organism's physical appearance is its <u>genotype</u>.

8. In <u>codominance</u>, neither of the alleles is dominant or recessive.

9. <u>Heredity</u> is the process by which sex cells form.

10. Proteins are made in the <u>nucleus</u> of the cell.

Checking Concepts

11. Describe what happened when Mendel crossed purebred tall pea plants with purebred short pea plants.

12. You toss a coin five times and it lands heads up each time. What is the probability that it will land heads up on the sixth toss? Explain your answer.

13. In guinea pigs, the allele for black fur (*B*) is dominant over the allele for white fur (*b*). In a cross between a heterozygous black guinea pig (*Bb*) and a homozygous white guinea pig (*bb*), what is the probability that an offspring will have white fur? Use a Punnett square to answer the question.

14. In your own words, describe the sequence of steps in the process of meiosis.

15. Describe the role of transfer RNA in protein synthesis.

16. **Writing to Learn** Imagine that you are a student in the 1860s visiting Gregor Mendel in his garden. Write a letter to a friend describing Mendel's experiments.

Thinking Critically

17. **Applying Concepts** In rabbits, the allele for a spotted coat is dominant over the allele for a solid-colored coat. A spotted rabbit was crossed with a solid-colored rabbit. The offspring all had spotted coats. What were the genotypes of the parents? Explain.

18. **Problem Solving** Suppose you are growing purebred green-skinned watermelons. One day you find a mutant striped watermelon. You cross the striped watermelon with a purebred green watermelon. Fifty percent of the offspring are striped, while fifty percent are green. Is the allele for the striped trait dominant or recessive? Explain.

19. **Predicting** A new mutation in mice causes the coat to be twice as thick as normal. In what environments would this mutation be helpful?

Applying Skills

In peas, the allele for green pods (G) is dominant over the allele for yellow pods (g). The table shows the phenotypes of the offspring produced from a cross of two plants with green pods. Use the data to answer Questions 20–22.

Phenotype	Number of Offspring
Green pods	9
Yellow pods	3

20. **Calculating** Calculate what percent of the offspring have green pods. Calculate what percent have yellow pods.
21. **Inferring** What is the genotype of the offspring with yellow pods? What are the possible genotypes of the offspring with green pods?
22. **Drawing Conclusions** What are the genotypes of the parents? How do you know?

CHAPTER PROJECT 3

Performance Assessment

Project Wrap Up Finalize your display of your pet's family. Be prepared to discuss the inheritance patterns in your pet's family. Examine your classmates' exhibits, and see which offspring look most like, and least like, their parents. Can you find any offspring that "break the laws" of inheritance?

Reflect and Record How did your paper pets help you learn about genetics? How do the inheritance patterns in your pet's family resemble real-life patterns? How could you use paper pets to help you understand other topics in genetics?

Test Preparation

Use these questions to prepare for standardized tests.

Use the information to answer Questions 23–26.
A pet store's customers prefer pet mice with black fur over mice with white fur. With this in mind, the owner crossed a female with black fur and a male with black fur. When the mice were born, she was surprised that three of the ten offspring had white fur. She did not know that the parents were heterozygous for fur color.

23. Which letters represent the genotype of the female parent?
    a. BB   b. Bb
    c. B   d. bb
24. Which letters represent the genotype of the male parent?
    a. BB   b. Bb
    c. B   d. bb

25. How could the pet store owner breed a litter of only white mice?
    a. by making sure that either the mother or the father has white fur
    b. by making sure that both the mother and the father have white fur
    c. by making sure that at least one of the grandparents has white fur
    d. She could not breed a litter of only white mice.
26. If the pet store owner were to cross one homozygous black mouse with a heterozygous black mouse, what percentage of the mice would you expect to have white fur?
    a. 0%   b. 25%
    c. 50%   d. 75%

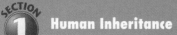

WEB ACTIVITY
www.phschool.com

A Family Portrait

A pedigree, or family tree, is a branched drawing that shows many generations of a family. In some cases, a pedigree may show centuries of a family's history.

In genetics, pedigrees are used to show how traits are passed from one generation to the next. In this project, you will create a genetic pedigree for an imaginary family. Although the family will be imaginary, your pedigree must show how real human traits are passed from parents to children.

Your Goal To create a pedigree for an imaginary family that shows the transfer of genetic traits from one generation to the next.

To complete the project you will
◆ choose two different genetic traits, and identify all the possible genotypes and phenotypes
◆ create pedigrees that trace each trait through three generations of your imaginary family
◆ prepare a family "photo" album to show what each family member looks like

Get Started With a partner, review the human traits described on page 86 in Chapter 3. List what you already know about human inheritance. For example, which human traits are controlled by dominant alleles? Which are controlled by recessive alleles? Then preview Section 1 of this chapter, and list the traits you'll be studying. Choose two traits that you would like to focus on in your project.

Check Your Progress You'll be working on this project as you study this chapter. To keep your project on track, look for Check Your Progress boxes at the following points.

Section 1 Review, page 118: Create a pedigree for the first trait you chose.

Section 2 Review, page 123: Create the second pedigree, and begin your family album.

Wrap Up At the end of the chapter (page 137), you will present your family's pedigrees and "photo" album to the class.

The children in this family
have some traits like their
mother's and some traits
like their father's.

DISCOVER · ACTIVITY · · · ·

How Tall Is Tall?

1. Choose a partner. Measure each other's height to the nearest 5 centimeters. Record your measurements on the chalkboard.

2. Create a bar graph showing the number of students at each height. Plot the heights on the horizontal axis and the number of students on the vertical axis.

Think It Over

Inferring If Gregor Mendel had graphed the heights of his pea plants, the graph would have had two bars—one for tall stems and one for short stems. Do you think height in humans is controlled by a single gene, as it is in peas? Explain your answer.

GUIDE FOR READING

◆ Why do some human traits show a large variety of phenotypes?

◆ Why are some sex-linked traits more common in males than in females?

◆ How do geneticists use pedigrees?

Reading Tip Before you read, rewrite the headings in this section as *how, why,* or *what* questions. As you read, write answers to the questions.

Have you ever heard someone say "He's the spitting image of his dad" or "She has her mother's eyes"? Children often resemble their parents. The reason for this is that alleles for eye color, hair color, and thousands of other traits are passed from parents to their children. People inherit some alleles from their mother and some from their father. This is why most people look a little like their mother and a little like their father.

Traits Controlled by Single Genes

In Chapter 3, you learned that many traits in peas and other organisms are controlled by a single gene with two alleles. Often one allele is dominant, while the other is recessive. Many human traits are also controlled by a single gene with one dominant allele and one recessive allele. As with tall and short pea plants, these human traits have two distinctly different phenotypes, or physical appearances.

For example, a widow's peak is a hairline that comes to a point in the middle of the forehead. The allele for a widow's peak is dominant over the allele for a straight hairline. The Punnett square in Figure 1 illustrates a cross between two parents who are heterozygous for a widow's peak. Trace the possible combinations of alleles that a child may inherit. Notice that each child has a 3 in 4, or 75 percent, probability of having a widow's peak. There is only a 1 in 4, or 25 percent, probability that a child will have a straight hairline. Recall from Chapter 3 that when Mendel crossed peas that were heterozygous for a trait, he obtained similar percentages in the offspring.

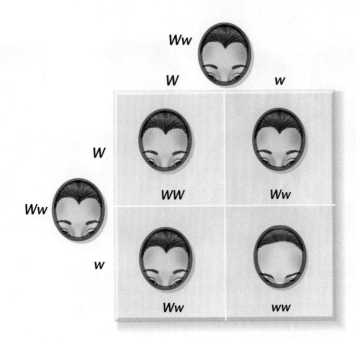

Figure 1 This Punnett square shows a cross between two parents with widow's peaks. *Interpreting Diagrams What are the possible genotypes of the offspring? What percent of the offspring will have each genotype?*

Do you have dimples when you smile? If so, then you have the dominant allele for this trait. Like having a widow's peak, having smile dimples is controlled by a single gene. People who have two recessive alleles do not have smile dimples.

Multiple Alleles

Some human traits are controlled by a single gene that has more than two alleles. Such a gene is said to have **multiple alleles**—three or more forms of a gene that code for a single trait. You can think of multiple alleles as being like flavors of pudding. Pudding usually comes in more flavors than just chocolate and vanilla!

Even though a gene may have multiple alleles, a person can carry only two of those alleles. This is because chromosomes exist in pairs. Each chromosome in a pair carries only one allele for each gene.

One human trait that is controlled by a gene with multiple alleles is blood type. There are four main blood types—A, B, AB, and O. Three alleles control the inheritance of blood types. The allele for blood type A and the allele for blood type B are codominant. The codominant alleles are written as capital letters with superscripts—I^A for blood type A and I^B for blood type B. The allele for blood type O—written i—is recessive. Recall that when two codominant alleles are inherited, neither allele is masked. A person who inherits an I^A allele from one parent and an I^B allele from the other parent will have type AB blood. Figure 2 shows the allele combinations that result in each blood type. Notice that only people who inherit two i alleles have type O blood.

☑ *Checkpoint* *If a gene has multiple alleles, why can a person only have two of the alleles for the gene?*

Blood Types	
Blood Type	**Combination of Alleles**
A	$I^A I^A$ or $I^A i$
B	$I^B I^B$ or $I^B i$
AB	$I^A I^B$
O	ii

Figure 2 Blood type is determined by a single gene with three alleles. This chart shows which combinations of alleles result in each blood type.

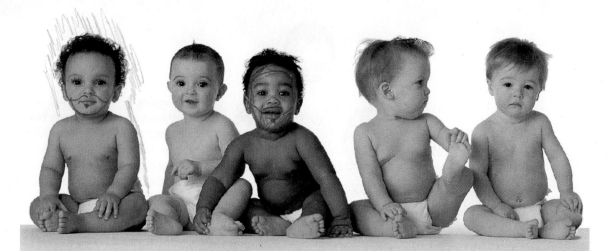

Figure 3 Skin color in humans is determined by three or more genes. Different combinations of alleles at each of the genes result in a wide range of possible skin colors.

Traits Controlled by Many Genes

If you did the Discover activity, you observed that height in humans has more than two distinct phenotypes. In fact, there is an enormous variety of phenotypes for height. What causes this wide range of phenotypes? **Some human traits show a large number of phenotypes because the traits are controlled by many genes. The genes act together as a group to produce a single trait.** At least four genes control height in humans, so there are many possible combinations of genes and alleles.

Like height, skin color is determined by many genes. Human skin color ranges from almost white to nearly black, with many shades in between. Skin color is controlled by at least three genes. Each gene, in turn, has at least two possible alleles. Various combinations of alleles at each of the genes determine the amount of pigment that a person's skin cells produce. Thus, a wide variety of skin colors is possible.

The Effect of Environment

The effects of genes are often altered by the environment—the organism's surroundings. For example, people's diets can affect their height. A diet lacking in protein, minerals, and vitamins can prevent a person from growing to his or her potential maximum height. Since the late 1800s, the average height of adults in the United States has increased by almost 10 centimeters. During that time, American diets have become more healthful. Other environmental factors, such as medical care and living conditions, have also improved since the late 1800s.

✓ *Checkpoint* *How can environmental factors affect a person's height?*

Male or Female?

"Congratulations, Mr. and Mrs. Gonzales. It's a baby girl!" What factors determine whether a baby is a boy or a girl? As with other traits, the sex of a baby is determined by genes on chromosomes. Among the 23 pairs of chromosomes in each body cell is a single pair of chromosomes called the sex chromosomes. The sex chromosomes determine whether a person is male or female.

The sex chromosomes are the only pair of chromosomes that do not always match. If you are female, your two sex chromosomes match. The two chromosomes are called X chromosomes. If you are male, your sex chromosomes do not match. One of your sex chromosomes is an X chromosome. The other chromosome is a Y chromosome. The Y chromosome is much smaller than the X chromosome.

What happens to the sex chromosomes when egg and sperm cells form? As you know, each egg and sperm cell has only one chromosome from each pair. Since both of a female's sex chromosomes are X chromosomes, all eggs carry one X chromosome. Males, however, have two different sex chromosomes. This means that half of a male's sperm cells carry an X chromosome, while half carry a Y chromosome.

When a sperm cell with an X chromosome fertilizes an egg, the egg has two X chromosomes. The fertilized egg will develop into a girl. When a sperm with a Y chromosome fertilizes an egg, the egg has one X chromosome and one Y chromosome. The fertilized egg will develop into a boy. Thus it is the sperm that determines the sex of the child, as you can see in Figure 4.

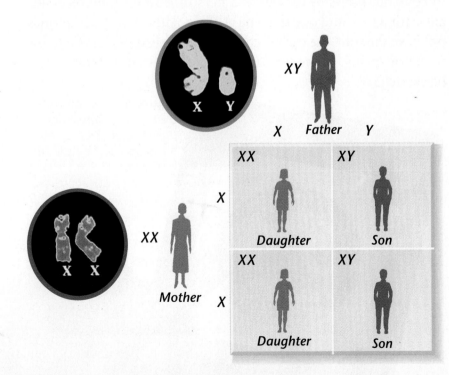

Figure 4 As this Punnett square shows, there is a 50 percent probability that a child will be a girl and a 50 percent probability that a child will be a boy. *Interpreting Diagrams* What sex will the child be if a sperm with a Y chromosome fertilizes an egg?

Girl or Boy?

You can model how the sex of an offspring is determined.

1. Label one paper bag "female." Label another paper bag "male."

2. Place two red marbles in the bag labeled "female." The red marbles represent X chromosomes.

3. Place one red marble and one white marble in the bag labeled "male." The white marble represents a Y chromosome.

4. Without looking, pick one marble from each bag. Two red marbles represent a female offspring. One red marble and one white marble represent a male offspring. Record the sex of the "offspring."

5. Put the marbles back in the correct bags. Repeat Step 4 nine more times.

Making Models How many males were produced? How many females? How close were your results to the expected probabilities for male and female offspring?

Sex-Linked Genes

Some human traits occur more often in one sex than the other. The genes for these traits are often carried on the sex chromosomes. Genes on the X and Y chromosomes are often called **sex-linked genes** because their alleles are passed from parent to child on a sex chromosome. Traits controlled by sex-linked genes are called sex-linked traits.

Like other genes, sex-linked genes can have dominant and recessive alleles. Recall that females have two X chromosomes, whereas males have one X chromosome and one Y chromosome. In females, a dominant allele on one X chromosome will mask a recessive allele on the other X chromosome. The situation is not the same in males, however. In males, there is no matching allele on the Y chromosome to mask, or hide, the allele on the X chromosome. As a result, any allele on the X chromosome—even a recessive allele—will produce the trait in a male who inherits it. **Because males have only one X chromosome, males are more likely than females to have a sex-linked trait that is controlled by a recessive allele.**

One example of a sex-linked trait that is controlled by a recessive allele is red-green colorblindness. A person with red-green colorblindness cannot distinguish between red and green. A common test for red-green colorblindness is shown in Figure 5.

Many more males than females have red-green colorblindness. You can understand why this is the case by examining the Punnett square in Figure 6. Both parents in this example have normal color vision. Notice, however, that the mother is a carrier of colorblindness. A **carrier** is a person who has one recessive allele for a trait and one dominant allele. Although a carrier does not have the trait, the carrier can pass the recessive allele on to his or her offspring. In the case of sex-linked traits, only females can be carriers.

Figure 5 A person with red-green colorblindness cannot see the loop of red and pink dots in this test chart.

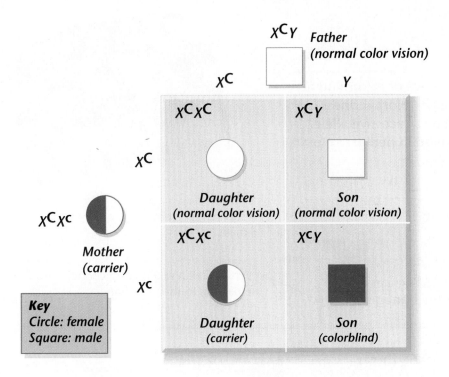

Figure 6 Red-green color-blindness is a sex-linked trait. A girl who receives only one recessive allele (written X^c) for red-green colorblindness will not have the trait. However, a boy who receives one recessive allele will be colorblind. *Applying Concepts What allele combination would a daughter need to inherit to be colorblind?*

As you can see in Figure 6, there is a 25 percent probability that this couple will have a colorblind child. Notice that none of the couple's daughters will be colorblind. On the other hand, the sons have a 50 percent probability of being colorblind. For a female to be colorblind, she must inherit two recessive alleles for colorblindness, one from each parent. A male needs to inherit only one recessive allele. This is because there is no gene for color vision on the Y chromosome. Thus, there is no allele that could mask the recessive allele on the X chromosome.

Pedigrees

Imagine that you are a geneticist interested in studying inheritance patterns in humans. What would you do? You can't set up crosses with people as Mendel did with peas. Instead, you would need to trace the inheritance of traits through many generations in a number of families.

One important tool that geneticists use to trace the inheritance of traits in humans is a pedigree. A **pedigree** is a chart or "family tree" that tracks which members of a family have a particular trait. The trait recorded in a pedigree can be an ordinary trait such as widow's peak, or it could be a sex-linked trait such as colorblindness. In *Exploring a Pedigree* on page 118, you can trace the inheritance of colorblindness through three generations of a family.

☑ *Checkpoint* How is a pedigree like a "family tree"?

EXPLORING *a Pedigree*

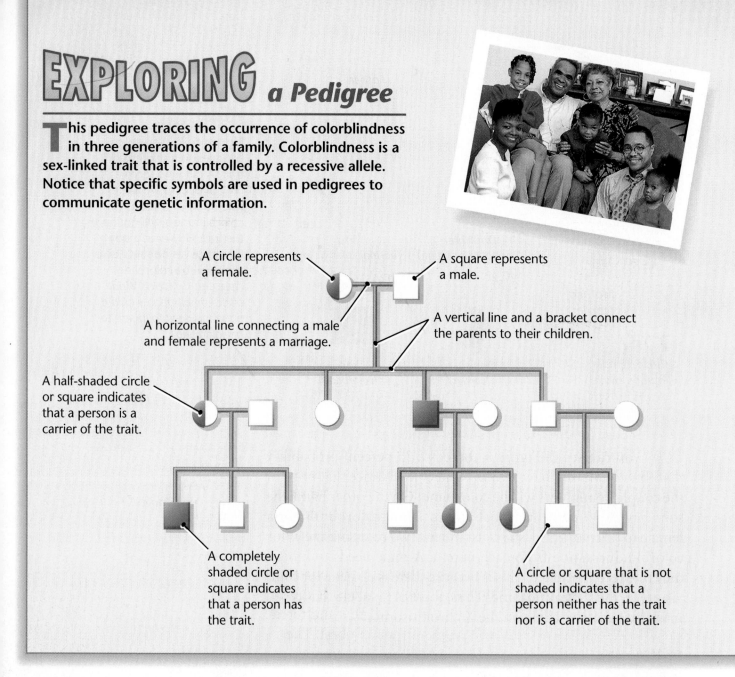

This pedigree traces the occurrence of colorblindness in three generations of a family. Colorblindness is a sex-linked trait that is controlled by a recessive allele. Notice that specific symbols are used in pedigrees to communicate genetic information.

A circle represents a female.

A square represents a male.

A horizontal line connecting a male and female represents a marriage.

A vertical line and a bracket connect the parents to their children.

A half-shaded circle or square indicates that a person is a carrier of the trait.

A completely shaded circle or square indicates that a person has the trait.

A circle or square that is not shaded indicates that a person neither has the trait nor is a carrier of the trait.

Section 1 Review

1. Why do human traits such as height and skin color have many different phenotypes?

2. Explain why red-green colorblindness is more common in males than in females.

3. What is a pedigree? How are pedigrees used?

4. **Thinking Critically Predicting** Could two people with widow's peaks have a child with a straight hairline? Could two people with straight hairlines have a child with a widow's peak? Explain.

Check Your Progress

CHAPTER PROJECT 4

By now, you should be creating your pedigree for the first trait you chose. Start with one couple, and show two generations of offspring. The couple should have five children. It is up to you to decide how many children each of those children has. Use Punnett squares to make sure that your imaginary family's inheritance pattern follows the laws of genetics.

2 Human Genetic Disorders

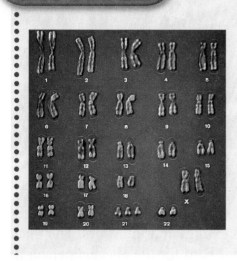

How Many Chromosomes?

The photo at the left shows the chromosomes from a cell of a person with Down syndrome, a genetic disorder. The chromosomes have been sorted into pairs.

1. Count the number of chromosomes in the photo.
2. How does the number of chromosomes compare to the usual number of chromosomes in human cells?

Think It Over

Inferring How do you think a cell could have ended up with this number of chromosomes? (*Hint:* Think about the events that occur during meiosis.)

The air inside the stadium was hot and still. The crowd cheered loudly as eight runners approached the starting blocks. The runners shook out their arms and legs to loosen up their muscles and calm their jitters. When the starter raised the gun, all eyes focused on the runners. At the crack of the starter's gun, the runners leaped into motion and sprinted down the track.

Seconds later, the race was over. The runners, bursting with pride, hugged each other and their coaches. It didn't matter where each of the runners placed. All that mattered was that they had finished the race and done their best. These athletes were running in the Special Olympics, a competition for people with disabilities.

Many of the athletes who compete in the Special Olympics have disabilities that result from genetic disorders. A **genetic disorder** is an abnormal condition that a person inherits through genes or chromosomes. **Genetic disorders are caused by mutations, or changes in a person's DNA.** In some cases, a mutation occurs when sex cells form during meiosis. In other cases, a mutation that is already present in a parent's cells is passed on to the offspring. In this section, you will learn about some common genetic disorders.

GUIDE FOR READING

◆ What causes genetic disorders?

◆ How are genetic disorders diagnosed?

Reading Tip As you read, make a list of different types of genetic disorders. Write a sentence about each disorder.

A runner at the Special Olympics ▶

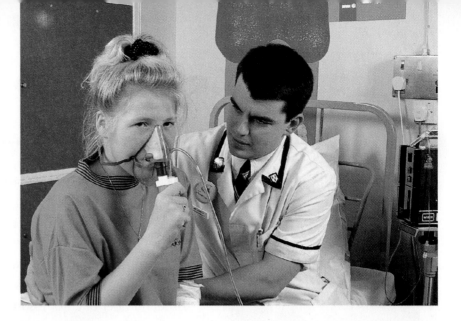

Figure 7 Cystic fibrosis is a genetic disorder that causes thick mucus to build up in a person's lungs and intestines. This patient is inhaling a fine mist that will help loosen the mucus in her lungs.

Figure 8 Normally, red blood cells are shaped like round disks (top). In a person with sickle-cell disease, red blood cells can become sickle-shaped (bottom). *Relating Cause and Effect What combination of alleles leads to sickle-cell disease?*

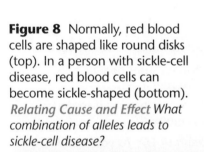

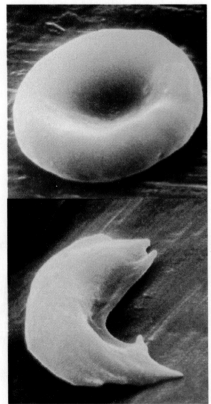

Cystic Fibrosis

Cystic fibrosis is a genetic disorder in which the body produces abnormally thick mucus in the lungs and intestines. The thick mucus fills the lungs, making it hard for the affected person to breathe. Bacteria that grow in the mucus can cause infections and, eventually, lung damage. In the intestines, the mucus makes it difficult for digestion to occur.

The mutation that leads to cystic fibrosis is carried on a recessive allele. The cystic fibrosis allele is most common among people whose ancestors are from Northern Europe. Every day in this country, four babies are born with cystic fibrosis.

Currently there is no cure for cystic fibrosis. Medical treatments include drugs to prevent infections and physical therapy to break up mucus in the lungs. Recent advances in scientists' understanding of the disease may lead to better treatments and longer lifespans for people with cystic fibrosis.

✓ *Checkpoint* *What are some symptoms of cystic fibrosis?*

Sickle-Cell Disease

Sickle-cell disease is a genetic disorder that affects the blood. The mutation that causes the disorder affects the production of an important protein called hemoglobin. Hemoglobin is the protein in red blood cells that carries oxygen. People with sickle-cell disease produce an abnormal form of hemoglobin. When oxygen concentrations are low, their red blood cells have an unusual sickle shape, as you can see in Figure 8.

Sickle-shaped red blood cells cannot carry as much oxygen as normal-shaped cells. Because of their shape, the cells become stuck in narrow blood vessels, blocking them. People with sickle-cell disease suffer from lack of oxygen in the blood and experience pain and weakness.

The allele for the sickle-cell trait is most common in people of African ancestry. About 9 percent of African Americans carry the sickle-cell allele. The allele for the sickle-cell trait is codominant with the normal allele. A person with two sickle-cell alleles will have the disease. A person with one sickle-cell allele will produce both normal hemoglobin and abnormal hemoglobin. This person usually will not have symptoms of the disease.

Currently, there is no cure for sickle-cell disease. People with sickle-cell disease are given drugs to relieve their painful symptoms and to prevent blockages in blood vessels. As with cystic fibrosis, scientists are hopeful that new, successful treatments will soon be found.

Hemophilia

Hemophilia is a genetic disorder in which a person's blood clots very slowly or not at all. People with the disorder do not produce one of the proteins needed for normal blood clotting. A person with hemophilia can bleed to death from a minor cut or scrape. The danger of internal bleeding from small bumps and bruises is also very high.

Hemophilia is an example of a disorder that is caused by a recessive allele on the X chromosome. Because hemophilia is a sex-linked disorder, it occurs more frequently in males than in females. **INTEGRATING HEALTH** People with hemophilia must get regular doses of the missing clotting protein. In general, people with hemophilia can lead normal lives. However, they are advised to avoid contact sports and other activities that could cause internal injuries.

Figure 9 Empress Alexandra of Russia (center row, left) passed the allele for hemophilia to her son Alexis (front).

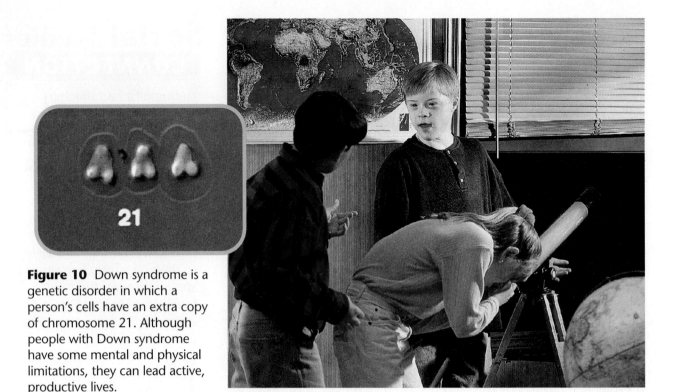

Figure 10 Down syndrome is a genetic disorder in which a person's cells have an extra copy of chromosome 21. Although people with Down syndrome have some mental and physical limitations, they can lead active, productive lives.

Down Syndrome

Some genetic disorders are the result of too many or too few chromosomes. In one such disorder, called Down syndrome, a person's cells have an extra copy of chromosome 21. The extra chromosome is the result of an error during meiosis. Recall that in meiosis, cells divide and chromosomes separate to produce sex cells with half the normal chromosome number. Down syndrome most often occurs when chromosomes fail to separate properly during meiosis.

People with Down syndrome have a distinctive physical appearance, and have some degree of mental retardation. Heart defects are also common, but can be treated. Despite their limitations, many people with Down syndrome lead full, active lives.

Diagnosing Genetic Disorders

INTEGRATING TECHNOLOGY Years ago, doctors had only Punnett squares and pedigrees to help them predict whether a child might have a genetic disorder. **Today doctors use tools such as amniocentesis and karyotypes to help detect genetic disorders.**

Before a baby is born, doctors can use a procedure called **amniocentesis** (am nee oh sen TEE sis) to determine whether the baby will have some genetic disorders. During amniocentesis, a doctor uses a very long needle to remove a small amount of the fluid that surrounds the developing baby. The fluid contains cells from the baby.

The doctor then examines the chromosomes from the cells. To do this, the doctor creates a karyotype. A **karyotype** (KA ree uh typ) is a picture of all the chromosomes in a cell. The chromosomes in a karyotype are arranged in pairs. A karyotype can reveal whether a developing baby has the correct number of chromosomes in its cells and whether it is a boy or a girl. If you did the Discover activity, you saw a karyotype from a girl with Down syndrome.

Genetic Counseling

A couple that has a family history or concern about a genetic disorder may turn to a genetic counselor for advice. Genetic counselors help couples understand their chances of having a child with a particular genetic disorder. Genetic counselors use tools such as karyotypes, pedigree charts, and Punnett squares to help them in their work.

Suppose, for example, that a husband and wife both have a history of cystic fibrosis in their families. If they are considering having children, they might seek the advice of a genetic counselor. The genetic counselor might order a test to determine whether they are carriers of the allele for cystic fibrosis. The genetic counselor would then apply the same principles of probability that you learned about in Chapter 3 to calculate the couple's chances of having a child with cystic fibrosis.

Figure 11 Couples may meet with a genetic counselor and their doctor in order to understand their chances of having a child with a genetic disorder.

Section 2 Review

1. Explain how genetic disorders occur in humans. Give two examples of genetic disorders.
2. Describe two tools that doctors use to detect genetic disorders.
3. How do the cells of people with Down syndrome differ from those of others? How might this difference arise?
4. **Thinking Critically** **Problem Solving** A couple with a family history of hemophilia is about to have a baby girl. What information about the parents would you want to know? How would this information help you determine whether the baby will have hemophilia?

Check Your Progress
CHAPTER PROJECT 4

At this point, you should begin to trace the inheritance of another trait through the same family members that are in your first pedigree. Also, start making your family "photo" album. Will you use drawings or some other method to show what the family members look like? (*Hint:* Photo albums show phenotypes. Remember that more than one genotype can have the same phenotype.)

Family Puzzles

Imagine that you are a genetic counselor. Two couples come to you for advice. Their family histories are summarized in the boxes labeled *Case Study 1* and *Case Study 2*. They want to understand the probability that their children might inherit certain genetic disorders. In this lab, you will find answers to their questions.

Problem

How can you investigate inheritance patterns in families?

Materials

12 index cards
scissors
marker

Procedure

Part 1 Investigating Case Study 1

1. Read over Case Study 1. In your notebook, draw a pedigree that shows all the family members. Use circles to represent the females, and squares to represent the males. Shade in the circles or squares representing the individuals who have cystic fibrosis.

Case Study 1: Joshua and Bella
- Joshua and Bella have a son named Ian. Ian has been diagnosed with cystic fibrosis.
- Joshua and Bella are both healthy.
- Bella's parents are both healthy.
- Joshua's parents are both healthy.
- Joshua's sister, Sara, has cystic fibrosis.

2. You know that cystic fibrosis is controlled by a recessive allele. To help you figure out Joshua and Bella's family pattern, create a set of cards to represent the alleles. Cut each of six index cards into four smaller cards. On 12 of the small cards, write *N* to represent the dominant normal allele. On the other 12 small cards, write *n* for the recessive allele.

3. Begin by using the cards to represent Ian's alleles. Since he has cystic fibrosis, what alleles must he have? Write in this genotype next to the pedigree symbol for Ian.

4. Joshua's sister, Sara, also has cystic fibrosis. What alleles does she have? Write in this genotype next to the pedigree symbol that represents Sara.

Case Study 2: Li and Mai

◆ The father, Li, has a skin condition. The mother, Mai, has normal skin.

◆ Li and Mai's first child, a girl named Gemma, has the same skin condition as Li.

◆ Mai's sister has a similar skin condition, but Mai's parents do not.

◆ Li has one brother whose skin is normal, and one sister who has the skin condition.

◆ Li's mother has the skin condition. His father does not.

◆ Li's family lives in a heavily wooded area. His family has always thought the skin condition was a type of allergy.

5. Now use the cards to figure out what genotypes Joshua and Bella must have. Write their genotypes next to their symbols in the pedigree.

6. Work with the cards to figure out the genotypes of all other family members. Fill in each person's genotype next to his or her symbol in the pedigree. If more than one genotype is possible, write in both genotypes.

Part 2 Investigating Case Study 2

7. Read over Case Study 2.

8. You suspect that Gemma and Li's skin condition is caused by an inherited recessive allele. Begin to investigate this possibility by drawing a family pedigree in your notebook. Use shading to indicate which individuals have the skin condition.

9. Fill in the genotype *ss* beside each individual who has the skin condition. Then use cards as you did in Case Study 1 to figure out each family member's genotype. If more than one genotype is possible, fill in both genotypes.

Analyze and Conclude

1. In Case Study 1, what were the genotypes of Joshua's parents? What were the genotypes of Bella's parents?

2. In Case Study 1, Joshua also has a brother. What is the probability that he has cystic fibrosis? Explain.

3. Can you conclude that the skin condition in Case Study 2 is most likely an inherited trait controlled by a recessive allele? Explain.

4. What is the probability that Mai and Li's next child will have the skin condition? Explain.

5. **Apply** Why do genetic counselors need information about many generations of a family in order to draw conclusions about a hereditary condition?

More to Explore

Review the two pedigrees that you just studied. What data suggests that the traits are not sex-linked? Explain.

SECTION 3 Advances in Genetics

DISCOVER ....ACTIVITY....

What Do Fingerprints Reveal?

1. Label a sheet of paper with your name. Then roll one of your fingers from side to side on an ink pad. Make a fingerprint by carefully rolling your inked finger from side to side on the paper.

2. Divide into groups. Each group should choose one member to use the same finger to make a second fingerprint on a sheet of paper. Leave the paper unlabeled.

3. Exchange your group's fingerprints with those from another group. Compare each labeled fingerprint with the fingerprint on the unlabeled paper. Decide whose fingerprint it is.

4. Wash your hands after completing this activity.

Think It Over
Observing Why are fingerprints a useful tool for identifying people?

GUIDE FOR READING

◆ What are three ways in which an organism's traits can be altered?

◆ What is the goal of the Human Genome Project?

Reading Tip As you read, make a concept map of the methods used to produce organisms with desirable traits. Include at least one example of each technique.

Dolly ▼

In the summer of 1996, a lamb named Dolly was born in Scotland. Dolly was an ordinary lamb in every way except one. The fertilized cell that developed into Dolly was produced in a laboratory by geneticists using experimental techniques. You will learn more about the techniques used by the geneticists later in the section.

Although the techniques used to create Dolly are new, the idea of producing organisms with specific traits is not. For thousands of years, people have tried to produce plants and animals with desirable traits. **Three methods that people have used to develop organisms with desirable traits are selective breeding, cloning, and genetic engineering.**

Selective Breeding

More than 5,000 years ago, people living in what is now central Mexico discovered that a type of wild grass could be used as food. They saved the seeds from those plants that produced the best food, and planted them to grow new plants. By repeating this process over many generations of plants, they developed an early variety of the food crop we now call corn. The process of selecting a few organisms with desired traits to serve as parents of the next generation is called **selective breeding.**

People have used selective breeding with many different plants and animals. Breeding programs usually focus on increasing the value of the plant or animal to people. For

Figure 12 For thousands of years, people have used selective breeding to produce plants and animals with desirable traits. *Making Generalizations* What are some traits for which corn may be bred?

example, dairy cows are bred to produce larger quantities of milk. Many varieties of fruits and vegetables are bred to resist diseases and insect pests.

Inbreeding One useful selective breeding technique is called inbreeding. **Inbreeding** involves crossing two individuals that have identical or similar sets of alleles. The organisms that result from inbreeding have alleles that are very similar to those of their parents. Mendel used inbreeding to produce purebred pea plants to use in his experiments.

One goal of inbreeding is to produce breeds of animals with specific traits. For example, by only crossing horses with exceptional speed, breeders can produce purebred horses that can run very fast. Purebred dogs, such as Labrador retrievers and German shepherds, were produced by inbreeding.

Unfortunately, because inbred organisms are genetically very similar, inbreeding reduces an offspring's chances of inheriting new allele combinations. Inbreeding also increases the probability that organisms may inherit alleles that lead to genetic disorders. For example, inherited hip problems are common in many breeds of dogs.

Hybridization Another selective breeding technique is called hybridization. In **hybridization** (hy brid ih ZAY shun), breeders cross two genetically different individuals. The hybrid organism that results is bred to have the best traits from both parents. For example, a farmer might cross corn that produces many kernels with corn that is resistant to disease. The result might be a hybrid corn plant with both of the desired traits. Today, most crops grown on farms and in gardens were produced by hybridization.

Figure 13 Plants can be easily cloned by making a cutting. Once the cutting has grown roots, it can be planted and will grow into a new plant. *Applying Concepts Why is the new plant considered to be a clone of the original plant?*

Cloning

One problem with selective breeding is that the breeder cannot control whether the desired allele will be passed from the parent to its offspring. This is because the transmission of alleles is determined by probability, as you learned in Chapter 3. For some organisms, another technique, called cloning, can be used to produce offspring with desired traits. A **clone** is an organism that is genetically identical to the organism from which it was produced. This means that a clone has exactly the same genes as the organism from which it was produced. Cloning can be done in plants and animals, as well as other organisms.

Cloning Plants One way to produce a clone of a plant is through a cutting. A cutting is a small part of a plant, such as a leaf or a stem, that is cut from the plant. The cutting can grow into an entire new plant. The new plant is genetically identical to the plant from which the cutting was taken.

Cloning Animals Remember Dolly, the lamb described at the beginning of this section? Dolly was the first clone of an adult mammal ever produced. To create Dolly, researchers removed an egg cell from one sheep. The cell's nucleus was replaced with the nucleus from a cell of a six-year-old sheep. The egg was then implanted into the uterus of a third sheep. Five months later, Dolly was born. Dolly is genetically identical to the six-year-old sheep that supplied the nucleus. Dolly is a clone of that sheep.

Since scientists first cloned Dolly, pigs and calves have also been cloned. Scientists hope that cloning animals will allow humans to live healthier lives. For example, pigs that are being cloned have genes that will make their organs suitable for organ transplant into humans.

Checkpoint How can a clone of a plant be produced?

Genetic Engineering

In the past few decades, geneticists have developed another powerful technique for producing organisms with desired traits. In this process, called **genetic engineering,** genes from one organism are transferred into the DNA of another organism. Genetic engineering is sometimes called "gene splicing" because a DNA molecule is cut open and a gene from another organism is spliced into it. Genetic engineering can produce medicines and improve food crops, and may cure human genetic disorders.

EXPLORING Genetic Engineering

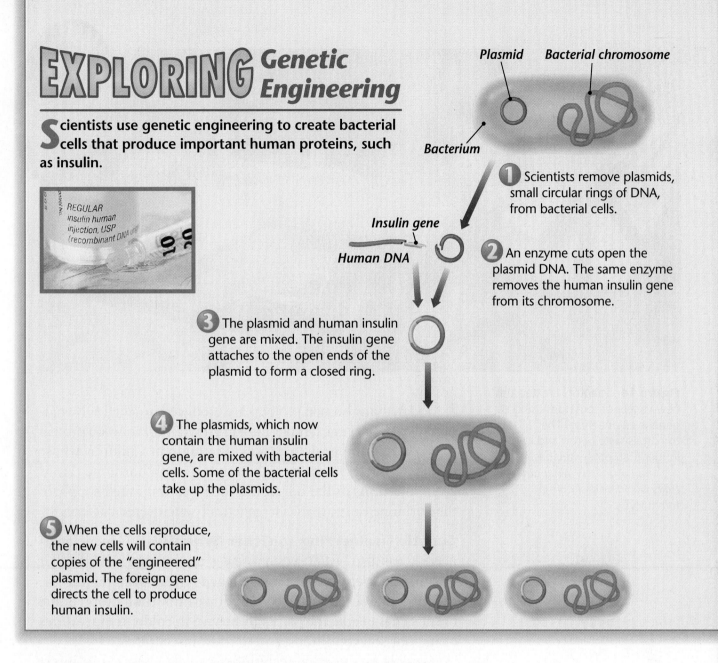

Scientists use genetic engineering to create bacterial cells that produce important human proteins, such as insulin.

REGULAR insulin human injection, USP (recombinant DNA...)

Plasmid **Bacterial chromosome**

Bacterium

Insulin gene

Human DNA

1 Scientists remove plasmids, small circular rings of DNA, from bacterial cells.

2 An enzyme cuts open the plasmid DNA. The same enzyme removes the human insulin gene from its chromosome.

3 The plasmid and human insulin gene are mixed. The insulin gene attaches to the open ends of the plasmid to form a closed ring.

4 The plasmids, which now contain the human insulin gene, are mixed with bacterial cells. Some of the bacterial cells take up the plasmids.

5 When the cells reproduce, the new cells will contain copies of the "engineered" plasmid. The foreign gene directs the cell to produce human insulin.

Genetic Engineering in Bacteria Researchers had their first successes with genetic engineering when they inserted DNA from other organisms into bacteria. Recall that the single DNA molecule of bacterial cells is found in the cytoplasm. Some bacterial cells also contain small circular pieces of DNA called plasmids.

In *Exploring Genetic Engineering,* you can see how scientists insert a human gene into the plasmid of a bacterium. Once the DNA is spliced into the plasmid, the bacterial cell and all its offspring will contain this human gene. As a result, the bacteria produce the protein that the human gene codes for, in this case insulin. Because bacteria reproduce quickly, large amounts of insulin can be produced in a short time. The insulin can be collected and used to treat people with diabetes, a disorder in which the body does not produce enough of this protein.

Figure 14 Scientists created this new variety of tomatoes using genetic engineering. The tomatoes taste better and keep longer than other varieties. *Making Judgments What other traits would be desirable in tomatoes?*

Today, many human proteins are produced in genetically engineered bacteria. For example, human growth hormone is a protein that controls the growth process in children. Children whose bodies do not produce enough human growth hormone can be given injections of the hormone. Today, an unlimited supply of the hormone exists, thanks to genetically engineered bacteria.

Genetic Engineering in Other Organisms Genetic engineering has also been used to insert genes into the cells of other organisms. Scientists have inserted genes from bacteria into the cells of tomatoes, wheat, rice, and other important crops. Some of the genes enable the plants to survive in colder temperatures or in poor soil conditions, and to resist insect pests.

Genetic engineering techniques can also be used to insert genes into animals, which then produce important medicines for humans. For example, scientists can insert human genes into the cells of cows. The cows then produce the human protein for which the gene codes. Scientists have used this technique to produce the blood clotting protein needed by people with hemophilia. The protein is produced in the cows' milk, and can easily be extracted and used to treat people with the disorder.

Gene Therapy Researchers are also using genetic engineering to try to correct some genetic disorders. This process, called **gene therapy,** involves inserting working copies of a gene directly into the cells of a person with a genetic disorder. For example, people with cystic fibrosis do not produce a protein that is needed for proper lung function. Both copies of the gene that codes for the protein are defective in these people.

Scientists can insert working copies of the gene into harmless viruses. The "engineered" viruses can then be sprayed into the lungs of patients with cystic fibrosis. Researchers hope that the working copies of the gene in the viruses will function in the patient to produce the protein. Gene therapy is still an experimental method for treating genetic disorders. Researchers are working hard to improve this promising technique.

DNA Fingerprinting

In courtrooms across the country, a genetic technique called DNA fingerprinting is being used to help solve crimes. If you did the Discover activity, you know that fingerprints can help to identify people. No two people have the same fingerprints. Detectives routinely use fingerprints found at a crime scene to help identify the person who committed the crime. In a similar way, DNA from samples of hair, skin, and blood can also be used to identify a person. No two people, except for identical twins, have the same DNA.

In DNA fingerprinting, enzymes are used to cut the DNA in the sample found at a crime scene into fragments. An electrical current then separates the fragments by size to form a pattern of bands, like the ones you see in Figure 15. Each person's pattern of DNA bands is unique. The DNA pattern can then be compared to the pattern produced by DNA taken from people suspected of committing the crime.

☑ *Checkpoint* *In what way is DNA like fingerprints?*

Figure 15 This scientist is explaining how DNA fingerprinting can be used to help solve crimes. DNA from blood or other substances collected at a crime scene can be compared to DNA from a suspect's blood.

The Human Genome Project

Imagine trying to crack a code that is 3 billion characters long. Then imagine working with people all over the world to accomplish this task. That's exactly what scientists working on the Human Genome Project are doing. A **genome** is all the DNA in one cell of an organism. Researchers estimate that the 23 pairs of chromosomes that make up the human genome contain about 3 billion DNA base pairs—or about 30,000 to 35,000 genes.

The main goal of the Human Genome Project is to identify the DNA sequence of every gene in the human genome. The Human Genome Project will provide scientists with an encyclopedia of genetic information about humans. Scientists will know the DNA sequence of every human gene, and thus the amino acid sequence of every protein.

Figure 16 The goal of the Human Genome Project is to identify the sequence of every DNA base pair in the human genome.

With the information from the Human Genome Project, researchers may gain a better understanding of how humans develop from a fertilized egg to an adult. They may also learn more about what makes the body work, and what causes things to go wrong. New understandings may lead to new treatments and prevention strategies for many genetic disorders and for diseases such as cancer.

Section 3 Review

1. Name three techniques that people have used to produce organisms with desired traits.
2. Why do scientists want to identify the DNA sequence of every human gene?
3. What is genetic engineering? Describe three possible benefits of this technique.
4. Explain how a DNA fingerprint is produced. What information can a DNA fingerprint reveal?
5. **Thinking Critically Making Judgments** Do you think there should be any limitations on genetic engineering? Give reasons to support your position.

Science at Home

With a parent or other adult family member, go to a grocery store. Look at the different varieties of potatoes, apples, and other fruits and vegetables. Discuss how these varieties were created by selective breeding. Then chose one type of fruit or vegetable and make a list of different varieties. If possible, find out what traits each variety was bred for.

Who Should Have Access to Genetic Test Results?

Scientists working on the Human Genome Project have identified many alleles that put people at risk for certain diseases, such as breast cancer and Alzheimer's disease. Through techniques known as genetic testing, people can have their DNA analyzed to find out whether they have any of these alleles. If they do, they may be able to take steps to prevent the illness or to seek early treatment.

Some health insurance companies and employers want access to this type of genetic information. However, many people believe that genetic testing results should be kept private.

The Issues

Why Do Insurance Companies Want Genetic Information?
Health insurance companies set their rates based on a person's risk of health problems. To determine a person's insurance rate, insurance companies often require that a person have a physical examination. If the examination reveals a condition such as high blood pressure, the company may charge that person more for an insurance policy. This is because he or she would be more likely to need expensive medical care.

Insurance companies view genetic testing as an additional way to gather information about a person's health status. Insurers argue that if they were unable to gather this information, they would need to raise rates for everyone. This would be unfair to people who are in good health.

Why Do Employers Want Genetic Information?
Federal laws forbid employers with 15 or more workers from choosing job applicants based on their health status. These laws do not apply to smaller companies, however. Employers may not want to hire employees with health problems because they often miss more work time than other employees. In addition, employers who hire people with health problems may be charged higher health insurance rates. Many small companies cannot afford to pay these higher rates.

Should Genetic Information Be Kept Private?
Some people think that the government should prohibit all access to genetic information. Today, some people fear that they will be discriminated against as a result of genetic test results. Because of this fear, some people avoid genetic testing—even though testing might allow them to seek early treatment for a disorder. These people want tighter control of genetic information. They want to be sure that insurers and employers will not have access to genetic test results.

You Decide

1. Identify the Problem
In your own words, explain the problem of deciding who should have access to genetic test results.

2. Analyze the Options
Examine the pros and cons of keeping genetic test results private. List reasons to maintain privacy. List reasons why test results should be shared.

3. Find a Solution
Create a list of rules to control access to genetic information. Who should have access, and under what circumstances? Explain your reasoning.

 You Solve the Mystery

Guilty or Innocent?

In this lab, you will investigate how DNA fingerprinting can be used to provide evidence related to a crime.

Problem

How can DNA be used to identify individuals?

Skills Focus

observing, making models, drawing conclusions

Materials

4–6 bar codes   hand lens

Procedure

1. Look at the photograph of DNA band patterns shown at right. Each person's DNA produces a unique pattern of these bands.
2. Now look at the Universal Product Code, also called a bar code, shown below the DNA bands. A bar code can be used as a model of a DNA band pattern. Compare the bar code with the DNA bands to see what they have in common. Record your observations.
3. Suppose that a burglary has taken place, and you're the detective leading the investigation. Your teacher will give you a bar code that represents DNA from blood found at the crime scene. You arrange to have DNA samples taken from several suspects. Write a sentence describing what you will look for as you try to match each suspect's DNA to the DNA sample from the crime scene.
4. You will now be given bar codes representing DNA samples taken from the suspects. Compare those bar codes with the bar code that represents DNA from the crime scene.

5. Use your comparisons to determine whether any of the suspects was present at the crime scene.

Analyze and Conclude

1. Based on your findings, were any of the suspects present at the crime scene? Support your conclusion with specific evidence.
2. Why do people's DNA patterns differ so greatly?
3. How would your conclusions be affected if you learned that the suspect whose DNA matched the evidence had an identical twin?
4. **Apply** In everyday life, do you think that DNA evidence is enough to determine that a suspect committed the crime? Explain.

More to Explore

Do you think the DNA fingerprints of a parent and a child would show any similarities? Draw what you think they would look like. Then explain your thinking.

CHAPTER 4 STUDY GUIDE

1 Human Inheritance

Key Ideas

- Some human traits are controlled by a single gene that has multiple alleles—three or more forms.
- Some human traits show a wide range of phenotypes because these traits are controlled by many genes. The genes act together as a group to produce a single trait.
- Traits are often influenced by the organism's environment.
- Males have one X chromosome and one Y chromosome. Females have two X chromosomes. Males are more likely than females to have a sex-linked trait controlled by a recessive allele.
- Geneticists use pedigrees to trace the inheritance pattern of a particular trait through a number of generations of a family.

Key Terms

multiple alleles   carrier
sex-linked gene   pedigree

2 Human Genetic Disorders

Key Ideas

- Genetic disorders are abnormal conditions that are caused by mutations, or DNA changes, in genes or chromosomes.
- Common genetic disorders include cystic fibrosis, sickle-cell disease, hemophilia, and Down syndrome.
- Amniocentesis and karyotypes are tools used to diagnose genetic disorders.
- Genetic counselors help couples understand their chances of having a child with a genetic disorder.

Key Terms

genetic disorder   karyotype
amniocentesis

3 Advances in Genetics

INTEGRATING TECHNOLOGY

Key Ideas

- Selective breeding is the process of selecting a few organisms with desired traits to serve as parents of the next generation.
- Cloning is a technique used to produce genetically identical organisms.
- Genetic engineering can be used to produce medicines and to improve food crops. Researchers are also using genetic engineering to try to cure human genetic disorders.
- DNA fingerprinting can be used to help determine whether material found at a crime scene came from a particular suspect.
- The goal of the Human Genome Project is to identify the DNA sequence of every gene in the human genome.

Key Terms

selective breeding   genetic engineering
inbreeding   gene therapy
hybridization   genome
clone

Organizing Information

Concept Map Copy the concept map about human traits onto a separate sheet of paper. Then complete it and add a title. (For more on concept maps, see the Skills Handbook.)

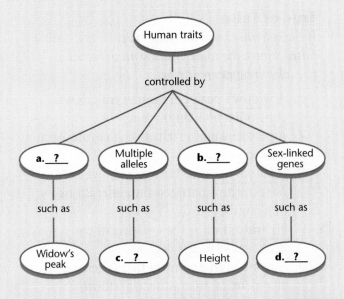

Chapter 4 **C ◆ 135**

Reviewing Content

 For more review of key concepts, see the Interactive Student Tutorial CD-ROM.

Multiple Choice

Choose the letter of the best answer.

1. A human trait that is controlled by multiple alleles is
   a. dimples.   b. blood type.
   c. height.   d. skin color.
2. A genetic disorder caused by a sex-linked gene is
   a. cystic fibrosis.
   b. sickle-cell disease.
   c. hemophilia.
   d. Down syndrome.
3. Sickle-cell disease is characterized by
   a. abnormally shaped red blood cells.
   b. abnormally thick body fluids.
   c. abnormal blood clotting.
   d. an extra copy of chromosome 21.
4. Inserting a human gene into a bacterial plasmid is an example of
   a. inbreeding.
   b. selective breeding.
   c. DNA fingerprinting.
   d. genetic engineering.
5. DNA fingerprinting is a way to
   a. clone organisms.
   b. breed organisms with desirable traits.
   c. identify people.
   d. map and sequence human genes.

True or False

If the statement is true, write true. If it is false, change the underlined word or words to make the statement true.

6. A <u>widow's peak</u> is a human trait that is controlled by a single gene.
7. A person who inherits two X chromosomes will be <u>male</u>.
8. A <u>karyotype</u> is a chart that shows the relationships between the generations of a family.
9. <u>Hybridization</u> is the crossing of two genetically similar organisms.
10. A <u>clone</u> is an organism that is genetically identical to another organism.

Checking Concepts

11. Explain how both genes and the environment determine how tall a person will be.
12. Explain why traits controlled by recessive alleles on the X chromosome are more common in males than in females.
13. What is sickle-cell disease? How is this disorder inherited?
14. How can amniocentesis be used to detect a disorder such as Down syndrome?
15. Explain how a horse breeder might use selective breeding to produce horses that have golden coats.
16. Describe how gene therapy might be used in the future to treat a person with hemophilia.
17. **Writing to Learn** As the webmaster for a national genetics foundation, you must create a Web site to inform the public about genetic disorders. Choose one human genetic disorder discussed in this chapter. Write a description of the disorder that you will use for the Web site.

Thinking Critically

18. **Applying Concepts** Why can a person be a carrier of a trait caused by a recessive allele but not of a trait caused by a dominant allele?
19. **Problem Solving** A woman with normal color vision has a colorblind daughter. What are the genotypes and phenotypes of both parents?
20. **Calculating** If a mother is a carrier of hemophilia, what is the probability that her son will have the trait? Explain your answer.
21. **Inferring** How could ancient people selectively breed corn if they didn't know about genes and inheritance?
22. **Comparing and Contrasting** How are selective breeding and genetic engineering different? How are they similar?

Applying Skills

Use the information below to answer Questions 23–25.

- Bob and Helen have three children.
- Bob and Helen have one son who has albinism, an inherited condition in which the skin does not have brown pigments.
- Bob and Helen have two daughters who do not have albinism.
- Neither Bob nor Helen has albinism.
- Albinism is neither sex-linked nor codominant.

23. Interpreting Data Use the information to construct a pedigree. If you don't know whether someone is a carrier, leave their symbol empty. If you decide later that a person is a carrier, change your pedigree.

24. Drawing Conclusions Is albinism controlled by a dominant allele or by a recessive allele? Explain your answer.

25. Predicting Suppose Bob and Helen were to have another child. What is the probability that the child will have albinism? Explain.

Performance ▽ CHAPTER PROJECT 4 Assessment

Project Wrap Up Before displaying your project, exchange it with another group to check each other's work. Make any necessary corrections, and then display your materials to the class. Be ready to explain the inheritance patterns shown in your pedigrees.

Reflect and Record In your journal, describe what you learned by creating the pedigrees. What questions do you have as a result of the project?

Test Preparation
Use these questions to prepare for standardized tests.

Use the information to answer Questions 26–29. The Punnett square below shows how muscular dystrophy, a sex-linked recessive disorder, is inherited.

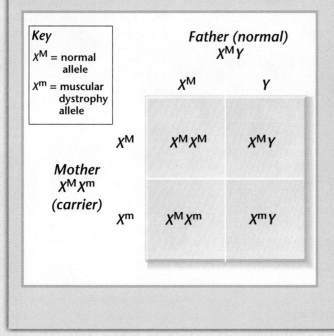

Key
X^M = normal allele
X^m = muscular dystrophy allele

Father (normal)
$X^M Y$

	X^M	Y
X^M	$X^M X^M$	$X^M Y$
X^m	$X^M X^m$	$X^m Y$

Mother
$X^M X^m$
(carrier)

26. What is the probability that a daughter of these parents will have muscular dystrophy?
a. 0%   **b.** 25%
c. 50%   **d.** 100%

27. What is the probability that a son of these parents will have muscular dystrophy?
a. 0%   **b.** 25%
c. 50%   **d.** 100%

28. What is the probability that a daughter of these parents will be a carrier of the disease?
a. 0%   **b.** 25%
c. 50%   **d.** 100%

29. Which of the following statements is true of muscular dystrophy?
a. More men than women have muscular dystrophy.
b. More women than men have muscular dystrophy.
c. More men than women are carriers of muscular dystrophy.
d. No women can have muscular dystrophy.

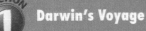

www.phschool.com

Life's Long Calendar

How far back in your life can you remember? How far can the adults you know remember? Think of how life has changed in the last ten, fifty, or one hundred years. This chapter looks back in time as well. But instead of looking back hundreds of years, you'll explore millions, hundreds of millions, and even billions of years.

The time frame of Earth's history is so large that it can be overwhelming. This chapter project will help you understand it. In this project, you'll find a way to convert enormous time periods into a more familiar scale.

Your Goal To use a familiar measurement scale to create two time lines for Earth's history.

To complete the project you will
- represent Earth's history using a familiar scale, such as hours on a clock, months on a calendar, or yards on a football field
- use your chosen scale twice, once to plot out 5 billion years of history, and then to focus on the past 600 million years
- include markers on both scales to show important events in the history of life

Get Started Preview *Exploring Life's History* on pages 156–157 to see what events occurred during the two time periods. In a small group, discuss some familiar scales you might use for your time lines. You could select a time interval such as a year or a day. Alternatively, you could choose a distance interval such as the length of your schoolyard or the walls in your classroom. Decide on the kind of time lines you will make.

Check Your Progress You will be working on this project as you study this chapter. To keep your project on track, look for Check Your Progress boxes at the following points.
  Section 1 Review, page 150: Plan your time lines.
  Section 3 Review, page 163: Construct your time lines.

Wrap Up At the end of the chapter (page 167), you'll display your time lines for the class.

This *Triceratops* lived in western North America about 70 million years ago. It used its sharp horns to defend itself against predators.

① Darwin's Voyage

DISCOVER · ACTIVITY····

How Do Living Things Vary?

1. Use a ruler to measure the length and width of 10 sunflower seeds. Record each measurement.

2. Now use a hand lens to carefully examine each seed. Record each seed's shape, color, and number of stripes.

Think It Over

Classifying In what ways are the seeds in your sample different from one another? In what ways are they similar? How could you group the seeds based on their similarities and differences?

GUIDE FOR READING

◆ How did Darwin explain the differences between species on the Galapagos Islands and on mainland South America?

◆ How does natural selection lead to evolution?

◆ How do new species form?

Reading Tip As you read, make a list of main ideas and supporting details about evolution.

In December 1831, the British naval ship HMS *Beagle* set sail from England on a five-year-long trip around the world. On board was a 22-year-old named Charles Darwin. Darwin eventually became the ship's naturalist—a person who studies the natural world. His job was to learn as much as he could about the living things he saw on the voyage.

During the voyage, Darwin observed plants and animals he had never seen before. He wondered why they were so different from those in England. Darwin's observations led him to develop one of the most important scientific theories of all time: the theory of evolution by natural selection.

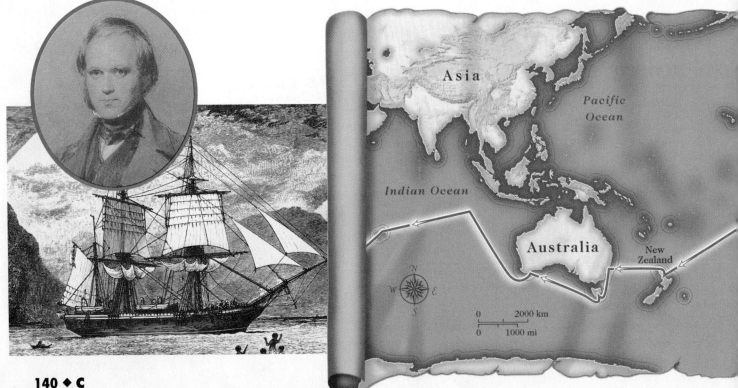

Darwin's Observations

One of the *Beagle's* first stops was the coast of South America. In Brazil, Darwin saw insects that looked like flowers, and ants that marched across the forest floor like huge armies. In Argentina, he saw armadillos—burrowing animals covered with small, bony plates. He also saw sloths, animals that moved very slowly and spent much of their time hanging upside down in trees.

Darwin was amazed by the tremendous diversity, or variety, of living things he saw. Today scientists know that living things are even more diverse than Darwin could ever have imagined. Scientists have identified more than 1.7 million species of organisms on Earth. A **species** is a group of similar organisms that can mate with each other and produce fertile offspring.

Darwin saw something else in Argentina that puzzled him: the bones of animals that had died long ago. From the bones, Darwin inferred that the animals had looked like the sloths he had seen. However, the bones were much larger than those of the living sloths. He wondered why only smaller sloths were alive today. What had happened to the giant creatures from the past?

In 1835, the *Beagle* reached the Galapagos Islands, a group of small islands in the Pacific Ocean off the west coast of South America. It was on the Galapagos Islands that Darwin observed some of the greatest diversity of life forms. He saw large numbers of giant tortoises, or land turtles, which he described as immense in size. There were also seals covered with fur, and lizards that ate cactus for food and water.

Figure 1 Charles Darwin sailed on HMS *Beagle* from England to South America and then to the Galapagos Islands. He saw many unusual organisms on the Galapagos Islands.

Galapagos hawk ▼

▲ *Giant tortoise*

▲ *Sally light-foot crab*

◄ *Blue-footed booby*

Similarities and Differences

Darwin was surprised that many of the plants and animals on the Galapagos Islands were similar to organisms on mainland South America. For example, many of the birds on the islands, including hawks, mockingbirds, and finches, resembled those on the mainland. Many of the plants were also similar to plants Darwin had collected on the mainland.

However, there were also important differences between the organisms on the islands and those on the mainland. Large sea birds called cormorants, for example, lived in both places. The cormorants on the mainland were able to fly, while those on the Galapagos Islands were unable to fly. The iguanas on the Galapagos Islands had large claws that allowed them to keep their grip on slippery rocks, where they fed on seaweed. The iguanas on the mainland had smaller claws. Smaller claws allowed the mainland iguanas to climb trees, where they ate leaves.

From his observations, Darwin inferred that a small number of different plant and animal species had come to the Galapagos Islands from the mainland. They might have been blown out to sea during a storm or set adrift on a fallen log. Once the plants and animals reached the islands, they reproduced. Eventually, their offspring became different from their mainland relatives.

Darwin also noticed many differences among similar organisms as he traveled from one Galapagos island to the next. For example, the tortoises on one island had dome-shaped shells. Those on another island had saddle-shaped shells. The governor of one of the islands told Darwin that he could tell which island a tortoise came from just by looking at its shell.

☑ *Checkpoint* *How did Darwin think plants and animals had originally come to the Galapagos Islands?*

Figure 2 Darwin observed many differences between organisms in South America and similar organisms on the Galapagos Islands. For example, green iguanas (left) live in South America. Marine iguanas (right) live on the Galapagos Islands. *Comparing and Contrasting How are the two species similar? How are they different?*

Figure 3 Darwin made these drawings of four species of Galapagos finches. The beak of each finch is adapted to the type of food it eats.

Adaptations

Like the tortoises, the finches on the Galapagos Islands were noticeably different from one island to another. The most obvious differences were the varied sizes and shapes of the birds' beaks. As Darwin studied the different finches, he noticed that each species was well suited to the life it led. Finches that ate insects had sharp, needlelike beaks. Finches that ate seeds had strong, wide beaks. Beak shape is an example of an **adaptation,** a trait that helps an organism survive and reproduce.

Evolution

After he returned home to England, Darwin continued to think about what he had seen during his voyage on the *Beagle.* Darwin spent the next 20 years consulting with many other scientists, gathering more information, and thinking through his ideas. He especially wanted to understand how the variety of organisms with different adaptations arose on the Galapagos Islands.

Darwin reasoned that plants or animals that arrived on one of the Galapagos Islands faced conditions that were different from those on the mainland. **Perhaps, Darwin thought, the species gradually changed over many generations and became better adapted to the new conditions.** The gradual change in a species over time is called **evolution.**

Darwin's ideas are often referred to as the theory of evolution. A **scientific theory** is a well-tested concept that explains a wide range of observations.

It was clear to Darwin that evolution had occurred on the Galapagos Islands. He did not know, however, how this process had occurred. Darwin had to draw on other examples of changes in living things to help him understand how evolution occurs.

Bird Beak Adaptations

Use this activity to explore adaptations in birds.

1. Scatter a small amount of bird seed on a paper plate. Scatter 20 raisins on the plate to represent insects.

2. Obtain a variety of objects such as tweezers, hair clips, clothes pins, and hairpins. Pick one object to use as a "beak."

3. See how many seeds you can pick up and drop into a cup in 10 seconds.

4. Now see how many "insects" you can pick up and drop into a cup in 10 seconds.

5. Use a different "beak" and repeat Steps 3 and 4.

Inferring What type of beak worked well for seeds? For insects? How are different-shaped beaks useful for eating different foods?

Darwin knew that people used selective breeding to produce organisms with desired traits. For example, English farmers used selective breeding to produce sheep with fine wool. Darwin himself had bred pigeons with large, fan-shaped tails. By repeatedly allowing only those pigeons with many tail feathers to mate, Darwin produced pigeons with two or three times the usual number of tail feathers. Darwin thought that a process similar to selective breeding must happen in nature. But he wondered why certain traits were selected for, and how.

✓ *Checkpoint* *What observations led Darwin to propose his theory of evolution?*

Natural Selection

In 1858, Darwin and another British biologist, Alfred Russel Wallace, proposed an explanation for how evolution occurs. The next year, Darwin described this mechanism in a book entitled *The Origin of Species.* In his book, Darwin explained that evolution occurs by means of natural selection. **Natural selection** is the process by which individuals that are better adapted to their environment are more likely to survive and reproduce than other members of the same species. Darwin identified a number of factors that affect the process of natural selection: overproduction, competition, and variations.

Overproduction Most species produce far more offspring than can possibly survive. In many species, so many offspring are produced that there are not enough resources—food, water, and living space—for all of them. For example, each year a female sea turtle may lay more than 100 eggs. If all the young turtles survived, the sea would soon be full of turtles. Darwin knew that this doesn't happen. Why not?

Figure 4 Most newborn loggerhead sea turtles will not survive to adulthood. *Making Generalizations What factors limit the number of young that survive?*

Figure 5 The walruses lying on this rocky beach in Alaska must compete for resources. All organisms compete for limited resources such as food.

Competition Since food and other resources are limited, the offspring must compete with each other to survive. Competition does not usually involve direct physical fights between members of a species. Instead, competition is usually indirect. For example, some turtles may fail to find enough to eat. Others may not be able to escape from predators. Only a few turtles will survive long enough to reproduce.

Variations As you learned in your study of genetics, members of a species differ from one another in many of their traits. Any difference between individuals of the same species is called a **variation.** For example, some newly hatched turtles are able to swim faster than other turtles.

Selection Some variations make certain individuals better adapted to their environment. Those individuals are more likely to survive and reproduce. When those individuals reproduce, their offspring may inherit the allele for the helpful trait. The offspring, in turn, will be more likely to survive and reproduce, and thus pass on the allele to their offspring. After many generations, more members of the species will have the helpful trait. In effect, the environment has "selected" organisms with helpful traits to be the parents of the next generation—hence the term "natural selection." **Over a long period of time, natural selection can lead to evolution. Helpful variations gradually accumulate in a species, while unfavorable ones disappear.**

For example, suppose a new fast-swimming predator moves into the turtles' habitat. Turtles that are able to swim faster would be more likely to escape from the new predator. The faster turtles would thus be more likely to survive and reproduce. Over time, more and more turtles in the species would have the "fast-swimmer" trait.

Inferring Scatter 15 black buttons and 15 white buttons on a sheet of white paper. Have a partner time you to see how many buttons you can pick up in 10 seconds. Pick up the buttons one at a time.

Did you collect more buttons of one color than the other? Why? How can a variation such as color affect the process of natural selection?

Nature at Work

In this lab, you will investigate how natural selection can lead to changes in a species over time. You'll explore how both genetic and environmental factors play a part in natural selection.

Problem

How do species change over time?

Materials

scissors
marking pen
construction paper, 2 colors

Procedure

1. Work on this lab with two other students. One student should choose construction paper of one color and make the team's 50 "mouse" cards, as described in Table 1. The second student should choose a different color construction paper and make the team's 25 "event" cards, as described in Table 2. The third student should copy the data table and record all the data.

Part 1 A White Sand Environment

2. Mix up the mouse cards.
3. Begin by using the cards to model what might happen to a group of mice in an environment of white sand dunes. Choose two mouse cards. Allele pairs *WW* and *Ww* produce a white mouse. Allele pair *ww* produces a brown mouse. Record the color of the mouse with a tally mark in the data table.

4. Choose an event card. An "S" card means the mouse survives. A "D" or a "P" card means the mouse dies. A "C" card means the mouse dies if its color contrasts with the white sand dunes. (Only brown mice will die when a "C" card is drawn.) Record each death with a tally mark in the data table.
5. If the mouse lives, put the two mouse cards in a "live mice" pile. If the mouse dies, put the cards in a "dead mice" pile. Put the event card at the bottom of its pack.
6. Repeat Steps 3 through 5 with the remaining mouse cards to study the first generation of mice. Record your results.
7. Leave the dead mice cards untouched. Mix up the cards from the live mice pile. Mix up the events cards.
8. Repeat Steps 3 through 7 for the second generation. Then repeat Steps 3 through 6 for the third generation.

Table 1: "Mouse" Cards

Number	Label	Meaning
25	W	Dominant allele for white fur
25	w	Recessive allele for brown fur

Table 2: "Event" Cards

Number	Label	Meaning
5	S	Mouse survives.
1	D	Disease kills mouse.
1	P	Predator kills mice of all colors.
18	C	Predator kills mice that contrast with the environment.

DATA TABLE				
Type of Environment:				
Generation	White Mice	Brown Mice	Deaths	
			White Mice	Brown Mice
1				
2				
3				

Part 2 A Forest Floor Environment

9. How would the data differ if the mice in this model lived on a dark brown forest floor? Record your prediction in your notebook.

10. Make a new copy of the data table. Then use the cards to test your prediction. Remember that a "C" card now means that any mouse with white fur will die.

Analyze and Conclude

1. In Part 1, how many white mice were there in each generation? How many brown mice? In each generation, which color mouse had the higher death rate? (*Hint:* To calculate the death rate for white mice, divide the number of white mice that died by the total number of white mice, then multiply by 100%.)

2. If the events in Part 1 occurred in nature, how would the group of mice change over time?

3. How did the results in Part 2 differ from those in Part 1?

4. What are some ways in which this investigation models natural selection? What are some ways in which natural selection differs from this model?

5. **Think About It** How would it affect your model if you increased the number of "C" cards? If you decreased the number?

Design an Experiment

Choose a different species with a trait that interests you. Make a set of cards similar to these cards to investigate how natural selection might bring about the evolution of that species.

The case of the English peppered moth is an example of how human actions can affect natural selection. In the late 1700s, most English peppered moths were light gray in color. The light-colored moths had an advantage over black peppered moths because birds could not see them against the light-gray trees. Natural selection favored the light-colored moths over the black moths.

The Industrial Revolution began in England in the late 1700s. People built factories to make cloth and other goods. Over time, smoke from the factories blackened the trunks of the trees. Now the light-colored moths were easier to see than the black ones. As a result, birds caught more light-colored moths. Natural selection favored the black moths. By about 1850, almost all the peppered moths were black.

In Your Journal

Since the 1950s, strict pollution laws have reduced the amount of smoke released into the air in England. Predict how this has affected the trees and the moths.

Figure 6 The Industrial Revolution affected natural selection in peppered moths in England. As pollution blackened the tree trunks, black moths became more likely to survive and reproduce.

The Role of Genes in Evolution

Without variations, all the members of a species would have the same traits. Evolution by natural selection would not occur because all individuals would have an equal chance of surviving and reproducing. But where do variations come from? How are they passed on from parents to offspring? Darwin could not answer these questions.

Darwin did not know anything about genes or mutations. It is not surprising that he could not explain what caused variations or how they were passed on. As scientists later learned, variations can result from mutations in genes or from the shuffling of alleles during meiosis. Only genes are passed from parents to their offspring. Because of this, only traits that are inherited, or controlled by genes, can be acted upon by natural selection.

Evolution in Action

Since Darwin published his book, scientists have observed many examples of evolution in action. In a 1977 study of the finches on Daphne Major, one of the Galapagos Islands, scientists observed that beak size could change very quickly by natural selection. That year, little rain fell on the island—only 25 millimeters instead of the usual 130 millimeters or so. Because of the lack of rain, many plants died. Fewer of the seeds that the finches usually ate were available. Instead, the birds had to eat large seeds that were enclosed in tough, thorny seed pods.

Finches with larger and stronger beaks were better able to open the tough pods than were finches with smaller, weaker beaks. Many of the finches with smaller beaks did not survive the drought. The next year, more finches on the island had larger and stronger beaks. Evolution by natural selection had occurred in just one year.

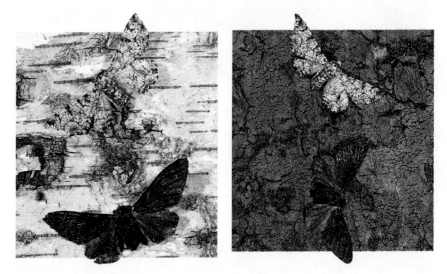

How Do New Species Form?

Darwin's theory of evolution by natural selection explains how variations can lead to changes in a species. But how does an entirely new species evolve? Since Darwin's time, scientists have come to understand that geographic isolation is one of the main ways that new species form. Isolation, or complete separation, occurs when some members of a species become cut off from the rest of the species.

Sometimes a group is separated from the rest of its species by a river, volcano, or mountain range. Even an ocean wave can separate a few individuals from the rest of their species by sweeping them out to sea and later washing them ashore on an island. This may have happened on the Galapagos Islands. Once a group becomes isolated, members of the isolated group can no longer mate with members of the rest of the species.

A new species can form when a group of individuals remains separated from the rest of its species long enough to evolve different traits. The longer the group remains isolated from the rest of the species, the more likely it is to evolve into a new species. For example, the Abert's squirrel and the Kaibab squirrel live in forests in the Southwest. About 10,000 years ago both types of squirrels were members of the same species. About that time, however, a small group of squirrels became isolated in a forest on the north side of the Grand Canyon in Arizona. Over time, this group evolved into the Kaibab squirrel, which has a distinctive black belly. Scientists are not sure whether the Kaibab squirrel has become different enough from the Abert's squirrel to be considered a separate species.

Checkpoint *How did geographic isolation affect the Kaibab squirrel?*

KEY

Range of Kaibab squirrel

Range of Abert's squirrel

Figure 7 About 10,000 years ago, a group of squirrels became isolated from the rest of the species. As a result, the Kaibab squirrel (left) has evolved to become different from the Abert's squirrel (right).
Interpreting Maps *What geographic feature separates the range of the Kaibab squirrel from that of the Abert's squirrel?*

Continental Drift

Geographic isolation has also occurred on a worldwide scale. For example, hundreds of millions of years ago all of Earth's landmasses were connected as one landmass. It formed a supercontinent called Pangaea. Organisms could migrate from one part of the supercontinent to another. Over millions of years, Pangaea gradually split apart in a process called continental drift. As the continents separated, species became isolated from one another and began to evolve independently.

Perhaps the most striking example of how continental drift affected the evolution of species is on the continent of Australia. The organisms living in Australia have been isolated from all other organisms on Earth for millions of years. Because of this, unique organisms have evolved in Australia. For example, most mammals in Australia belong to the group known as marsupials. Unlike other mammals, a marsupial gives birth to very small young that continue to develop in a pouch on the mother's body. Figure 8 shows two of the many marsupial species that exist in Australia. In contrast, few species of marsupials exist on other continents.

Figure 8 As a result of continental drift, many species of marsupials evolved in Australia. Australian marsupials include the numbat (top) and the spotted cuscus (bottom).

Section 1 Review

1. What is evolution? What did Darwin observe on the Galapagos Islands that he thought was the result of evolution?
2. Explain why variations are needed for natural selection to occur.
3. Describe how geographic isolation can result in the formation of a new species.
4. **Thinking Critically** Applying Concepts Some insects look just like sticks. How could this be an advantage to the insects? How could this trait have evolved through natural selection?

Check Your Progress

CHAPTER PROJECT 5

You should now be ready to submit your plans for your time lines to your teacher. Include a list of the major events you will include on your time lines. Remember, you want to emphasize the life forms that were present at each period. When your plans are approved, begin to construct your time lines. (*Hint:* You will need to divide your time lines into equal-sized intervals. For example, if you use a 12-month calendar to represent 5 billion years, calculate how many months will represent 1 billion years.)

SECTION 2 The Fossil Record

DISCOVER

ACTIVITY

What Can You Learn From Fossils?

1. Look at the fossil in the photograph. Describe the fossil's characteristics in as much detail as you can.

2. From your description in Step 1, try to figure out how the organism lived. How did it move? Where did it live?

Think It Over
Inferring What type of present-day organism do you think is related to the fossil? Why?

A crime has been committed. You and another detective arrive at the crime scene after the burglar has fled. To piece together what happened, you begin searching for clues. First you notice a broken first-floor window. Leading up to the window are footprints in the mud. From the prints, you can infer the size and type of shoes the burglar wore. As you gather these and other clues, you slowly piece together a picture of what happened and who the burglar might be.

To understand events that occurred long ago, scientists act like detectives. Some of the most important clues to Earth's past are fossils. A **fossil** is the preserved remains or traces of an organism that lived in the past. A fossil can be formed from a bone, tooth, shell, or other part of an organism. Other fossils can be traces of the organism, such as footprints or worm burrows left in mud that later turned to stone.

How Do Fossils Form?

Very few fossils are of complete organisms. Often when an animal dies, the soft parts of its body either decay or are eaten before a fossil can form. Usually only the hard parts of the animal, such as the bones or shells, remain. Plants also form fossils. The parts of plants that are most often preserved as fossils include leaves, stems, roots, and seeds.

The formation of any fossil is a rare event. The conditions must be just right for a fossil to form. **Most fossils form when organisms that die become buried in sediments.** Sediments are

GUIDE FOR READING

◆ How do most fossils form?

◆ How can scientists determine a fossil's age?

Reading Tip Before you read, preview *Exploring Life's History* on pages 156–157. Make a list of questions you have about geologic time and the evolution of life.

A fossilized shark tooth ▼

1. Two dinosaurs are buried by ash from an erupting volcano.

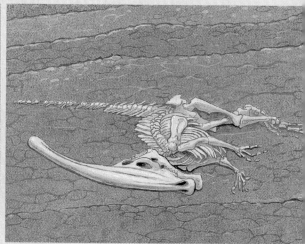

2. Minerals gradually replace the remains. Over millions of years, the fossils become buried by sediments.

Figure 9 Fossils are the preserved remains or traces of organisms that lived in the past. Fossils can form when organisms that die become buried in sediments.
Interpreting Diagrams What is one way in which a buried fossil can become uncovered?

particles of soil and rock. When a river flows into a lake or ocean, the sediments carried by the river settle to the bottom. Layers of sediments build up and cover the dead organisms. Over millions of years, the layers harden to become **sedimentary rock.**

Petrified Fossils Some remains that become buried in sediments are actually changed to rock. Minerals dissolved in the water soak into the buried remains. Gradually, the minerals replace the remains, changing them into rock. Fossils that form in this way are called **petrified fossils.**

Molds and Casts Sometimes shells or other hard parts buried by sediments are gradually dissolved. An empty space remains in the place the part once occupied. A hollow space in sediment in the shape of an organism or part of an organism is called a **mold.**

Sometimes a mold becomes filled in with hardened minerals, forming a **cast.** A cast is a copy of the shape of the organism that made the mold. If you have ever made a gelatin dessert in a plastic mold, then you can understand how a cast forms.

Preserved Remains Organisms can also be preserved in substances other than sediments. Entire organisms, such as the huge elephant-like mammoths that lived thousands of years ago, have been preserved in ice. The low temperatures preserved the mammoths' soft parts.

The bones and teeth of other ancient animals have been preserved in tar pits. Tar is a dark, sticky form of oil. Tar pits formed when tar seeped up from under the ground to the surface. The tar pits were often covered with water. Animals that came to drink the water became stuck in the tar.

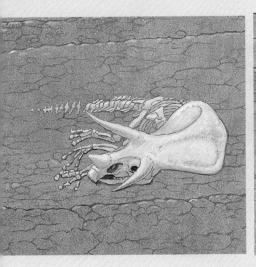
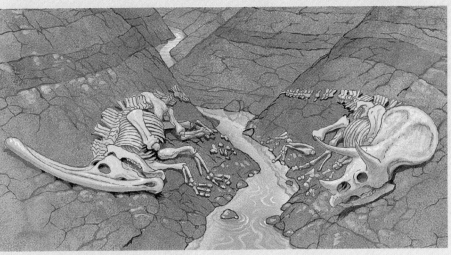

3. Running water cuts through the sedimentary rock layers, exposing the fossils.

Insects and some other organisms can become stuck in the sticky sap that some evergreen trees produce. The sap then hardens, forming amber. The amber protects the organism's body from decay.

Determining a Fossil's Age

To understand how living things have changed through time, scientists need to be able to determine the ages of fossils. They can then determine the sequence in which past events occurred. This information can be used to reconstruct the history of life on Earth. **Scientists can determine a fossil's age in two ways: relative dating and absolute dating.**

Relative Dating Scientists use **relative dating** to determine which of two fossils is older. To understand how relative dating works, imagine that a river has cut down through layers of sedimentary rock to form a canyon. If you look at the canyon walls, you can see the layers of sedimentary rock piled up one on top of another. The layers near the top of the canyon were formed most recently. These layers are the youngest rock layers. The lower down the canyon wall you go, the older the layers are. Therefore, fossils found in layers near the top of the canyon are younger than fossils found near the bottom of the canyon.

Relative dating can only be used when the rock layers have been preserved in their original sequence. Relative dating can help scientists determine whether one fossil is older than another. However, relative dating does not tell scientists the fossil's actual age.

✓ *Checkpoint* *Which rock layers contain younger fossils?*

Preservation in Ice

1. Place fresh fruit, such **ACTIVITY** as apple slices, strawberries, and blueberries, in an open plastic container.
2. Completely cover the fruit with water. Put the container in a freezer.
3. Place the same type and amount of fresh fruit in another open container. Leave it somewhere where no one will disturb it.
4. After three days, observe the fruit in both containers.

Inferring Use your observations to explain why fossils preserved in ice are more likely to include soft, fleshy body parts.

Figure 10 The half-life of potassium-40, a radioactive element, is 1.3 billion years. This means that half of the potassium-40 in a sample will break down into argon-40 every 1.3 billion years. *Interpreting Charts If a sample contains one fourth of the original amount of potassium-40, how old is the sample?*

Decay of Potassium-40 (Half-life = 1.3 billion years)		
Time	**Amount of Potassium-40**	**Amount of Argon-40**
2.6 billion years ago	1 g	0 g
1.3 billion years ago	0.5 g	0.5 g
Present	0.25 g	0.75 g

Absolute Dating Another technique, called **absolute dating,** allows scientists to determine the actual age of fossils. The rocks that fossils are found near contain **radioactive elements,** unstable elements that decay, or break down, into different elements. The **half-life** of a radioactive element is the time it takes for half of the atoms in a sample to decay. Figure 10 shows how a sample of potassium-40, a radioactive element, breaks down into argon-40 over time.

INTEGRATING CHEMISTRY

Scientists can compare the amount of a radioactive element in a sample to the amount of the element into which it breaks down. As you can see in Figure 10, this information can be used to calculate the age of the rock, and thus the age of the fossil.

✔ *Checkpoint* What is a half-life?

What Do Fossils Reveal?

Like pieces in a jigsaw puzzle, fossils help scientists piece together information about Earth's past. The millions of fossils that scientists have collected are called the **fossil record.** The fossil record, however, is incomplete. Many organisms die without leaving fossils behind. Despite gaps in the fossil record, it has given scientists a lot of important information about past life on Earth.

Almost all of the species preserved as fossils are now extinct. A species is **extinct** if no members of that species are still alive. Most of what scientists know about extinct species is based on the fossil record. Scientists use fossils of bones and teeth to build models of extinct animals. Fossil footprints provide clues about how fast an animal could move and how tall it was.

Sharpen your Skills

Calculating

ACTIVITY

A radioactive element has a half-life of 713 million years. After 2,139 million years, how many half-lives will have gone by?

Calculate how much of a 16-gram sample of the element will remain after 2,139 million years.

The fossil record also provides clues about how and when new groups of organisms evolved. The first animals appeared in the seas about 540 million years ago. These animals included worms, sponges, and other invertebrates—animals without backbones. About 500 million years ago, fishes evolved. These early fishes were the first vertebrates—animals with backbones.

The first land plants, which were similar to mosses, evolved around 410 million years ago. Land plants gradually evolved strong stems that held them upright. These plants were similar to modern ferns and cone-bearing trees. Look at *Exploring Life's History* on pages 156 and 157 to see when other groups of organisms evolved.

The Geologic Time Scale

Using absolute dating, scientists have calculated the ages of many different fossils and rocks. From this information, scientists have created a "calendar" of Earth's history that spans more than 4.6 billion years. Scientists have divided this large time period into smaller units called eras and periods. This calendar of Earth's history is sometimes called the Geologic Time Scale.

The largest span of time in the Geologic Time Scale is Precambrian Time, also called the Precambrian (pree KAM bree un). It covers the first 4 billion years of Earth's history. Scientists know very little about the Precambrian because there are few fossils from these ancient times. After the Precambrian, the Geologic Time Scale is divided into three major blocks of time, or eras. Each era is further divided into shorter periods. In *Exploring Life's History,* you can see the events that occurred during each time period.

Figure 11 Complete skeletons of animals that lived thousands of years ago have been found in the Rancho La Brea tar pits in Los Angeles, California. The photo shows a model of an elephant-like animal. Scientists created the model based on information learned from the fossils.

EXPLORING Life's History

Take a trip through time to see how life on Earth has changed.

PRECAMBRIAN TIME The Precambrian covers about 87 percent of Earth's history.

4.6 billion years ago

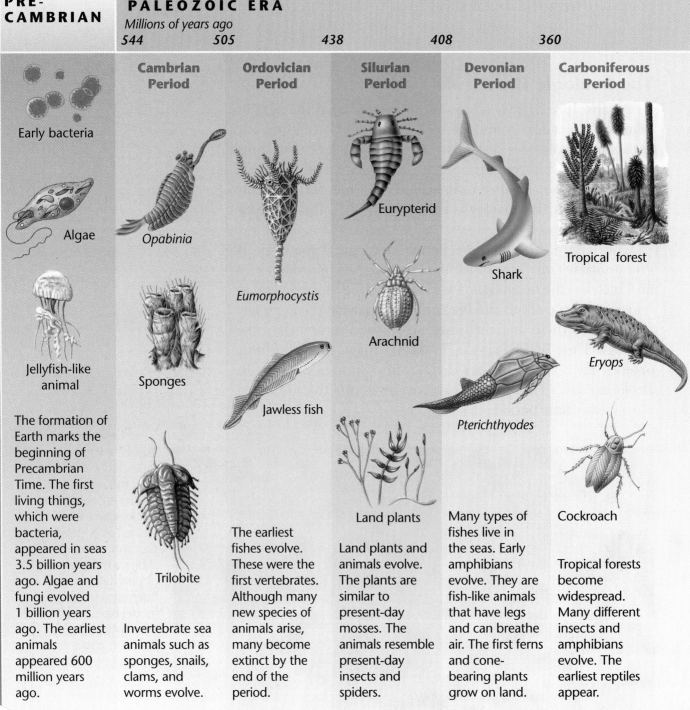

PRE-CAMBRIAN	PALEOZOIC ERA

Millions of years ago

544   505   438   408   360

Cambrian Period — Opabinia, Sponges, Trilobite

Ordovician Period — Eumorphocystis, Jawless fish

Silurian Period — Eurypterid, Arachnid, Land plants

Devonian Period — Shark, Pterichthyodes

Carboniferous Period — Tropical forest, Eryops, Cockroach

Early bacteria

Algae

Jellyfish-like animal

The formation of Earth marks the beginning of Precambrian Time. The first living things, which were bacteria, appeared in seas 3.5 billion years ago. Algae and fungi evolved 1 billion years ago. The earliest animals appeared 600 million years ago.

Invertebrate sea animals such as sponges, snails, clams, and worms evolve.

The earliest fishes evolve. These were the first vertebrates. Although many new species of animals arise, many become extinct by the end of the period.

Land plants and animals evolve. The plants are similar to present-day mosses. The animals resemble present-day insects and spiders.

Many types of fishes live in the seas. Early amphibians evolve. They are fish-like animals that have legs and can breathe air. The first ferns and cone-bearing plants grow on land.

Tropical forests become widespread. Many different insects and amphibians evolve. The earliest reptiles appear.

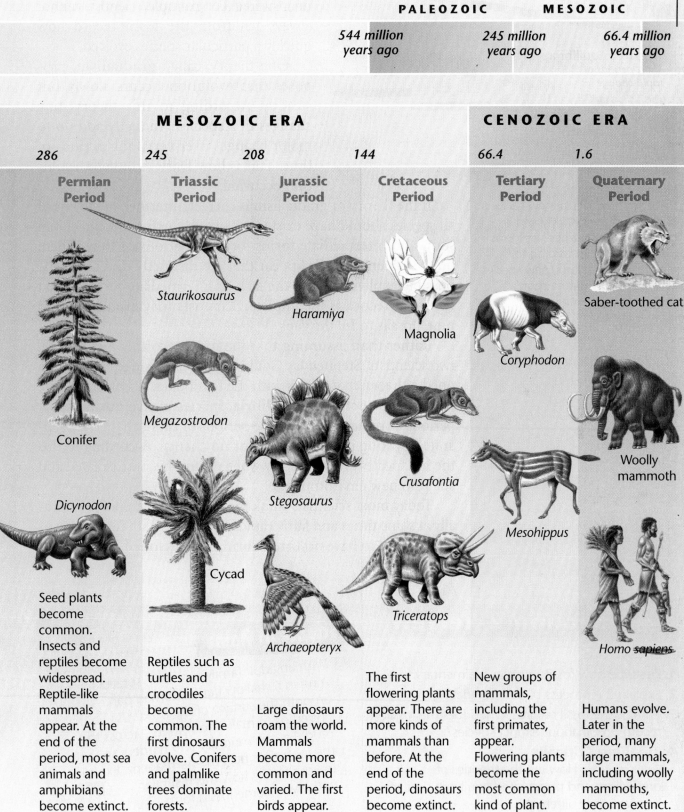

				CENOZOIC
	PALEOZOIC		MESOZOIC	
	544 million years ago	245 million years ago	66.4 million years ago	

MESOZOIC ERA

CENOZOIC ERA

286	245	208	144	66.4	1.6
Permian Period	**Triassic Period**	**Jurassic Period**	**Cretaceous Period**	**Tertiary Period**	**Quaternary Period**

Staurikosaurus

Haramiya

Magnolia

Saber-toothed cat

Conifer

Megazostrodon

Coryphodon

Dicynodon

Stegosaurus

Crusafontia

Woolly mammoth

Cycad

Mesohippus

Triceratops

Archaeopteryx

Homo sapiens

Seed plants become common. Insects and reptiles become widespread. Reptile-like mammals appear. At the end of the period, most sea animals and amphibians become extinct.

Reptiles such as turtles and crocodiles become common. The first dinosaurs evolve. Conifers and palmlike trees dominate forests.

Large dinosaurs roam the world. Mammals become more common and varied. The first birds appear.

The first flowering plants appear. There are more kinds of mammals than before. At the end of the period, dinosaurs become extinct.

New groups of mammals, including the first primates, appear. Flowering plants become the most common kind of plant.

Humans evolve. Later in the period, many large mammals, including woolly mammoths, become extinct.

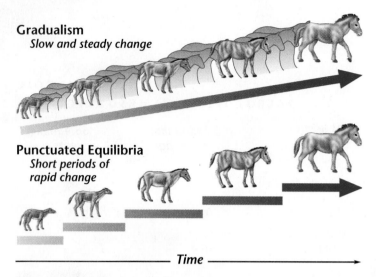

Gradualism
Slow and steady change

Punctuated Equilibria
Short periods of rapid change

———— *Time* ————→

Figure 12 According to the theory of gradualism, new species of horses evolved slowly and continuously. Intermediate forms were common. According to punctuated equilibria, new species evolved rapidly during short periods of time. Intermediate forms were rare.

How Fast Does Evolution Occur?

Because the fossil record is incomplete, many questions about evolution remain unanswered. For example, scientists cannot always tell from the fossil record how quickly a particular species evolved.

One theory, called **gradualism,** proposes that evolution occurs slowly but steadily. According to this theory, tiny changes in a species gradually add up to major changes over very long periods of time. This is how Darwin thought evolution occurred.

If the theory of gradualism is correct, intermediate forms of all species should have existed. However, the fossil record often shows no intermediate forms for long periods of time. Then, quite suddenly, fossils appear that are distinctly different. One possible explanation for the lack of intermediate forms is that the fossil record is incomplete. Scientists may eventually find more fossils to fill the gaps.

Rather than assuming that the fossil record is incomplete, two scientists, Stephen Jay Gould and Niles Eldridge, have developed a theory that agrees with the fossil data. According to the theory of **punctuated equilibria,** species evolve during short periods of rapid change. These periods of rapid change are separated by long periods of little or no change. According to this theory, species evolve quickly when groups become isolated and adapt to new environments.

Today most scientists think that evolution can occur gradually at some times and fairly rapidly at others. Both forms of evolution seem to have occurred during Earth's long history.

Section 2 Review

1. Describe how fossils form in sedimentary rock.
2. Explain the process of absolute dating.
3. What is the fossil record? What does the fossil record reveal about extinct species?
4. **Thinking Critically** *Comparing and Contrasting* How are the theories of gradualism and punctuated equilibria similar? How are they different?

Science at Home

With an adult family member, spread some mud in a shallow flat-bottomed pan. Smooth the surface of the mud. Use your fingertips to make "footprints" across the mud. Let the mud dry and harden, so that the footprints become permanent. Explain to your family how this is similar to the way some fossils form.

SECTION 3 Other Evidence for Evolution

How Can You Classify Species?

1. Collect six to eight different pens. Each pen will represent a different species of similar organisms.

2. Choose a trait that varies among your pen species, such as size or ink color. Using this trait, try to divide the pen species into two groups.

3. Now choose another trait. Divide each group into two smaller groups.

Think It Over

Classifying Which of the pen species share the most characteristics? What might the similarities suggest about how the pen species evolved?

Do you know anyone who has had their appendix out? The appendix is a tiny organ attached to the large intestine. You might think that having a part of the body removed might cause a problem. After all, you need your heart, lungs, stomach and other body parts to live. However, this is not the case with the appendix. In humans, the appendix does not seem to have much function. In some other species of mammals, though, the appendix is much larger and plays an important role in digestion. To scientists, this information about modern-day organisms provides clues about their ancestors and their relationships.

The appendix is just one example of how modern-day organisms can provide clues about evolution. By comparing organisms, scientists can infer how closely related the organisms are in an evolutionary sense. **Scientists compare body structures, development before birth, and DNA sequences to determine the evolutionary relationships among organisms.**

Similarities in Body Structure

Scientists long ago began to compare the body structures of living species to look for clues about evolution. In fact, this is how Darwin came to understand that evolution had occurred on the Galapagos Islands. An organism's body structure is its basic body plan, such as how its bones are arranged. Fishes, amphibians, reptiles, birds, and mammals, for example, all have a similar body

GUIDE FOR READING

◆ What evidence from modern-day organisms can help scientists determine evolutionary relationships among groups?

Reading Tip As you read, use the headings to make an outline about the different types of evidence for evolution.

Sharpen your Skills

Drawing Conclusions

Look at the drawing **ACTIVITY** below of the bones in a crocodile's leg. Compare this drawing to Figure 13. Do you think that crocodiles share a common ancestor with birds, dolphins, and dogs? Support your answer with evidence.

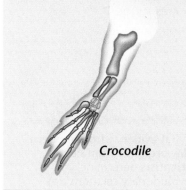

Crocodile

structure—an internal skeleton with a backbone. This is why scientists classify all five groups of animals together as vertebrates. Presumably, these groups all inherited these similarities in structure from an early vertebrate ancestor that they shared.

Look closely at the structure of the bones in the bird's wing, dolphin's flipper, and dog's leg shown in Figure 13. Notice that the bones in the forelimbs of these three animals are arranged in a similar way. These similarities provide evidence that these three organisms all evolved from a common ancestor. Similar structures that related species have inherited from a common ancestor are called **homologous structures** (hoh MAHL uh gus).

Sometimes scientists find fossil evidence that supports the evidence provided by homologous structures. For example, scientists have recently found fossils of ancient whale-like creatures. The fossils show that the ancestors of today's whales had legs and walked on land. This evidence supports other evidence that whales and humans share a common ancestor.

☑ *Checkpoint* *What information do homologous structures reveal?*

Similarities in Early Development

Scientists can also make inferences about evolutionary relationships by comparing the early development of different organisms. Suppose you were asked to compare an adult turtle, a chicken, and a rat. You would probably say they look quite different from each other. However, during early development, these three organisms go through similar stages, as you can see

Figure 13 A bird's wing, dolphin's flipper, and dog's leg are all adapted to performing different tasks. However, the structure of the bones in each forelimb is very similar. These homologous structures provide evidence that these animals evolved from a common ancestor. *Observing What similarities in structure do the three forelimbs share?*

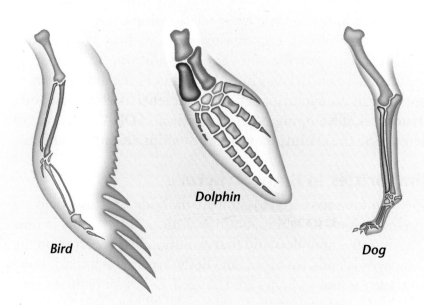

Bird

Dolphin

Dog

 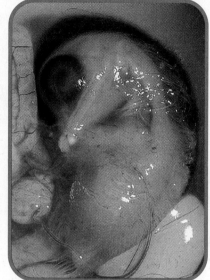 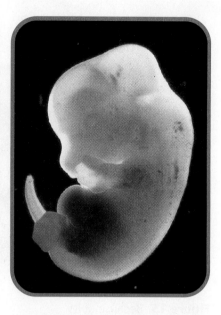

Figure 14 Turtles (left), chickens (center), and rats (right) look similar during the earliest stages of development. These similarities provide evidence that these three animals evolved from a common ancestor.

in Figure 14. For example, during the early stages of development all three organisms have a tail and tiny gill slits in their throats. These similarities suggest that these three vertebrate species are related and share a common ancestor.

When scientists study early development more closely, they notice that the turtle appears more similar to the chicken than it does to the rat. This evidence supports the conclusion that turtles are more closely related to chickens than they are to rats.

Similarities in DNA

Why do related species have similar body structures and development patterns? Scientists infer that the species inherited many of the same genes from a common ancestor. Recently, scientists have begun to compare the genes of different species to determine how closely related the species are.

Recall that genes are made of DNA. By comparing the sequence of nitrogen bases in the DNA of different species, scientists can infer how closely related the species are. The more similar the sequences, the more closely related the species are.

Recall also that the DNA bases along a gene specify what type of protein will be produced. Thus, scientists can also compare the order of amino acids in a protein to see how closely related two species are.

Sometimes DNA evidence does not confirm earlier conclusions about relationships between species. For example, aside from its long nose, the tiny elephant shrew looks very similar to rodents such as mice. Because of this, biologists used to think that the elephant shrew was closely related to rodents. But when scientists compared DNA from elephant shrews to that of both

Figure 15 Because of its appearance, the tiny elephant shrew was thought to be closely related to mice and other rodents. Surprisingly, DNA comparisons showed that the elephant shrew is actually more closely related to elephants.

rodents and elephants, they got a surprise. The elephant shrew's DNA was more similar to the elephant's DNA than it was to the rodent's DNA. Scientists now think that elephant shrews are more closely related to elephants than to rodents.

INTEGRATING TECHNOLOGY Recently, scientists have developed techniques that allow them to extract, or remove, DNA from fossils. Using these techniques, scientists have now extracted DNA from fossils of bones, teeth, and plants, and from insects trapped in amber. The DNA from fossils has provided scientists with new evidence about evolution.

Combining the Evidence

Scientists have combined evidence from fossils, body structures, early development, and DNA and protein sequences to determine the evolutionary relationships among species. In most cases, DNA and protein sequences have confirmed conclusions based on earlier evidence. For example, recent DNA comparisons show that dogs are more similar to wolves than they are to coyotes. Scientists had already reached this conclusion based on similarities in the structure and development of these three species.

Another example of how scientists combined evidence from different sources is shown in the branching tree in Figure 16. A **branching tree** is a diagram that shows how scientists think different groups of organisms are related. Based on similar body structures, lesser pandas were thought to be closely related to giant pandas. The two panda species also resemble both bears and raccoons. Until recently, scientists were not sure how these four groups were related. DNA analysis and other methods have shown that giant pandas and lesser pandas are not closely related. Instead, giant pandas are more closely related to bears, while lesser pandas are more closely related to raccoons.

Raccoons

Lesser pandas

Giant pandas

Bears

Present

10 million
years ago

25 million
years ago

40 million
years ago

Common ancestor

Figure 16 This branching tree shows how scientists now think that lesser pandas, giant pandas, bears, and raccoons are related.
Interpreting Diagrams Are giant pandas more closely related to lesser pandas or to bears?

Section 3 Review

1. Name three types of evidence from modern-day organisms that scientists use to determine evolutionary relationships.
2. What are homologous structures?
3. What information did scientists learn by comparing the early developmental stages of turtles, chickens, and rats?
4. If two species are closely related, what would you expect a comparison of their DNA base sequences to reveal?
5. **Thinking Critically** **Making Judgments** Most scientists today consider similarities in DNA to be the best indicator of how closely two species are related. Why do you think this is the case?

Check Your Progress
CHAPTER PROJECT 5
You should be completing construction of the time line that covers 5 billion years. Now begin work on the time line showing 600 million years. This version is a magnified view of one part of the first time line. It will give you additional space to show what happened in the more recent years of Earth's history. (*Hint:* Prepare drawings to show how life forms on Earth were changing. Also, try to include three or more events not mentioned in the text.)

TELLTALE MOLECULES

In this lab, you will compare the structure of one protein in a variety of animals. You'll use the data to draw conclusions about how closely related those animals are.

Problem

What information can protein structure reveal about evolutionary relationships among organisms?

Procedure

1. Examine the table below. It shows the sequence of amino acids in one region of a protein, cytochrome c, for six different animals. Each letter represents a different amino acid.

2. Predict which of the five other animals is most closely related to the horse. Which animal do you think is most distantly related?

3. Compare the amino acid sequence of the horse to that of the donkey. How many amino acids differ between the two species? Record that number in your notebook.

4. Compare the amino acid sequences of each of the other animals to that of the horse. Record the number of differences in your notebook.

Analyze and Conclude

1. Which animal's amino acid sequence was most similar to that of the horse? What similarities and difference(s) did you observe?

2. How did the amino acid sequences of each of the other animals compare with that of the horse?

3. Based on this data, which species is the most closely related to the horse? Which is the most distantly related?

4. For the entire cytochrome c protein, the horse's amino acid sequence differs from the other animals as follows: donkey, 1 difference; rabbit, 6; snake, 22; turtle, 11; and whale, 5. How do the relationships indicated by the entire protein compare with those for the region you examined?

5. **Think About It** Explain why data about amino acid sequences can provide information about evolutionary relationships among organisms.

More to Explore

Use the amino acid data to construct a branching tree that includes horses, donkeys, and snakes. The tree should show one way that the three species could have evolved from a common ancestor.

Section of Cytochrome c Protein in Animals														
Amino Acid Position														
Animal	**39**	**40**	**41**	**42**	**43**	**44**	**45**	**46**	**47**	**48**	**49**	**50**	**51**	**52**	**53**
Horse	A	B	C	D	E	F	G	H	I	J	K	L	M	N	O
Donkey	A	B	C	D	E	F	G	H	Z	J	K	L	M	N	O
Rabbit	A	B	C	D	E	Y	G	H	Z	J	K	L	M	N	O
Snake	A	B	C	D	E	Y	G	H	Z	J	K	W	M	N	O
Turtle	A	B	C	D	E	V	G	H	Z	J	K	U	M	N	O
Whale	A	B	C	D	E	Y	G	H	Z	J	K	L	M	N	O

SECTION 1 Darwin's Voyage

Key Ideas

◆ Darwin thought that species gradually changed over many generations as they became better adapted to new conditions. This process is called evolution.

◆ Darwin's observations led him to propose that evolution occurs through natural selection. Natural selection occurs due to overproduction, competition, and variations.

◆ Only traits controlled by genes can change over time as a result of natural selection.

◆ If a group of individuals remains separated from the rest of its species long enough to evolve different traits, a new species can form.

Key Terms

species evolution natural selection
adaptation scientific theory variation

SECTION 2 The Fossil Record

INTEGRATING EARTH SCIENCE

Key Ideas

◆ Most fossils form when organisms die and sediments bury them. The sediments harden, preserving parts of the organisms.

◆ Relative dating determines which of two fossils is older and which is younger. Absolute dating determines the actual age of a fossil.

◆ Fossils help scientists understand how extinct organisms looked and evolved.

◆ The Geologic Time Scale shows when during Earth's 4.6-billion-year history major groups of organisms evolved.

◆ Evolution has occurred gradually at some times and fairly rapidly at other times.

Key Terms

fossil   radioactive element
sedimentary rock half-life
petrified fossil fossil record
mold   extinct
cast   gradualism
relative dating punctuated equilibria
absolute dating

SECTION 3 Other Evidence for Evolution

Key Ideas

◆ By comparing modern-day organisms, scientists can infer how closely related they are in an evolutionary sense.

◆ Homologous structures can provide evidence of how species are related and of how they evolved from a common ancestor.

◆ Similarities in early developmental stages are evidence that species are related and shared a common ancestor.

◆ Scientists can compare DNA and protein sequences to determine more precisely how species are related.

◆ A branching tree is a diagram that shows how scientists think different groups of organisms are related.

Key Terms

homologous structure
branching tree

Organizing Information

Flowchart Copy the flowchart about natural selection onto a separate sheet of paper. Complete the flowchart by writing a sentence describing each factor that leads to natural selection. Then add a title. (For more on flowcharts, see the Skills Handbook.)

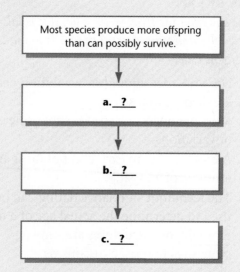

Reviewing Content

 For more review of key concepts, see the Interactive Student Tutorial CD-ROM.

Multiple Choice

Choose the letter of the best answer.

1. Changes in a species over long periods of time are called
   a. relative dating.
   b. evolution.
   c. homologous structures.
   d. developmental stages.

2. A trait that helps an organism survive and reproduce is called a(n)
   a. variation.   b. adaptation.
   c. species.   d. selection.

3. The type of fossil formed when an organism dissolves and leaves an empty space in a rock is called a
   a. cast.   b. mold.
   c. trace.   d. petrified fossil.

4. The rate of decay of a radioactive element is measured by its
   a. year.   b. era.
   c. half-life.   d. period.

5. Which of these is *not* used as evidence for evolution?
   a. DNA sequences
   b. stages of development
   c. body size
   d. body structures

True or False

If the statement is true, write true. If it is false, change the underlined word or words to make the statement true.

6. Darwin's idea about how evolution occurs is called <u>natural selection</u>.

7. Most members of a species show differences, or <u>variations</u>.

8. A footprint of an extinct dinosaur is an example of a <u>fossil</u>.

9. The technique of <u>relative dating</u> can be used to determine the actual age of a fossil.

10. <u>Homologous structures</u> are similar structures in related organisms.

Checking Concepts

11. What role does the overproduction of offspring play in the process of natural selection?

12. Use an example to explain how natural selection can lead to evolution.

13. How are rock layers used to determine the relative ages of fossils?

14. According to the theory of punctuated equilibria, why does the fossil record include very few intermediate forms?

15. Explain why similarities in the early development of different species suggest that the species are related.

16. **Writing to Learn** You are a young reporter for a local newspaper near the home of Charles Darwin. You have been asked to interview Darwin about his theory of evolution. Write three questions that you would ask Darwin. Then choose one question and answer it as Darwin would have.

Thinking Critically

17. **Applying Concepts** Why did Darwin's visit to the Galapagos Islands have such an important influence on his development of the theory of evolution by natural selection?

18. **Predicting** Predict how an extreme change in climate might affect natural selection in a species.

19. **Relating Cause and Effect** What is the role of geographic isolation in the formation of new species?

20. **Comparing and Contrasting** How does relative dating differ from absolute dating?

21. **Applying Concepts** A seal's flipper and a human arm have very different functions. What evidence might scientists look for to determine whether both structures evolved from the forelimb of a common ancestor?

Applying Skills

Radioactive carbon-14 decays to nitrogen with a half-life of 5,730 years. Use this information and the table below to answer Questions 22–24.

Fossil	Amount of Carbon-14 in Fossil	Amount of Nitrogen in Fossil	Position of Fossil in Rock Layers
A	1 gram	7 grams	bottom layer
B	4 grams	4 grams	top layer
C	2 grams	6 grams	middle layer

22. Inferring Use the positions of the fossils in the rock layers to put the fossils in order from youngest to oldest.

23. Calculating Calculate the age of each fossil using the data about carbon-14 and nitrogen.

24. Drawing Conclusions Do your answers to Questions 22 and 23 agree or disagree with each other? Explain.

Performance ▼ Assessment

CHAPTER PROJECT 5

Project Wrap Up Display your completed time lines for the class. Be prepared to explain why you chose the scale that you did. Also, describe how your time lines are related to each other.

Reflect and Record In your notebook, describe how the time lines helped you understand the long periods involved in the evolution of life. Were you surprised to see how far apart some of the events were? What surprised you the most? What did making two time lines enable you to see that you might have missed with only one?

Test Preparation Use these questions to prepare for standardized tests.

Use the illustration to answer Questions 25–28.

25. What is the best title for this illustration?
   a. Plant Growth Over Time
   b. Branching Tree of Plant Evolution
   c. Mosses and Ferns, the Oldest Plants
   d. Flowering Plants, the Youngest Plants

26. About how long ago did mosses evolve?
   a. 100 million years ago
   b. 150 million years ago
   c. 350 million years ago
   d. 450 million years ago

27. Which group of plants would have DNA that is most similar to the DNA of flowering plants?
   a. mosses
   b. ferns
   c. conifers
   d. They would all be equally alike.

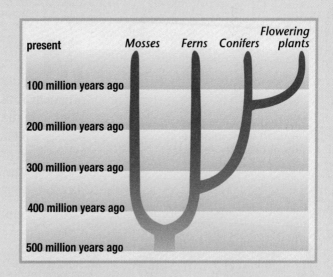

28. Which group of plants would have DNA that is least similar to the DNA of flowering plants?
   a. mosses
   b. ferns
   c. conifers
   d. They would all be equally alike.

DOGS

LOYAL COMPANIONS

WHAT'S YOUR IMAGE OF A **DOG**?

✦ A small, floppy-eared spaniel?

✦ A large, powerful Great Dane?

✦ A protective German shepherd guide dog?

✦ A shaggy sheepdog?

✦ A tiny, lively Chihuahua?

✦ A friendly, lovable mutt?

The gray wolf is the ancestor of most modern breeds of dogs.

More than 3,000 years ago, an artist in ancient Egypt drew three dogs chasing a hyena. ▼

Most dogs are descendants of the gray wolf, which was originally found throughout Europe, Asia, and North America. Dogs were the first animals to be domesticated, or tamed. As far back as 9,000 years ago, farmers who raised sheep, cattle, and goats tamed dogs to herd and guard the livestock.

After taming dogs, people began to breed them for traits that people valued. Early herding dogs helped shepherds. Speedy hunting dogs learned to chase deer and other game. Strong, sturdy working dogs pulled sleds and even rescued people. Small, quick terriers hunted animals, such as rats. "Toy" dogs were companions to people of wealth and leisure. More recently, sporting dogs were trained to flush out and retrieve birds. Still others were bred to be guard dogs. But perhaps the real reason people bred dogs was for their loyalty and companionship.

From Wolf to Purebred

About ten thousand years ago, some wolves may have been attracted to human settlements. They may have found it easier to feed on food scraps than to hunt for themselves. Gradually the wolves came to depend on people for food. The wolves, in turn, kept the campsites clean and safe. They ate the garbage and barked to warn of approaching strangers. These wolves were the ancestors of the dogs you know today.

Over time dogs became more and more a part of human society. People began to breed dogs for the traits needed for tasks such as herding sheep and hunting. Large, aggressive dogs, for example, were bred to be herding dogs, while fast dogs with a keen sense of smell were bred to be hunting dogs. Today there are hundreds of breeds. They range from the tiny Chihuahua to the massive Saint Bernard, one of which can weigh as much as fifty Chihuahuas.

Today, people breed dogs mostly for their appearance and personality. Physical features such as long ears or a narrow snout are valued in particular breeds of dogs. To create "pure" breeds of dogs, breeders use a method known as inbreeding. Inbreeding involves mating dogs that are genetically very similar. Inbreeding is the surest way to produce dogs with a uniform physical appearance.

One undesirable result of inbreeding is an increase in genetic disorders. Experts estimate that 25 percent of all purebred dogs have a genetic disorder. Dalmatians, for example, often inherit deafness. German shepherds may develop severe hip problems. Mixed-breed dogs, in contrast, are less likely to inherit genetic disorders.

Science Activity

Most traits that dogs are bred for are controlled by more than one gene. A few traits, however, show simpler inheritance patterns. For example, in Labrador retrievers, a single gene with one dominant and one recessive allele determines whether the dog's fur will be dark or yellow. The allele for dark fur (*D*) is dominant over the allele for yellow fur (*d*).

◆ Construct a Punnett square for a cross between 2 Labrador retrievers that are both heterozygous for dark fur (*Dd*).

◆ Suppose there were 8 puppies in the litter. Predict how many would have dark fur and how many would have yellow fur.

◆ Construct a second Punnett square for a cross between a Labrador retriever with yellow fur (*dd*) and one with dark fur (*Dd*). In a litter with 6 puppies, predict how many would have dark fur and how many would have yellow fur.

In Labrador retrievers, the allele for dark-colored fur is dominant over the allele for yellow fur.

Golden Retriever
Great Britain, A.D. 1870s
Lord Tweedsmouth developed this breed to help hunters retrieve waterfowl and other small animals.

Border Collie
Great Britain, after A.D. 1100
This breed was developed in the counties near the border of England and Scotland for herding sheep. The Border collie's ancestors were cross-breeds of local sheepdogs and dogs brought to Scotland by the Vikings.

Dachshund
Germany, A.D. 1700s
These dogs were bred to catch badgers or rats. Their short legs and long body can fit into a badger's burrow. In fact, in German the word *Dachshund* means "badger dog."

Basset Hound
France, A.D. 1600s
Second only to the bloodhound at following a scent, the basset hound has short legs and a compact body that help it run through underbrush.

Greyhound
Egypt, 3500 B.C.
These speedy, slender hounds were bred for chasing prey. Today, greyhounds are famous as racers.

Dogs and People

Over thousands of years, people have developed many different breeds of dogs. Each of the dogs shown on the map was bred for a purpose—hunting, herding, guarding, pulling sleds—as well as companionship. Every breed has its own story.

Siberian Husky
Siberia, 1000 B.C.
The Chukchi people of northeastern Siberia used these strong working dogs to pull sleds long distances across the snow.

Pekingese
China, A.D. 700s
These lapdogs were bred as pets in ancient China. One Chinese name for a Pekingese means "lion dog," which refers to the dog's long, golden mane.

Chow Chow
China, 150 B.C.
Chow chows, the working dogs of ancient China, worked as hunters, herders, and guard dogs.

Akita
Japan, A.D. 1600s
This breed was developed in the cold mountains of northern Japan as a guard dog and hunting dog. The Akita is able to hunt in deep snow and is also a powerful swimmer.

Lhasa Apso
Tibet, A.D. 1100
This breed has a long, thick coat to protect it from the cold air of the high Tibetan plateau. In spite of its small size, the Lhasa apso guarded homes and temples.

Social Studies Activity

Draw a time line that shows the approximate date of origin of different breeds of domestic dogs from 7000 B.C. to the present. Use the information on the map to fill out your time line. Include information about where each breed was developed.

Picking a Puppy

People look for different traits in the dogs they choose. Here is how one expert selected his dog based on good breeding and personality.

James Herriot, a veterinarian in England, had owned several dogs during his lifetime. But he had always wanted a Border terrier. These small, sturdy dogs are descendants of working terrier breeds that lived on the border of England and Scotland. For centuries they were used to hunt foxes, rats, and other small animals. In this story, Herriot and his wife Helen follow up on an advertisement for Border terrier puppies.

Border terrier ▶

She [Helen, his wife] turned to me and spoke agitatedly, "I've got Mrs. Mason on the line now. There's only one pup left out of the litter and there are people coming from as far as eighty miles away to see it. We'll have to hurry. What a long time you've been out there!"

We bolted our lunch and Helen, Rosie, granddaughter Emma and I drove out to Bedale. Mrs. Mason led us into the kitchen and pointed to a tiny brindle creature twisting and writhing under the table.

"That's him," she said.

I reached down and lifted the puppy as he curled his little body round, apparently trying to touch his tail with his nose. But that tail wagged furiously and the pink tongue was busy at my hand. I knew he was ours before my quick examination for hernia and overshot jaw.

The deal was quickly struck and we went outside to inspect the puppy's relations. His mother and grandmother were out there. They lived in little barrels which served as kennels and both of them darted out and stood up at our legs, tails lashing, mouths panting in delight. I felt vastly reassured. With happy, healthy ancestors like those I knew we had every chance of a first rate dog.

As we drove home with the puppy in Emma's arms, the warm thought came to me. The wheel had indeed turned. After nearly fifty years I had my Border terrier.

James Herriot was a country veterinarian in Yorkshire, England. In several popular books published in the 1970s and 1980s, he wrote warm, humorous stories about the animals he cared for. His book *All Creatures Great and Small* was the basis for a television series.

Breed	1970	1980	1990	1997
Poodle	265,879	92,250	71,757	54,773
Labrador Retriever	25,667	52,398	99,776	158,366
Cocker Spaniel	21,811	76,113	105,642	41,439

Poodles in the U.S., 1970–1997

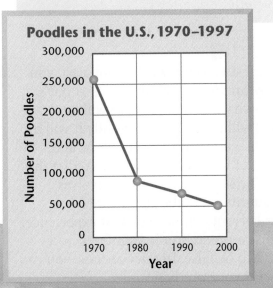

Math Activity

The popularity of different breeds of dogs changes over time. For example, the line graph shows how the number of poodles registered with the American Kennel Club changed between 1970 and 1997. Use the table to create your own line graph for Labrador retrievers and cocker spaniels.

Which breed was more popular in 1980, Labrador retrievers or cocker spaniels? How has the number of Labrador retrievers changed from 1970 to 1997? How has the number of cocker spaniels changed over the same time?

Tie It Together

Best of Breed Show

In many places proud dog owners of all ages bring their animals to compete in dog shows. Organize your own dog show. With a partner, choose one specific breed of dog. Pick a breed shown on the map on pages 170–171, or use library resources to research another breed.

- Find out what the breed looks like, the time and place where it originated, and what traits it was first bred for.
- List your breed's characteristics, height, weight, and coloring.
- Research the breed's personality and behavior.
- Find out your breed's strengths. Learn what weakness may develop as a result of inbreeding.
- Make a poster for your breed. Include a drawing or photo and the information that you researched.
- With your class, organize the dog displays into categories of breeds, such as hunting dogs, herding dogs, and toy dogs.

Think Like a Scientist

*A*lthough you may not know it, you think like a scientist every day. Whenever you ask a question and explore possible answers, you use many of the same skills that scientists do. Some of these skills are described on this page.

Observing

When you use one or more of your five senses to gather information about the world, you are **observing.** Hearing a dog bark, counting twelve green seeds, and smelling smoke are all observations. To increase the power of their senses, scientists sometimes use microscopes, telescopes, or other instruments that help them make more detailed observations.

An observation must be an accurate report of what your senses detect. It is important to keep careful records of your observations in science class by writing or drawing in a notebook. The information collected through observations is called evidence, or data.

Inferring

When you interpret an observation, you are **inferring,** or making an inference. For example, if you hear your dog barking, you may infer that someone is at your front door. To make this inference, you combine the evidence—the barking dog—and your experience or knowledge—you know that your dog barks when strangers approach—to reach a logical conclusion.

Notice that an inference is not a fact; it is only one of many possible interpretations for an observation. For example, your dog may be barking because it wants to go for a walk. An inference may turn out to be incorrect even if it is based on accurate observations and logical reasoning. The only way to find out if an inference is correct is to investigate further.

Predicting

When you listen to the weather forecast, you hear many predictions about the next day's weather—what the temperature will be, whether it will rain, and how windy it will be. Weather forecasters use observations and knowledge of weather patterns to predict the weather. The skill of **predicting** involves making an inference about a future event based on current evidence or past experience.

Because a prediction is an inference, it may prove to be false. In science class, you can test some of your predictions by doing experiments. For example, suppose you predict that larger paper airplanes can fly farther than smaller airplanes. How could you test your prediction?

ACTIVITY Use the photograph to answer the questions below.

Observing Look closely at the photograph. List at least three observations.

Inferring Use your observations to make an inference about what has happened. What experience or knowledge did you use to make the inference?

Predicting Predict what will happen next. On what evidence or experience do you base your prediction?

Classifying

Could you imagine searching for a book in the library if the books were shelved in no particular order? Your trip to the library would be an all-day event! Luckily, librarians group together books on similar topics or by the same author. Grouping together items that are alike in some way is called **classifying.** You can classify items in many ways: by size, by shape, by use, and by other important characteristics.

Like librarians, scientists use the skill of classifying to organize information and objects. When things are sorted into groups, the relationships among them become easier to understand.

ACTIVITY

Classify the objects in the photograph into two groups based on any characteristic you choose. Then use another characteristic to classify the objects into three groups.

Making Models

Have you ever drawn a picture to help someone understand what you were saying? Such a drawing is one type of model. A model is a picture, diagram, computer image, or other representation of a complex object or process. **Making models** helps people understand things that they cannot observe directly.

Scientists often use models to represent things that are either very large or very small, such as the planets in the solar system, or the parts of a cell. Such models are physical models—drawings or three-dimensional structures that look like the real thing. Other models are mental models—mathematical equations or words that describe how something works.

ACTIVITY

This student is using a model to demonstrate what causes day and night on Earth. What do the flashlight and the tennis ball in the model represent?

Communicating

Whenever you talk on the phone, write a letter, or listen to your teacher at school, you are communicating. **Communicating** is the process of sharing ideas and information with other people. Communicating effectively requires many skills, including writing, reading, speaking, listening, and making models.

Scientists communicate to share results, information, and opinions. Scientists often communicate about their work in journals, over the telephone, in

letters, and on the Internet. They also attend scientific meetings where they share their ideas with one another in person.

ACTIVITY

On a sheet of paper, write out clear, detailed directions for tying your shoe. Then exchange directions with a partner. Follow your partner's directions exactly. How successful were you at tying your shoe? How could your partner have communicated more clearly?

Making Measurements

When scientists make observations, it is not sufficient to say that something is "big" or "heavy." Instead, scientists use instruments to measure just how big or heavy an object is. By measuring, scientists can express their observations more precisely and communicate more information about what they observe.

Measuring in SI

The standard system of measurement used by scientists around the world is known as the International System of Units, which is abbreviated as SI (in French, *Système International d'Unités*). SI units are easy to use because they are based on multiples of 10. Each unit is ten times larger than the next smallest unit and one tenth the size of the next largest unit. The table lists the prefixes used to name the most common SI units.

Common SI Prefixes		
Prefix	**Symbol**	**Meaning**
kilo-	k	1,000
hecto-	h	100
deka-	da	10
deci-	d	0.1 (one tenth)
centi-	c	0.01 (one hundredth)
milli-	m	0.001 (one thousandth)

Length To measure length, or the distance between two points, the unit of measure is the **meter (m).** The distance from the floor to a doorknob is approximately one meter. Long distances, such as the distance between two cities, are measured in kilometers (km). Small lengths are measured in centimeters (cm) or millimeters (mm). Scientists use metric rulers and meter sticks to measure length.

Common Conversions
1 km = 1,000 m
1 m = 100 cm
1 m = 1,000 mm
1 cm = 10 mm

Liquid Volume To measure the volume of a liquid, or the amount of space it takes up, you will use a unit of measure known as the **liter (L).** One liter is the approximate volume of a medium-size carton of milk. Smaller volumes are measured in milliliters (mL). Scientists use graduated cylinders to measure liquid volume.

Common Conversion
1 L = 1,000 mL

The larger lines on the metric ruler in the picture show centimeter divisions, while the smaller, unnumbered lines show millimeter divisions. How many centimeters long is the shell? How many millimeters long is it?

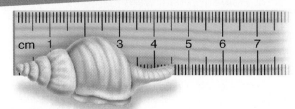

The graduated cylinder in the picture is marked in milliliter divisions. Notice that the water in the cylinder has a curved surface. This curved surface is called the *meniscus*. To measure the volume, you must read the level at the lowest point of the meniscus. What is the volume of water in this graduated cylinder?

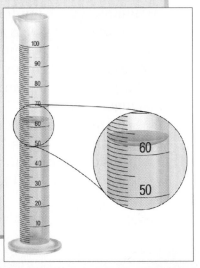

Mass To measure mass, or the amount of matter in an object, you will use a unit of measure known as the **gram (g)**. One gram is approximately the mass of a paper clip. Larger masses are measured in kilograms (kg). Scientists use a scale to find the mass of an object.

Common Conversion

1 kg = 1,000 g

The electronic scale displays the mass of an apple in kilograms. What is the mass of the apple? Suppose a recipe for applesauce called for one kilogram of apples. About how many apples would you need?

ACTIVITY

Temperature
To measure the temperature of a substance, you will use the **Celsius scale**. Temperature is measured in degrees Celsius (°C) using a Celsius thermometer. Water freezes at 0°C and boils at 100°C.

ACTIVITY

What is the temperature of the liquid in degrees Celsius?

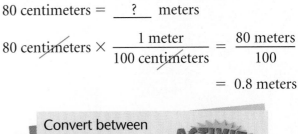

Converting SI Units

To use the SI system, you must know how to convert between units. Converting from one unit to another involves the skill of **calculating**, or using mathematical operations. Converting between SI units is similar to converting between dollars and dimes because both systems are based on multiples of ten.

Suppose you want to convert a length of 80 centimeters to meters. Follow these steps to convert between units.

1. Begin by writing down the measurement you want to convert—in this example, 80 centimeters.
2. Write a conversion factor that represents the relationship between the two units you are converting. In this example, the relationship is *1 meter = 100 centimeters*. Write this conversion factor as a fraction, making sure to place the units you are converting from (centimeters, in this example) in the denominator.

3. Multiply the measurement you want to convert by the fraction. When you do this, the units in the first measurement will cancel out with the units in the denominator. Your answer will be in the units you are converting to (meters, in this example).

Example

80 centimeters = ___?__ meters

$$80 \text{ centimeters} \times \frac{1 \text{ meter}}{100 \text{ centimeters}} = \frac{80 \text{ meters}}{100}$$

$$= 0.8 \text{ meters}$$

ACTIVITY

Convert between the following units.
1. 600 millimeters = _?_ meters
2. 0.35 liters = _?_ milliliters
3. 1,050 grams = _?_ kilograms

Conducting a Scientific Investigation

In some ways, scientists are like detectives, piecing together clues to learn about a process or event. One way that scientists gather clues is by carrying out experiments. An experiment tests an idea in a careful, orderly manner. Although experiments do not all follow the same steps in the same order, many follow a pattern similar to the one described here.

Posing Questions

Experiments begin by asking a scientific question. A scientific question is one that can be answered by gathering evidence. For example, the question "Which freezes faster—fresh water or salt water?" is a scientific question because you can carry out an investigation and gather information to answer the question.

Developing a Hypothesis

The next step is to form a hypothesis. A **hypothesis** is a possible explanation for a set of observations or answer to a scientific question. In science, a hypothesis must be something that can be tested. A hypothesis can be worded as an *If…then…* statement. For example, a hypothesis might be *"If I add salt to fresh water, then the water will take longer to freeze."* A hypothesis worded this way serves as a rough outline of the experiment you should perform.

Designing an Experiment

Next you need to plan a way to test your hypothesis. Your plan should be written out as a step-by-step procedure and should describe the observations or measurements you will make.

Two important steps involved in designing an experiment are controlling variables and forming operational definitions.

Controlling Variables In a well-designed experiment, you need to keep all variables the same except for one. A **variable** is any factor that can change in an experiment. The factor that you change is called the **manipulated variable.** In this experiment, the manipulated variable is the amount of salt added to the water. Other factors, such as the amount of water or the starting temperature, are kept constant.

The factor that changes as a result of the manipulated variable is called the responding variable. The **responding variable** is what you measure or observe to obtain your results. In this experiment, the responding variable is how long the water takes to freeze.

An experiment in which all factors except one are kept constant is a **controlled experiment.** Most controlled experiments include a test called the control. In this experiment, Container 3 is the control. Because no salt is added to Container 3, you can compare the results from the other containers to it. Any difference in results must be due to the addition of salt alone.

Forming Operational Definitions
Another important aspect of a well-designed experiment is having clear operational definitions. An **operational definition** is a statement that describes how a particular variable is to be measured or how a term is to be defined. For example, in this experiment, how will you determine if the water has frozen? You might decide to insert a stick in each container at the start of the experiment. Your operational definition of "frozen" would be the time at which the stick can no longer move.

EXPERIMENTAL PROCEDURE

1. Fill 3 containers with 300 milliliters of cold tap water.

2. Add 10 grams of salt to Container 1; stir. Add 20 grams of salt to Container 2; stir. Add no salt to Container 3.

3. Place the 3 containers in a freezer.

4. Check the containers every 15 minutes. Record your observations.

Interpreting Data

The observations and measurements you make in an experiment are called data. At the end of an experiment, you need to analyze the data to look for any patterns or trends. Patterns often become clear if you organize your data in a data table or graph. Then think through what the data reveal. Do they support your hypothesis? Do they point out a flaw in your experiment? Do you need to collect more data?

Drawing Conclusions

A conclusion is a statement that sums up what you have learned from an experiment. When you draw a conclusion, you need to decide whether the data you collected support your hypothesis or not. You may need to repeat an experiment several times before you can draw any conclusions from it. Conclusions often lead you to pose new questions and plan new experiments to answer them.

Is a ball's bounce affected by the height from which it is dropped? Using the steps just described, plan a controlled experiment to investigate this problem. **ACTIVITY**

Thinking Critically

Has a friend ever asked for your advice about a problem? If so, you may have helped your friend think through the problem in a logical way. Without knowing it, you used critical-thinking skills to help your friend. Critical thinking involves the use of reasoning and logic to solve problems or make decisions. Some critical-thinking skills are described below.

Comparing and Contrasting

When you examine two objects for similarities and differences, you are using the skill of **comparing and contrasting.** Comparing involves identifying similarities, or common characteristics. Contrasting involves identifying differences. Analyzing objects in this way can help you discover details that you might otherwise overlook.

ACTIVITY

Compare and contrast the two animals in the photo. First list all the similarities that you see. Then list all the differences.

Applying Concepts

When you use your knowledge about one situation to make sense of a similar situation, you are using the skill of **applying concepts.** Being able to transfer your knowledge from one situation to another shows that you truly understand a concept. You may use this skill in answering test questions that present different problems from the ones you've reviewed in class.

ACTIVITY

You have just learned that water takes longer to freeze when other substances are mixed into it. Use this knowledge to explain why people need a substance called antifreeze in their car's radiator in the winter.

Interpreting Illustrations

Diagrams, photographs, and maps are included in textbooks to help clarify what you read. These illustrations show processes, places, and ideas in a visual manner. The skill called **interpreting illustrations** can help you learn from these visual elements. To understand an illustration, take the time to study the illustration along with all the written information that accompanies it. Captions identify the key concepts shown in the illustration. Labels point out the important parts of a diagram or map, while keys identify the symbols used in a map.

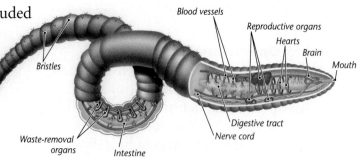

Bristles   Blood vessels   Reproductive organs   Hearts   Brain   Mouth

Waste-removal organs   Intestine   Digestive tract   Nerve cord

▲ Internal anatomy of an earthworm

ACTIVITY

Study the diagram above. Then write a short paragraph explaining what you have learned.

Relating Cause and Effect

If one event causes another event to occur, the two events are said to have a cause-and-effect relationship. When you determine that such a relationship exists between two events, you use a skill called **relating cause and effect.** For example, if you notice an itchy, red bump on your skin, you might infer that a mosquito bit you. The mosquito bite is the cause, and the bump is the effect.

It is important to note that two events do not necessarily have a cause-and-effect relationship just because they occur together. Scientists carry out experiments or use past experience to determine whether a cause-and-effect relationship exists.

ACTIVITY You are on a camping trip and your flashlight has stopped working. List some possible causes for the flashlight malfunction. How could you determine which cause-and-effect relationship has left you in the dark?

Making Generalizations

When you draw a conclusion about an entire group based on information about only some of the group's members, you are using a skill called **making generalizations.** For a generalization to be valid, the sample you choose must be large enough and representative of the entire group. You might, for example, put this skill to work at a farm stand if you see a sign that says, "Sample some grapes before you buy." If you sample a few sweet grapes, you may conclude that all the grapes are sweet—and purchase a large bunch.

ACTIVITY A team of scientists needs to determine whether the water in a large reservoir is safe to drink. How could they use the skill of making generalizations to help them? What should they do?

Making Judgments

When you evaluate something to decide whether it is good or bad, or right or wrong, you are using a skill called **making judgments.** For example, you make judgments when you decide to eat healthful foods or to pick up litter in a park. Before you make a judgment, you need to think through the pros and cons of a situation, and identify the values or standards that you hold.

ACTIVITY Should children and teens be required to wear helmets when bicycling? Explain why you feel the way you do.

Problem Solving

When you use critical-thinking skills to resolve an issue or decide on a course of action, you are using a skill called **problem solving.** Some problems, such as how to convert a fraction into a decimal, are straightforward. Other problems, such as figuring out why your computer has stopped working, are complex. Some complex problems can be solved using the trial and error method—try out one solution first, and if that doesn't work, try another. Other useful problem-solving strategies include making models and brainstorming possible solutions with a partner.

Organizing Information

As you read this textbook, how can you make sense of all the information it contains? Some useful tools to help you organize information are shown on this page. These tools are called *graphic organizers* because they give you a visual picture of a topic, showing at a glance how key concepts are related.

Concept Maps

Concept maps are useful tools for organizing information on broad topics. A concept map begins with a general concept and shows how it can be broken down into more specific concepts. In that way, relationships between concepts become easier to understand.

A concept map is constructed by placing concept words (usually nouns) in ovals and connecting them with linking words. Often, the most general concept word is placed at the top, and the words become more specific as you move downward. Often the linking words, which are written on a line extending between two ovals, describe the relationship between the two concepts they connect. If you follow any string of concepts and linking words down the map, it should read like a sentence.

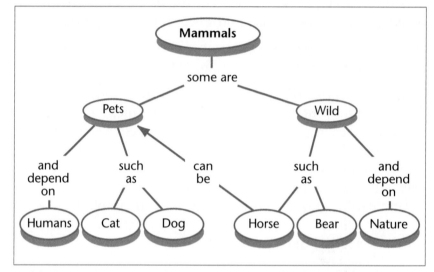

Some concept maps include linking words that connect a concept on one branch of the map to a concept on another branch. These linking words, called cross-linkages, show more complex interrelationships among concepts.

Compare/Contrast Tables

Compare/contrast tables are useful tools for sorting out the similarities and differences between two or more items. A table provides an organized framework in which to compare items based on specific characteristics that you identify.

To create a compare/contrast table, list the items to be compared across the top of a table. Then list the characteristics that will form the basis of your comparison in the left-hand column. Complete the table by filling in information about each characteristic, first for one item and then for the other.

Characteristic	Baseball	Basketball
Number of Players	9	5
Playing Field	Baseball diamond	Basketball court
Equipment	Bat, baseball, mitts	Basket, basketball

Venn Diagrams

Another way to show similarities and differences between items is with a Venn diagram. A Venn diagram consists of two or more circles that partially overlap. Each circle represents a particular concept or idea. Common characteristics, or similarities, are written within the area of overlap between the two circles. Unique characteristics, or differences, are written in the parts of the circles outside the area of overlap.

To create a Venn diagram, draw two overlapping circles. Label the circles with the names of the items being compared. Write the

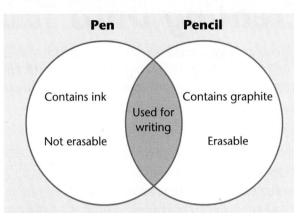

unique characteristics in each circle outside the area of overlap. Then write the shared characteristics within the area of overlap.

Flowcharts

A flowchart can help you understand the order in which certain events have occurred or should occur. Flowcharts are useful for outlining the stages in a process or the steps in a procedure.

To make a flowchart, write a brief description of each event in a box. Place the first event at the top of the page, followed by the second event, the third event, and so on. Then draw an arrow to connect each event to the one that occurs next.

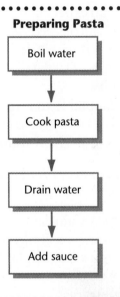

Cycle Diagrams

A cycle diagram can be used to show a sequence of events that is continuous, or cyclical. A continuous sequence does not have an end because, when the final event is over, the first event begins again. Like a flowchart, a cycle diagram can help you understand the order of events.

To create a cycle diagram, write a brief description of each event in a box. Place one event at the top of the page in the center. Then, moving in a clockwise direction around an imaginary circle, write each event in its proper sequence. Draw arrows that connect each event to the one that occurs next, forming a continuous circle.

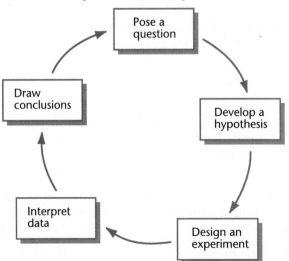

Creating Data Tables and Graphs

How can you make sense of the data in a science experiment? The first step is to organize the data to help you understand them. Data tables and graphs are helpful tools for organizing data.

Data Tables

You have gathered your materials and set up your experiment. But before you start, you need to plan a way to record what happens during the experiment. By creating a data table, you can record your observations and measurements in an orderly way.

Suppose, for example, that a scientist conducted an experiment to find out how many Calories people of different body masses burn while doing various activities. The data table shows the results.

Notice in this data table that the manipulated variable (body mass) is the heading of one column. The responding variable (for Experiment 1, the number of Calories burned while bicycling) is the heading of the next column. Additional columns were added for related experiments.

CALORIES BURNED IN 30 MINUTES OF ACTIVITY			
Body Mass	Experiment 1 Bicycling	Experiment 2 Playing Basketball	Experiment 3 Watching Television
30 kg	60 Calories	120 Calories	21 Calories
40 kg	77 Calories	164 Calories	27 Calories
50 kg	95 Calories	206 Calories	33 Calories
60 kg	114 Calories	248 Calories	38 Calories

Bar Graphs

To compare how many Calories a person burns doing various activities, you could create a bar graph. A bar graph is used to display data in a number of separate, or distinct, categories. In this example, bicycling, playing basketball, and watching television are three separate categories.

To create a bar graph, follow these steps.

1. On graph paper, draw a horizontal, or *x*-, axis and a vertical, or *y*-, axis.
2. Write the names of the categories to be graphed along the horizontal axis. Include an overall label for the axis as well.
3. Label the vertical axis with the name of the responding variable. Include units of measurement. Then create a scale along the axis by marking off equally spaced numbers that cover the range of the data collected.
4. For each category, draw a solid bar using the scale on the vertical axis to determine the

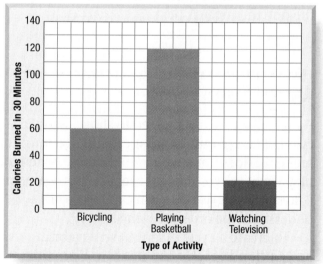

Calories Burned by a 30-kilogram Person in Various Activities

appropriate height. For example, for bicycling, draw the bar as high as the 60 mark on the vertical axis. Make all the bars the same width and leave equal spaces between them.
5. Add a title that describes the graph.

Line Graphs

To see whether a relationship exists between body mass and the number of Calories burned while bicycling, you could create a line graph. A line graph is used to display data that show how one variable (the responding variable) changes in response to another variable (the manipulated variable). You can use a line graph when your manipulated variable is *continuous*, that is, when there are other points between the ones that you tested. In this example, body mass is a continuous variable because there are other body masses between 30 and 40 kilograms (for example, 31 kilograms). Time is another example of a continuous variable.

Line graphs are powerful tools because they allow you to estimate values for conditions that you did not test in the experiment. For example, you can use the line graph to estimate that a 35-kilogram person would burn 68 Calories while bicycling.

To create a line graph, follow these steps.

1. On graph paper, draw a horizontal, or *x*-, axis and a vertical, or *y*-, axis.
2. Label the horizontal axis with the name of the manipulated variable. Label the vertical axis with the name of the responding variable. Include units of measurement.
3. Create a scale on each axis by marking off equally spaced numbers that cover the range of the data collected.
4. Plot a point on the graph for each piece of data. In the line graph above, the dotted lines show how to plot the first data point (30 kilograms and 60 Calories). Draw an imaginary vertical line extending up from the horizontal axis at the 30-kilogram mark. Then draw an imaginary horizontal line extending across from the vertical axis at the 60-Calorie mark. Plot the point where the two lines intersect.

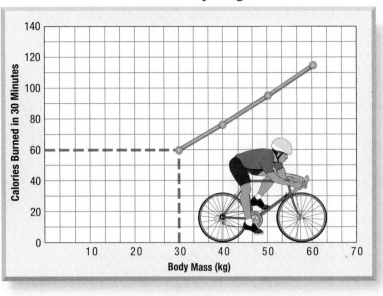

Effect of Body Mass on Calories Burned While Bicycling

5. Connect the plotted points with a solid line. (In some cases, it may be more appropriate to draw a line that shows the general trend of the plotted points. In those cases, some of the points may fall above or below the line. Also, not all graphs are linear. It may be more appropriate to draw a curve to connect the points.)
6. Add a title that identifies the variables or relationship in the graph.

Create line graphs to display the data from Experiment 2 and Experiment 3 in the data table.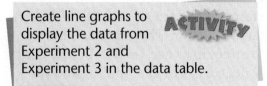

You read in the newspaper that a total of 4 centimeters of rain fell in your area in June, 2.5 centimeters fell in July, and 1.5 centimeters fell in August. What type of graph would you use to display these data? Use graph paper to create the graph.

Circle Graphs

Like bar graphs, circle graphs can be used to display data in a number of separate categories. Unlike bar graphs, however, circle graphs can only be used when you have data for *all* the categories that make up a given topic. A circle graph is sometimes called a pie chart because it resembles a pie cut into slices. The pie represents the entire topic, while the slices represent the individual categories. The size of a slice indicates what percentage of the whole a particular category makes up.

The data table below shows the results of a survey in which 24 teenagers were asked to identify their favorite sport. The data were then used to create the circle graph at the right.

Sports That Teens Prefer

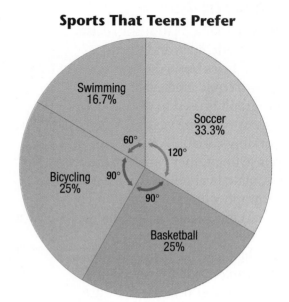

FAVORITE SPORTS	
Sport	Number of Students
Soccer	8
Basketball	6
Bicycling	6
Swimming	4

To create a circle graph, follow these steps.

1. Use a compass to draw a circle. Mark the center of the circle with a point. Then draw a line from the center point to the top of the circle.

2. Determine the size of each "slice" by setting up a proportion where x equals the number of degrees in a slice. (NOTE: A circle contains 360 degrees.) For example, to find the number of degrees in the "soccer" slice, set up the following proportion:

$$\frac{\text{students who prefer soccer}}{\text{total number of students}} = \frac{x}{\text{total number of degrees in a circle}}$$

$$\frac{8}{24} = \frac{x}{360}$$

Cross-multiply and solve for x.

$$24x = 8 \times 360$$
$$x = 120$$

The "soccer" slice should contain 120 degrees.

3. Use a protractor to measure the angle of the first slice, using the line you drew to the top of the circle as the 0° line. Draw a line from the center of the circle to the edge for the angle you measured.

4. Continue around the circle by measuring the size of each slice with the protractor. Start measuring from the edge of the previous slice so the wedges do not overlap. When you are done, the entire circle should be filled in.

5. Determine the percentage of the whole circle that each slice represents. To do this, divide the number of degrees in a slice by the total number of degrees in a circle (360), and multiply by 100%. For the "soccer" slice, you can find the percentage as follows:

$$\frac{120}{360} \times 100\% = 33.3\%$$

6. Use a different color to shade in each slice. Label each slice with the name of the category and with the percentage of the whole it represents.

7. Add a title to the circle graph.

ACTIVITY

In a class of 28 students, 12 students take the bus to school, 10 students walk, and 6 students ride their bicycles. Create a circle graph to display these data.

Laboratory Safety

Safety Symbols

These symbols alert you to possible dangers in the laboratory and remind you to work carefully.

Safety Goggles Always wear safety goggles to protect your eyes in any activity involving chemicals, flames or heating, or the possibility of broken glassware.

Lab Apron Wear a laboratory apron to protect your skin and clothing from damage.

Breakage You are working with materials that may be breakable, such as glass containers, glass tubing, thermometers, or funnels. Handle breakable materials with care. Do not touch broken glassware.

Heat-resistant Gloves Use an oven mitt or other hand protection when handling hot materials. Hot plates, hot glassware, or hot water can cause burns. Do not touch hot objects with your bare hands.

Heating Use a clamp or tongs to pick up hot glassware. Do not touch hot objects with your bare hands.

Sharp Object Pointed-tip scissors, scalpels, knives, needles, pins, or tacks are sharp. They can cut or puncture your skin. Always direct a sharp edge or point away from yourself and others. Use sharp instruments only as instructed.

Electric Shock Avoid the possibility of electric shock. Never use electrical equipment around water, or when the equipment is wet or your hands are wet. Be sure cords are untangled and cannot trip anyone. Disconnect the equipment when it is not in use.

Corrosive Chemical You are working with an acid or another corrosive chemical. Avoid getting it on your skin or clothing, or in your eyes. Do not inhale the vapors. Wash your hands when you are finished with the activity.

Poison Do not let any poisonous chemical come in contact with your skin, and do not inhale its vapors. Wash your hands when you are finished with the activity.

Physical Safety When an experiment involves physical activity, take precautions to avoid injuring yourself or others. Follow instructions from your teacher. Alert your teacher if there is any reason you should not participate in the activity.

Animal Safety Treat live animals with care to avoid harming the animals or yourself. Working with animal parts or preserved animals also may require caution. Wash your hands when you are finished with the activity.

Plant Safety Handle plants in the laboratory or during field work only as directed by your teacher. If you are allergic to certain plants, tell your teacher before doing an activity in which those plants are used. Avoid touching harmful plants such as poison ivy, poison oak, or poison sumac, or plants with thorns. Wash your hands when you are finished with the activity.

Flames You may be working with flames from a lab burner, candle, or matches. Tie back loose hair and clothing. Follow instructions from your teacher about lighting and extinguishing flames.

No Flames Flammable materials may be present. Make sure there are no flames, sparks, or other exposed heat sources present.

Fumes When poisonous or unpleasant vapors may be involved, work in a ventilated area. Avoid inhaling vapors directly. Only test an odor when directed to do so by your teacher, and use a wafting motion to direct the vapor toward your nose.

Disposal Chemicals and other laboratory materials used in the activity must be disposed of safely. Follow the instructions from your teacher.

Hand Washing Wash your hands thoroughly when finished with the activity. Use antibacterial soap and warm water. Lather both sides of your hands and between your fingers. Rinse well.

General Safety Awareness You may see this symbol when none of the symbols described earlier appears. In this case, follow the specific instructions provided. You may also see this symbol when you are asked to develop your own procedure in a lab. Have your teacher approve your plan before you go further.

Science Safety Rules

To prepare yourself to work safely in the laboratory, read over the following safety rules. Then read them a second time. Make sure you understand and follow each rule. Ask your teacher to explain any rules you do not understand.

Dress Code

1. To protect yourself from injuring your eyes, wear safety goggles whenever you work with chemicals, burners, glassware, or any substance that might get into your eyes. If you wear contact lenses, notify your teacher.
2. Wear a lab apron or coat whenever you work with corrosive chemicals or substances that can stain.
3. Tie back long hair to keep it away from any chemicals, flames, or equipment.
4. Remove or tie back any article of clothing or jewelry that can hang down and touch chemicals, flames, or equipment. Roll up or secure long sleeves.
5. Never wear open shoes or sandals.

General Precautions

6. Read all directions for an experiment several times before beginning the activity. Carefully follow all written and oral instructions. If you are in doubt about any part of the experiment, ask your teacher for assistance.
7. Never perform activities that are not assigned or authorized by your teacher. Obtain permission before "experimenting" on your own. Never handle any equipment unless you have specific permission.
8. Never perform lab activities without direct supervision.
9. Never eat or drink in the laboratory.
10. Keep work areas clean and tidy at all times. Bring only notebooks and lab manuals or written lab procedures to the work area. All other items, such as purses and backpacks, should be left in a designated area.
11. Do not engage in horseplay.

First Aid

12. Always report all accidents or injuries to your teacher, no matter how minor. Notify your teacher immediately about any fires.
13. Learn what to do in case of specific accidents, such as getting acid in your eyes or on your skin. (Rinse acids from your body with lots of water.)
14. Be aware of the location of the first-aid kit, but do not use it unless instructed by your teacher. In case of injury, your teacher should administer first aid. Your teacher may also send you to the school nurse or call a physician.
15. Know the location of emergency equipment, such as the fire extinguisher and fire blanket, and know how to use it.
16. Know the location of the nearest telephone and whom to contact in an emergency.

Heating and Fire Safety

17. Never use a heat source, such as a candle, burner, or hot plate, without wearing safety goggles.
18. Never heat anything unless instructed to do so. A chemical that is harmless when cool may be dangerous when heated.
19. Keep all combustible materials away from flames. Never use a flame or spark near a combustible chemical.
20. Never reach across a flame.
21. Before using a laboratory burner, make sure you know proper procedures for lighting and adjusting the burner, as demonstrated by your teacher. Do not touch the burner. It may be hot. And never leave a lighted burner unattended!
22. Chemicals can splash or boil out of a heated test tube. When heating a substance in a test tube, make sure that the mouth of the tube is not pointed at you or anyone else.
23. Never heat a liquid in a closed container. The expanding gases produced may blow the container apart.
24. Before picking up a container that has been heated, hold the back of your hand near it. If you can feel heat on the back of your hand, the container is too hot to handle. Use an oven mitt to pick up a container that has been heated.

Using Chemicals Safely

25. Never mix chemicals "for the fun of it." You might produce a dangerous, possibly explosive substance.

26. Never put your face near the mouth of a container that holds chemicals. Never touch, taste, or smell a chemical unless you are instructed by your teacher to do so. Many chemicals are poisonous.

27. Use only those chemicals needed in the activity. Read and double-check labels on supply bottles before removing any chemicals. Take only as much as you need. Keep all containers closed when chemicals are not being used.

28. Dispose of all chemicals as instructed by your teacher. To avoid contamination, never return chemicals to their original containers. Never simply pour chemicals or other substances into the sink or trash containers.

29. Be extra careful when working with acids or bases. Pour all chemicals over the sink or a container, not over your work surface.

30. If you are instructed to test for odors, use a wafting motion to direct the odors to your nose. Do not inhale the fumes directly from the container.

31. When mixing an acid and water, always pour the water into the container first and then add the acid to the water. Never pour water into an acid.

32. Take extreme care not to spill any material in the laboratory. Wash chemical spills and splashes immediately with plenty of water. Immediately begin rinsing with water any acids that get on your skin or clothing, and notify your teacher of any acid spill at the same time.

Using Glassware Safely

33. Never force glass tubing or thermometers into a rubber stopper or rubber tubing. Have your teacher insert the glass tubing or thermometer if required for an activity.

34. If you are using a laboratory burner, use a wire screen to protect glassware from any flame. Never heat glassware that is not thoroughly dry on the outside.

35. Keep in mind that hot glassware looks cool. Never pick up glassware without first checking to see if it is hot. Use an oven mitt. See rule 24.

36. Never use broken or chipped glassware. If glassware breaks, notify your teacher and dispose of the glassware in the proper broken-glassware container. Never handle broken glass with your bare hands.

37. Never eat or drink from lab glassware.

38. Thoroughly clean glassware before putting it away.

Using Sharp Instruments

39. Handle scalpels or other sharp instruments with extreme care. Never cut material toward you; cut away from you.

40. Immediately notify your teacher if you cut your skin when working in the laboratory.

Animal and Plant Safety

41. Never perform experiments that cause pain, discomfort, or harm to mammals, birds, reptiles, fishes, or amphibians. This rule applies at home as well as in the classroom.

42. Animals should be handled only if absolutely necessary. Your teacher will instruct you as to how to handle each animal species brought into the classroom.

43. If you know that you are allergic to certain plants, molds, or animals, tell your teacher before doing an activity in which these are used.

44. During field work, protect your skin by wearing long pants, long sleeves, socks, and closed shoes. Know how to recognize the poisonous plants and fungi in your area, as well as plants with thorns, and avoid contact with them.

45. Never eat any part of an unidentified plant or fungus.

46. Wash your hands thoroughly after handling animals or the cage containing animals. Wash your hands when you are finished with any activity involving animal parts, plants, or soil.

End-of-Experiment Rules

47. After an experiment has been completed, clean up your work area and return all equipment to its proper place.

48. Dispose of waste materials as instructed by your teacher.

49. Wash your hands after every experiment.

50. Always turn off all burners or hot plates when they are not in use. Unplug hot plates and other electrical equipment. If you used a burner, check that the gas-line valve to the burner is off as well.

Using the Microscope

The microscope is an essential tool in the study of life science. It allows you to see things that are too small to be seen with the unaided eye.

You will probably use a compound microscope like the one you see here. The compound microscope has more than one lens that magnifies the object you view.

Typically, a compound microscope has one lens in the eyepiece, the part you look through. The eyepiece lens usually magnifies 10 ×. Any object you view through this lens would appear 10 times larger than it is.

The compound microscope may contain one or two other lenses called objective lenses. If there are two objective lenses, they are called the low-power and high-power objective lenses. The low-power objective lens usually magnifies 10 ×. The high-power objective lens usually magnifies 40 ×.

To calculate the total magnification with which you are viewing an object, multiply the magnification of the eyepiece lens by the magnification of the objective lens you are using. For example, the eyepiece's magnification of 10 × multiplied by the low-power objective's magnification of 10 × equals a total magnification of 100 ×.

Use the photo of the compound microscope to become familiar with the parts of the microscope and their functions.

The Parts of the Compound Microscope

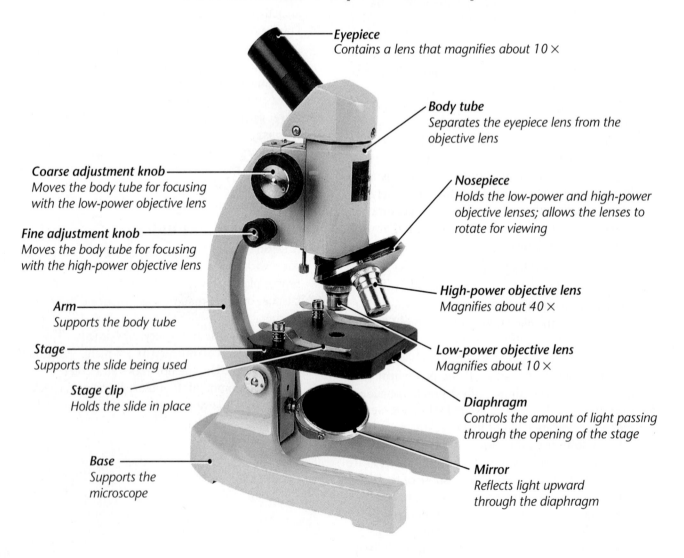

Eyepiece
Contains a lens that magnifies about 10 ×

Body tube
Separates the eyepiece lens from the objective lens

Coarse adjustment knob
Moves the body tube for focusing with the low-power objective lens

Nosepiece
Holds the low-power and high-power objective lenses; allows the lenses to rotate for viewing

Fine adjustment knob
Moves the body tube for focusing with the high-power objective lens

High-power objective lens
Magnifies about 40 ×

Arm
Supports the body tube

Stage
Supports the slide being used

Low-power objective lens
Magnifies about 10 ×

Stage clip
Holds the slide in place

Diaphragm
Controls the amount of light passing through the opening of the stage

Base
Supports the microscope

Mirror
Reflects light upward through the diaphragm

Using the Microscope

Use the following procedures when you are working with a microscope.

1. To carry the microscope grasp the microscope's arm with one hand. Place your other hand under the base.
2. Place the microscope on a table with the arm toward you.
3. Turn the coarse adjustment knob to raise the body tube.
4. Revolve the nosepiece until the low-power objective lens clicks into place.
5. Adjust the diaphragm. While looking through the eyepiece, also adjust the mirror until you see a bright white circle of light. **CAUTION:** *Never use direct sunlight as a light source.*
6. Place a slide on the stage. Center the specimen over the opening on the stage. Use the stage clips to hold the slide in place. **CAUTION:** *Glass slides are fragile.*
7. Look at the stage from the side. Carefully turn the coarse adjustment knob to lower the body tube until the low-power objective almost touches the slide.
8. Looking through the eyepiece, very slowly turn the coarse adjustment knob until the specimen comes into focus.
9. To switch to the high-power objective lens, look at the microscope from the side. Carefully revolve the nosepiece until the high-power objective lens clicks into place. Make sure the lens does not hit the slide.
10. Looking through the eyepiece, turn the fine adjustment knob until the specimen comes into focus.

Making a Wet-Mount Slide

Use the following procedures to make a wet-mount slide of a specimen.

1. Obtain a clean microscope slide and a coverslip. **CAUTION:** *Glass slides and coverslips are fragile.*
2. Place the specimen on the slide. The specimen must be thin enough for light to pass through it.
3. Using a plastic dropper, place a drop of water on the specimen.
4. Gently place one edge of the coverslip against the slide so that it touches the edge of the water drop at a 45° angle. Slowly lower the coverslip over the specimen. If air bubbles are trapped beneath the coverslip, tap the coverslip gently with the eraser end of a pencil.
5. Remove any excess water at the edge of the coverslip with a paper towel.

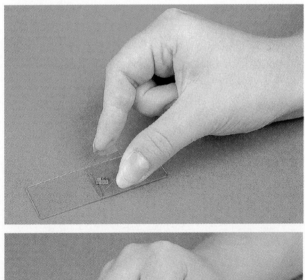

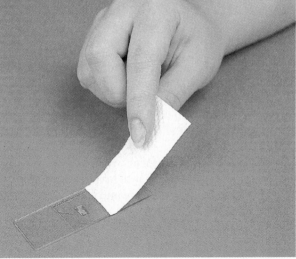

A

absolute dating A technique used to determine the actual age of a fossil. (p. 154)

active transport The movement of materials through a cell membrane using energy. (p. 43)

adaptation A trait that helps an organism survive and reproduce. (p. 143)

alleles The different forms of a gene. (p. 83)

amino acids Small molecules that are linked together chemically to form proteins. (p. 35)

amniocentesis A technique by which a small amount of the fluid that surrounds a developing baby is removed; the fluid is analyzed to determine whether the baby will have a genetic disorder. (p. 122)

atom The smallest unit of an element. (p. 33)

autotroph An organism that makes its own food. (p. 54)

B

branching tree A diagram that shows how scientists think different groups of organisms are related. (p. 162)

C

cancer A disease in which some body cells grow and divide uncontrollably, damaging the parts of the body around them. (p. 71)

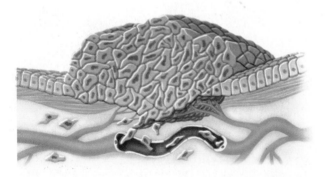

carbohydrates Energy-rich organic compounds, such as sugars and starches, that are made of the elements carbon, hydrogen, and oxygen. (p. 34)

carrier A person who has one recessive allele for a trait and one dominant allele, but does not have the trait. (p. 116)

cast A type of fossil that forms when a mold becomes filled in with minerals that then harden. (p. 152)

cell The basic unit of structure and function in living things. (p. 16)

cell cycle The regular sequence of growth and division that cells undergo. (p. 62)

cell membrane A cell structure that controls which substances can enter or leave the cell. (p. 24)

cell theory A widely accepted explanation of the relationship between cells and living things. (p. 20)

cell wall A rigid layer of nonliving material that surrounds the cells of plants and some other organisms. (p. 24)

chemotherapy The use of drugs to kill cancer cells. (p. 72)

chlorophyll A green pigment found in the chloroplasts of plants, algae, and some bacteria. (p. 52)

chloroplast A structure in the cells of plants and some other organisms that captures energy from sunlight and uses it to produce food. (p. 29)

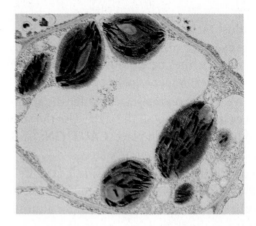

chromatid One of the identical rods of a chromosome. (p. 63)

chromatin Material in cells that contains DNA and carries genetic information. (p. 28)

chromosome A doubled rod of condensed chromatin; contains DNA that carries genetic information. (p. 63)

clone An organism that is genetically identical to the organism from which it was produced. (p. 128)

codominance A condition in which neither of two alleles of a gene is dominant or recessive. (p. 92)

compound Two or more elements that are chemically combined. (p. 33)

compound microscope A light microscope that has more than one lens. (p. 17)

controlled experiment An experiment in which all factors except one are kept constant. (p. 179)

convex lens A curved lens in which the center is thicker than the edges. (p. 21)

cytokinesis The final stage of the cell cycle, in which the cell's cytoplasm divides, distributing the organelles into each of the two new cells. (p. 66)

cytoplasm The region between the cell membrane and the nucleus; in organisms without a nucleus, the region located inside the cell membrane. (p. 28)

diffusion The process by which molecules move from an area of higher concentration to an area of lower concentration. (p. 41)

DNA Deoxyribonucleic acid; the genetic material that carries information about an organism and is passed from parent to offspring. (p. 36)

dominant allele An allele whose trait always shows up in the organism when the allele is present. (p. 83)

element Any substance that cannot be broken down into simpler substances. (p. 33)

endoplasmic reticulum A cell structure that forms a maze of passageways in which proteins and other materials are carried from one part of the cell to another. (p. 29)

enzyme A type of protein that speeds up a chemical reaction in a living thing. (p. 35)

evolution The gradual change in a species over time. (p. 143)

extinct A species that does not have any living members. (p. 154)

fermentation The process by which cells break down molecules to release energy without using oxygen. (p. 58)

fossil The preserved remains or traces of an organism that lived in the past. (p. 151)

fossil record The millions of fossils that scientists have collected. (p. 154)

gene therapy The insertion of working copies of a gene into the cells of a person with a genetic disorder in an attempt to correct the disorder. (p. 130)

gene A segment of DNA on a chromosome that codes for a specific trait. (p. 83)

genetic disorder An abnormal condition that a person inherits through genes or chromosomes. (p. 119)

genetic engineering The transfer of a gene from the DNA of one organism into another organism, in order to produce an organism with desired traits. (p. 128)

genetics The scientific study of heredity. (p. 80)

genome All of the DNA in one cell of an organism. (p. 132)

genotype An organism's genetic makeup, or allele combinations. (p. 92)

Golgi body A structure in a cell that receives proteins and other newly formed materials from the endoplasmic reticulum, packages them, and distributes them to other parts of the cell. (p. 29)

gradualism The theory that evolution occurs slowly but steadily. (p. 158)

half-life The time it takes for half of the atoms in a radioactive element to break down. (p. 154)

heredity The passing of traits from parents to offspring. (p. 80)

heterotroph An organism that cannot make its own food. (p. 54)

heterozygous Having two different alleles for a trait. (p. 92)

homologous structures Body parts that are structurally similar in related species; provide evidence that the structures were inherited from a common ancestor. (p. 160)

homozygous Having two identical alleles for a trait. (p. 92)

hybrid An organism that has two different alleles for a trait; an organism that is heterozygous for a particular trait. (p. 84)

hybridization A selective breeding method in which two genetically different individuals are crossed. (p. 127)

hypothesis A possible explanation for a set of observations or answer to a scientific question; must be testable. (p. 178)

I

inbreeding A selective breeding method in which two individuals with identical or similar sets of alleles are crossed. (p. 127)

inorganic compound A compound that does not contain carbon. (p. 34)

interphase The stage of the cell cycle that takes place before cell division occurs; during this stage, the cell grows, copies its DNA, and prepares to divide. (p. 62)

karyotype A picture of all the chromosomes in a cell arranged in pairs. (p. 123)

lipids Energy-rich organic compounds, such as fats, oils, and waxes, that are made of carbon, hydrogen, and oxygen. (p. 36)

lysosome A small round cell structure that contains chemicals that break down large food particles into smaller ones. (p. 30)

magnification The ability to make things look larger than they are. (p. 21)

manipulated variable The one factor that a scientist changes during an experiment. (p. 179)

meiosis The process that occurs in sex cells (sperm and egg) by which the number of chromosomes is reduced by half. (p. 98)

messenger RNA RNA that copies the coded message from DNA in the nucleus and carries the message into the cytoplasm. (p. 103)

microscope An instrument that makes small objects look larger. (p. 17)

mitochondria Rod-shaped cell structures that produce most of the energy needed to carry out the cell's functions. (p. 28)

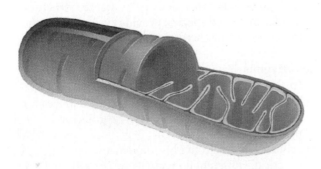

mitosis The stage of the cell cycle during which the cell's nucleus divides into two new nuclei and one copy of the DNA is distributed into each daughter cell. (p. 63)

mold A type of fossil formed when a shell or other hard part of an organism dissolves, leaving an empty space in the shape of the part. (p. 152)

molecule The smallest unit of most compounds. (p. 33)

multiple alleles Three or more forms of a gene that code for a single trait. (p. 113)

mutation A change in a gene or chromosome. (p. 71)

natural selection The process by which individuals that are better adapted to their environment are more likely to survive and reproduce than other members of the same species. (p. 144)

nucleic acid A very large organic molecule made of carbon, oxygen, hydrogen, nitrogen, and phosphorus, that contains instructions that cells need to carry out all the functions of life. (p. 36)

nucleus A cell structure that contains nucleic acids, the chemical instructions that direct all the cell's activities. (p. 25)

operational definition A statement that describes how a particular variable is to be measured or a term is to be defined. (p. 179)

organelle A tiny cell structure that carries out a specific function within the cell. (p. 24)

organic compound A compound that contains carbon. (p. 34)

osmosis The diffusion of water molecules through a selectively permeable membrane. (p. 42)

passive transport The movement of materials through a cell membrane without using energy. (p. 43)

pedigree A chart or "family tree" that tracks which members of a family have a particular trait. (p. 117)

petrified fossil A fossil formed when minerals replace all or part of an organism. (p. 152)

phenotype An organism's physical appearance, or visible traits. (p. 92)

photosynthesis The process by which plants and some other organisms capture the energy in sunlight and use it to make food. (p. 51)

pigment A colored chemical compound that absorbs light. (p. 52)

probability The likelihood that a particular event will occur. (p. 88)

proteins Large organic molecules made of carbon, hydrogen, oxygen, nitrogen, and sometimes sulfur. (p. 35)

punctuated equilibria The theory that species evolve during short periods of rapid change. (p. 158)

Punnett square A chart that shows all the possible combinations of alleles that can result from a genetic cross. (p. 90)

purebred An organism that always produces offspring with the same form of a trait as the parent. (p. 81)

radioactive element An unstable particle that breaks down into a different element. (p. 154)

recessive allele An allele that is masked when a dominant allele is present. (p. 83)

relative dating A technique used to determine which of two fossils is older. (p. 153)

replication The process by which a cell makes a copy of the DNA in its nucleus. (p. 62)

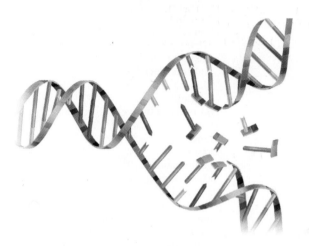

resolution The ability to clearly distinguish the individual parts of an object. (p. 22)

respiration The process by which cells break down simple food molecules to release the energy they contain. (p. 56)

responding variable The factor that changes as a result of changes to the manipulated variable in an experiment. (p. 179)

ribosome A small grain-like structure in the cytoplasm of a cell where proteins are made. (p. 29)

RNA Ribonucleic acid; a nucleic acid that plays an important role in the production of proteins. (p. 37)

scientific theory A well-tested concept that explains a wide range of observations. (p. 143)

sedimentary rock Rock formed when layers of sediments harden over millions of years. (p. 152)

selective breeding The process of selecting a few organisms with desired traits to serve as parents of the next generation. (p. 126)

selectively permeable A property of cell membranes that allows some substances to pass through, while others cannot. (p. 40)

sex-linked gene A gene that is carried on the X or Y chromosome. (p. 116)

species A group of similar organisms that can mate with each other and produce fertile offspring. (p. 141)

stomata Small openings on the underside of a leaf through which oxygen and carbon dioxide can move. (p. 52)

trait A characteristic that an organism can pass on to its offspring through its genes. (p. 80)

transfer RNA RNA in the cytoplasm that carries an amino acid to the ribosome and adds it to the growing protein chain. (p. 103)

tumor A mass of abnormal cells that develops when cancerous cells divide and grow uncontrollably. (p. 71)

V

vacuole A water-filled sac inside a cell that acts as a storage area. (p. 30)

variable Any factor that can change in an experiment. (p. 179)

variation Any difference between individuals of the same species. (p. 145)

Acknowledgments

Staff Credits

The people who made up the **Science Explorer** team—representing design services, editorial, editorial services, electronic publishing technology, manufacturing & inventory planning, marketing, marketing services, market research, online services & multimedia development, production services, product planning, project office, and publishing processes—are listed below.

Carolyn Belanger, Barbara A. Bertell, Suzanne Biron, Peggy Bliss, Peter W. Brooks, Christopher R. Brown, Greg Cantone, Jonathan Cheney, Todd Christy, Lisa J. Clark, Patrick Finbarr Connolly, Edward Cordero, Robert Craton, Patricia Cully, Patricia M. Dambry, Kathleen J. Dempsey, Judy Elgin, Gayle Connolly Fedele, Frederick Fellows, Barbara Foster, Paula Foye, Loree Franz, Donald P. Gagnon Jr., Paul J. Gagnon, Joel Gendler, Elizabeth Good, Robert M. Graham, Kerri Hoar, Joanne Hudson, Linda D. Johnson, Anne Jones, Toby Klang, Carolyn Langley, Russ Lappa, Carolyn Lock, Cheryl Mahan, Dotti Marshall, Meredith Mascola, Jeanne Y. Maurand, Karen McHugh, Eve Melnechuk, Natania Mlawer, Paul W. Murphy, Cindy A. Noftle, Julia F. Osborne, Judi Pinkham, Caroline M. Power, Robin L. Santel, Suzanne J. Schineller, Emily Soltanoff, Kira Thaler-Marbit, Mark Tricca, Diane Walsh, Pearl Weinstein, Merce Wilczek, Helen Young.

Illustration

Robert Fuller: 140–141
GeoSystems Global Corporation: 149, 170–171
Keith Kasnot: 26, 27, 28, 29, 63
Martucci Design: 66, 184, 185, 186
Matt Mayerchak: 45, 75, 135, 165, 182, 183,
Morgan Cain & Associates: 12–13, 20, 21, 33, 41, 43, 57, 64–65, 67, 68, 99, 102–103, 104–105, 154, 176, 177
J/B Woolsey Associates: 47, 53, 72–73, 87, 91, 93, 98, 113, 115, 118, 129, 137, 156–157, 158, 160, 163, 180

Photography

Photo Research by Sharon Donahue
Cover Image Tom Pantages/Phototake

Nature of Science
Page 10,11, Courtesy of Lydia Villa-Komaroff; **12t**, Biophoto Associates/ Science Source/Photo Researchers; **12b**, Howard Sochurek/The Stock Market; **13**, Will & Deni McIntyre/Photo Researchers.

Chapter 1
Pages 14–15, Julie Habel/Westlight; **16t**, Richard Haynes; **16bl**, Joseph Nettis/Photo Researchers; **16br**, John Coletti/Stock Boston; **17, 18t**The Granger Collection, NY; **18b**, Corbis-Bettmann; **19t**, H.R. Bramaz/Peter Arnold; **19bl**, Corbis-Bettmann; **19br**, Lawrence Migdale/Stock Boston; **20**, Anup Shah/Masterfile; **22**, CNRI/Science Photo Library/Photo Researchers; **23t**, Runk/Schoenberger/Grant Heilman Photography; **23b**, Doug Wilson/Westlight; **24t**, M. Abbey/Visuals Unlimited; **24b**, Runk/Schoenberger/Grant Heilman Photography; **25**, Dr. Dennis Kunkel/Phototake; **28**, Bill Longcore/Photo Researchers; **29**, K.G. Murtis/Visuals Unlimited; **30**, A.B. Dowsett/Photo Researchers; **31l**, Dr. David Scott/CNRI/Phototake; **31r**, Dr. Dennis Kunkel/Phototake; **32**, Runk/Schoenberger/Grant Heilman Photography; **33**, Russ Lappa; **34**, Okapia-Frankfurt/Photo Researchers; **34 inset**, Andrew Syred/Science Photo Library/Photo Researchers; **35**, Gary Bell/Masterfile; **36t**, Barry L. Runk/Grant Heilman Photography & Michael Mahovlich/Masterfile; **36l**, Lou Lainey; **36r** Barry L. Runk/Grant Heilman Photography; **36 inset**, Michael Mahovlich/Masterfile; **37**, Hans Blohm/Masterfile; **38**, James Holmes/Farmer Giles Foods/Science Photo Library/ Photo Researchers; **40**, NASA; **42l**, Stanley Flegler/Visuals Unlimited; **42m,r**, David M. Phillips/Visuals Unlimited; **44**, M. Abbey/Visuals Unlimited.

Chapter 2
Pages 48–49, Carr Clifton/Minden Pictures; **50t**, Russ Lappa; **50b**, Paul Barton/The Stock Market; **51r**, Cosmo Condina; **51 inset**, Biophoto Associates/Photo Researchers; **52t**, Russ Lappa; **52bl, br** , Dr. Jeremy Burgess/Science Photo Library/Photo Researchers; **54t**, Frans Lanting/Minden Pictures; **54b**, Tom J. Ulrich/Visuals Unlimited; **55**, William Johnson/Stock Boston; **56l**, Stephen Dalton/Photo Researchers; **56r**, Phil Dotson/Photo Researchers; **58**, Mark Newman/Visuals Unlimited; **59**, Terje Rakke/The Image Bank; **61t**, David Scharf/Peter Arnold; **61b**, Larry Lefever/Grant Heilman Photography; **62**, Art Wolfe/TSI; **63**, Biophoto Associates/Science Source/Photo Researchers; **64–65 all**, M. Abbey/Photo Researchers; **69**, Robert Knauft/Biology Media; **70t**, Richard Haynes; **70b**, Myrleen Ferguson/Photo Edit; **71**, National Cancer Institute/Science Photo Library/Photo Researchers; **74**, Joseph Sohm/Stock Boston; **75**, Frans Lanting/Minden Pictures.

Chapter 3
Pages 78–79, Ron Kimball; **80t**, Mike Rothwell/Stone; **80b**, Corbis-Bettmann; **81**, Barry Runk/Grant Heilman Photography; **84 both**, Meinrad Faltner/The Stock Market; **85**, Inga Spence/The Picture Cube; **88-89**, Image Stop/Phototake; **92**, Hans Reinhard/Bruce Coleman; **95**, Richard Haynes; **96l**, David M. Phillips/Photo Researchers; **96r**, University "La Sapienza," Rome/Science Photo Library/Photo Researchers; **97l**, Jonathan D. Speer/Visuals Unlimited; **97r**, M. Abbey/Photo Researchers; **101**, AP/Wide World Photos; **106**, William E. Ferguson; **107,** Mike Rothwell/Stone.

Chapter 4
Pages 110–111, Herb Snitzer/Stock Boston; **112**, Richard Haynes; **114**, Camille Tokerud/TSI; **115t,b**, Biophoto Associates/Science Source/Photo Researchers; **116**, Andrew McClenaghan/Science Photo Library/Photo Researchers; **118**, Superstock; **119t**, CNRI/Science Photo Library/Photo Researchers; **119b**, Lawrence Migdale/TSI; **120t**, Simon Fraser/RVI, Newcastle-upon-TYNE/Science Photo Library/Photo Researchers; **120b**, Stanley Flegler/Visuals Unlimited; **121**, Corbis-Bettmann; **122l**, CNRI/Science Photo Library/Photo Researchers; **122r**, Mugshots/The Stock Market; **123**, Will and Deni McIntyre/Photo Researchers Inc.; **124**, Richard Haynes; **126**, AP/Wide World Photos; **127**, Tim Barnwell/Stock Boston; **128**, Patricia J. Bruno/Positive Images; **129**, LeLand Bobbe/TSI; **130**, Gary Wagner/Stock Boston; **131**, AP/Wide World Photos; **132**, U.S. Department of Energy/Human Genome Management Information System, Oak Ridge National Laboratory; **133**, David Parker/Science Photo Library/Photo Researchers; **134**, Michael Newman/PhotoEdit.

Chapter 5
Pages 138–139, Bill Varie/Westlight; **140t**, Portrait by George Richmond/Down House, Downe/The Bridgeman Art Library; **140b**, Corbis-Bettmann; **141t,b**, Tui De Roy/Minden Pictures; **141m**, Frans Lanting/Minden Pictures; **142l**, Zig Leszczynski/Animals Animals; **142r**, Tui De Roy/Minden Pictures; **143**, Dr. Jeremy Burgess/Science Photo Library/Photo Researchers; **144**, Mitsuaki Iwago/Minden Pictures; **145**, Jeff Gnass Photography/The Stock Market; **147**, Richard Haynes; **148l,r**, Breck P. Kent; **149l,r**, Pat & Tom Leeson/Photo Researchers; **150t**, John Cancalosi/Tom Stack & Associates; **150b**, Tom McHugh/Photo Researchers; **151t**, James L. Amos/Photo Researchers; **151b** Sinclair Stammers/Science Photo Library/Photo Researchers; **155**, Robert Landau/Westlight; **159**, Richard Haynes; **161l**, Keith Gillett/Animals Animals; **161m**, George Whiteley/Photo Researchers; **161r**, David Spears Ltd./Science Photo Library/Photo Researchers; **162l**, Gary Milburn/Tom Stack & Associates; **162r**, Daryl Balfour/TSI.

Interdisciplinary Exploration
Page 168t, Tim Fitzharris/Minden Pictures; **168b**, Bridgeman Art Library; **169**, Ron Kimball; **170tr**, Charles Philip/Westlight; **170b**, Jack Daniels/TSI; **170tl, ml, mr**, Corel Corp.; **170ml**, C. Jeanne White/Photo Researchers; **171 all others**, Corel Corp.; **172t**, Peter Cade/TSI; **172b**, AP/ Wide World Photos; **172–173**, Nick Meers/Panoramic Images.

Skills Handbook
Page 174, Mike Moreland/Photo Network; **175t**, Foodpix; **175m**, Richard Haynes; **175b**, Russ Lappa; **178**, Richard Haynes; **180**, Ron Kimball; **181**, Renee Lynn/Photo Researchers.

Appendix B
Page 190, Russ Lappa; **191 both**, Russ Lappa.